The Harlot of Revelation
and the Great Tribulation

To Chris and Kathy

The HARLOT of REVELATION
and the Great Tribulation.

Fred V. Squillante

FRED V. SQUILLANTE

XULON PRESS

Xulon Press
2301 Lucien Way #415
Maitland, FL 32751
407.339.4217
www.xulonpress.com

© 2019 by Fred V. Squillante

All Underlined, Italicized, and Bold text in copied text is the work of "The Harlot" author.

All rights reserved solely by the author. The author guarantees all contents are original and do not infringe upon the legal rights of any other person or work. No part of this book may be reproduced in any form without the permission of the author. The views expressed in this book are not necessarily those of the publisher.

Unless otherwise indicated, Scripture quotations taken from the New American Standard Bible (NASB). Copyright © 1960, 1962, 1963, 1968, 1971, 1972, 1973, 1975, 1977, 1995 by The Lockman Foundation. Used by permission. All rights reserved.

Printed in the United States of America.

ISBN-13: 978-1-5456-7311-9

TABLE OF CONTENTS

PREMISE xv
PREFACE xix
ACKNOWLEDGMENTS xxiii
INTRODUCTION xxv

THE HARLOT

Part I–In the Old Testament 1
   Preamble 1
      Jeremiah 50:17-20
      Romans 13:1-7

   In the Time of the Exodus 6
      Exodus 34:10-17
      Leviticus 17:1-7
      Leviticus 20:4-6
      Deutercnomy 31:14-18

   In the Time of the Judges 11
      Judges 2:11-23
      Judges 8:22-35

   In the Time of the Kings 15
   Jezebel and Athaliah 17
      2 Kings 9:22
      2 Chronicles 21:1-5

   What the Prophets Said 23
      Isaiah 1:1-31

    Isaiah 23:13-17
    Jeremiah 2:20
    Jeremiah 3:6-10
    Ezekiel 6:1-14
    Ezekiel 16:1-63
    Ezekiel 23:1-49
    Hosea 4:1-19
    Micah 1:1-16
    Summary 43

Part II–In the Time of Our Lord 47
    "This Generation" and the End of the Age 47
        Matthew 23:1-39

    Jesus Speaks of Daniel 61
        Daniel 9:1-19

    Daniel Points to Jesus 67
        Daniel 9:24-27
        Daniel 12:1-4

    Daniel's Fourth Kingdom–First Century Rome 72

    Summary 78

Part III – In the Revelation 79
    Introduction 79
        Revelation 16:17-21
        Revelation 17:1-7
        Revelation 17:8-18
        Revelation 18:1-8
        Revelation 18:9-24
        Revelation 19:1-6

Part IV–The Early Witness – The Date of the Revelation . . . 113
    Irenaeus–Against Heresies 113

Book 5: Chapter 25 - The Fraud, Pride, and Tyrannical Kingdom of Antichrist, as Described by Daniel and Paul.
    Paragraphs 1, 2, & 4

Book 5: Chapter 28 - The Distinction to be made Between the Righteous and the Wicked. The Future Apostasy in the Time of Antichrist, and the End of the World
    Paragraph 2

Book 5: Chapter 30 - Although Certain as to the Number of the Name of Antichrist, yet we should come to no Rash Conclusions as to the Name Itself, because this Number is Capable of being Fitted to Many Names. Reasons for This Point being Reserved by the Holy Spirit. Antichrist's Reign and Death.
    Paragraphs 1-4

Eusebius–Ecclesiastical Histories 147
    Book 3: Chapter 18 – The Apostle John and the Apocalypse

    Book 3: Chapter 39 – The Writings of Papias
        Paragraphs 1-4

    Book 5: Chapter 8 – The Statements of Irenaeus in Regard to the Divine Scriptures
        Paragraphs 1-3

    Book 7: Chapter 25 – The Apocalypse of John
        Paragraphs 1-2

Article–Judaea in the Age of Nero .171

Part V–Persecution 179
    The Story of Stephen – We Meet Paul 179
        Acts 6:1-15

Acts 7:1-60
Acts 8:1-3

From Stephen to Nero.......................... 193
   From the Book of Acts

From Nero to Constantine........................ 212
   Eusebius–Ecclesiastical Histories
      Book 2 – Chapter 25–The Persecution under Nero (54-68) in which Paul and Peter were honored at Rome with Martyrdom in Behalf of Religion
      Book 3 – Chapter 5–The Last Siege of the Jews after Christ
      Book 3 – Chapter 20 -The Relatives of our Saviour
      Book 3 – Chapter 33–Trajan (98-117) Forbids the Christians to be Sought After
      Book 4 – Chapter 9–The Epistle of Adrian (Hadrian) 117-138, Decreeing That we Should Not be Punished Without a Trial
      Book 6 – Chapter 1–The Persecution Under Severus (193-211)
      Book 6 – Chapter 28–The Persecution Under Maximinus (235-238)
      Book 6 – Chapter 39–The Persecution Under Decius (249-251), and the Sufferings of Origen
      Book 6 – Chapter 41–The Martyrs in Alexandria
      Book 7 – Chapter 10–Valerian (253-260) and the Persecution Under Him
      Book 7 – Chapter 13–The Peace Under Gallienus (260-268)
      Book 8 – Chapter 2–The Destruction of the Churches
      Book 8 – Chapter 13–The Bishops of the Church That Evinced by Their Blood the Genuineness of the Religion Which They Preached

Table of Contents

    Book 9 – Chapter 9–The Victory of the God-Beloved Emperors

    Book 9 – Chapter 11–The Final Destruction of the Enemies of Religion

Appendices

Timeline of Events from the Birth of Christ to the End of the Persecution and Roman Empire 236

Table 1 – Kings & Prophets 238

Table 2 – The Captivity to the End of the Old Testament. . . . 242

Glossary of Names, Places. And Events. 245

Bibliography 269

End Notes 271

Scripture Verse Index 277

Subject Index 289

The Harlot of Revelation
and the
Great Tribulation

"Text without context is pretext"
–the father of Canadian theologian, D.A. Carson.

Premise

The premise of this book is to explain the theme whereby God chose a people for His own. He nurtured that people while entering into a covenant with them. He gave them the law, which spelled out His blessings for obedience and curses for disobedience. When the people rebelled, He sent His prophets to warn them and tell them to return to the law. When they killed the prophets, He came in judgment against them, while keeping a remnant to Himself. Then, when they rebelled a second time, He sent His Son. When they killed Him, too, God came in judgment against them again, once again keeping a remnant to Himself (this story is reminiscent of the Parable of the Landowner of Matthew 21:33-46). Those who claim Jesus Christ as Lord and Savior of their lives are that remnant. That is the Good News.

With that in mind, many have missed that message and misinterpreted what Jesus said in His Olivet Discourse. As a result of that, in perceiving that He was talking about things concerning the end of the world, they have accepted a false narrative about Revelation, prophecy, and eschatology.

I have come to appreciate that in order to understand people of differing languages, there must be (and there are) laws and rules of language. Taking all of that into consideration, it is my conclusion that much of that logic and structure is very much misplaced when it comes to "things of the end." After all, the overall message of the Bible itself is salvation, and it all points to Christ. Since it was God who gave us those laws and rules, He did not place them aside in the area of prophecy as that would be confusing to us.

This author has also come to the conclusion that much of what has been presented by some of the writers cited here has been largely ignored because those writers make their point and move on without contrasting their ideas with opposing views and exposing the weakness of those opposing views. Although it is not my intent to disparage anyone personally, the futurist view must be emphatically refuted.

In light of that, the fact that the Scriptures state that the great persecution has already occurred (Acts 8:1) has been overlooked in favor of a future Great Tribulation. Also, the harlot of Revelation chapters 16-19 has been looked upon as some mystical figure or city, rather than understanding the facts as they are presented in the Scriptures and applying man's own rules and laws of language and hermeneutical principles in interpreting those facts, ultimately coming to the conclusion that the harlot is an image of a continuing wayward people behaving in a manner which is consistent with the fathers of the Old Testament, and in fact were the sons of those very fathers.

All of that would depend, of course, on the Revelation being accepted as a vision seen and a document written before the destruction of Jerusalem and the Temple in 70AD, which is the preterist view. There have been many books and articles (some referenced here) written throughout the years that have focused on various aspects of the preterist view of eschatology. There have not, however, been any which have combined those various thoughts into a coherent treatise.

What is presented in this book is an attempt to present a coherent approach to the entirety of Scripture as it relates to eschatology. It is the desire of the author that this book will be used as a reference tool. It is also the desire of this author that future writers will improve upon the suggestions here and present their own in such a way that will show that God's plan is evident from Genesis to Revelation and it is not necessary to interpret every aspect of every prophecy. Some will remain unsolved until we meet the Lord in Heaven.

Pre or post 70AD is a binary choice. It either was or wasn't. What the reader believes in that regard makes all the difference in the world. By generally believing that the Revelation was received in the 90's, man has constructed a monstrosity of a ziggurat and has actually complicated his own life because he feels compelled to interpret the prophecies in a way that is centered on the here and now. The yearning for relevance in prophecy has prevented man from accepting the Scriptures at face value.

That is the theme of this story, His story, History. The question is, how is it relevant to today? Is it relevant to today? And if so, how would it be relevant to today? Will God judge us again? Why must man demand to have all the answers? There are some things we don't know and should leave to God. And some of those things are *all* the answers to Revelation. After 2,000 years, we still don't know. We will know when we get to Heaven.

Preface

I want to tell the world how and why I wrote this book, but I want to say first, here and now, that I hold no Master of Divinity or Doctor of Theology degree; nor any other college degree for that matter. What I can claim is a high school equivalency diploma, a couple or three years at Westchester Community College, one semester at Covenant Theological Seminary, and two years auditing Koine Greek at Knox Theological Seminary.

My boyhood dream was to become a Major League baseball player or a meteorologist, which is why, at thirty or so years of age, I took the hard courses like math through Calculus III; science courses in Astronomy, Chemistry, Geology, Oceanography, and Physics; and a correspondence course through Penn State in introductory Meteorology. I also worked in various trades, becoming a machine operator in the printing industry; as well, I worked in construction. Later I moved into Real Estate and mortgages where I learned sales technique. I believe God gave me a natural curiosity as to how and why things work, the motivation to become a good learner, and He prepared me and used all of that to do His will in writing this book.

I met the Lord in 1985 and I have been a student of the Bible ever since, beginning with a King James version. It spoke right to me; it was so vivid and contemporary, and I gobbled it up. I immediately became aware of a controversy about which version to read, so one of the first books that I bought, besides a Bible, was a book called, "So Many Versions." I was also introduced to a small church of the Christian and Missionary Alliance, where I grew as a Christian (see Acknowledgements) and remained there for three years or so.

My good friend Gail, and sister in the Lord, started hosting a Bible study which was on 1st Thessalonians, and I (naturally) wound up with Chapter 4, which many refer to as the chapter about the Rapture. I have been, from that moment on, pretty much consumed with the subject of eschatology, prophecy, Revelation, or anything related to "the end times." As time wore on, I started to see certain patterns or themes develop. There was something that God was saying, but it wasn't what everybody else was talking about, regarding things of the end.

I relocated to sunny, hot, and humid Florida in 1988 with my two children: Mark, who was six, and Kelly, four. Four years later, we again relocated, this time to St. Louis, where we remained for six months. During that time, I had bought a new Bible, a Master Study Bible (NASB), which I still have and use diligently, though it is literally falling apart. I also, as a result of being a single parent, spent a lot of time at home – and did I study! Finally, I moved back to Florida, with the children going back to their mom.

I cannot tell you when I actually started writing this book, but I can tell you that inside the back cover of my Bible are written these words: "Goals for 1993: 1. get my spiritual life in order; 2. get involved in CRPC (Coral Ridge Presbyterian Church); 3. take Greek at Knox; 4. *return to writing book*; 5. find a girlfriend (wife); and 6. become financially stable." Though I wouldn't actually take Greek at Knox Theological Seminary until 2006, my book was already in some stage of being written by 1993.

I had the honor of leading a Bible study on 1st & 2nd Kings during 2006 – 2008. It was an eye-opening experience as I began to see a certain pattern emerge–nearly every king was an idolater, and so were the people. I remembered that the first two commandments were about idolatry,[i] and I saw that the practice of idolatry was referred to as harlotry. I also saw that Revelation had something to say about "the harlot." That eventually narrowed my focus and the nugget of "The Harlot" was born.

I recall an online debate I had about who the harlot was with somebody on a blog about eschatology in 2007 or 2008. This guy pretty much blew me away because he was so proficient on the keyboard–I peck with my forefingers. He would respond with massive replies and he would just go off and was way out there. There was nothing believable in what he said, and I would feel helpless because it would take me so long to respond to him, and only on a point or two before he would hit me with another barrage.

At the end of one such debate about the prophet Daniel, he closed with – *there!* As though he had just laid it all out. "Wow," was all I could say to myself. This guy seemed to have it all figured out, and while there were a number of people who sympathized with my idea, even though it was still being formulated in my mind, I was speechless and didn't bother to respond in the end. That is what spurred me to go with The Harlot as an entity of its own instead of as a chapter in a larger book.

Acknowledgments

I want to thank, first and foremost, my wonderful wife Renee, who has spent many long hours listening to me go on about my thoughts about things of the harlot, eschatology, prophecy, Revelation or what have you. Lord bless her.

There are so many other people I want to thank, and for so many reasons. God is so good, and I thank the Lord for putting so many God-loving people in my life at so crucial a time. Special thanks to my first wife Sue, for allowing me to "escape" from my home city, raise a family, and start a new life. It was during that time that I first felt the Lord tugging at me. Thank you both for allowing me to beget two wonderful children, Mark and Kelly, and adopt a third, April.

Thank you, Pastor Charlie Harrah, my first pastor, who baptized me in the Hudson River in Ossining, New York in 1985. You are the one who introduced me to the idea of the early-date for Revelation and recommended David Chilton's, *The Days of Vengeance, An Exposition of the Book of Revelation,* Dominion Press, Ft. Worth, Tx. (1987). You were also instrumental in my spiritual growth by your leading in the Bible studies of the Gospel of John, the book of Acts, and Romans. Nothing could have prepared me more for this book than those spiritual, historical, and doctrinal books, respectively. Thank you again.

To me–that book, along with: Kenneth Gentry's, *Before Jerusalem Fell, Dating the Book of Revelation* (this was his doctoral dissertation at Whitefield Theological Seminary), Dominion

Press, Ft. Worth, Tx. (1989); J. Stuart Russel's, *The Parousia, A Study of the New Testament Doctrine of Our Lord's Second* Coming; Baker Book House; Grand Rapids, Mi. (1887); and Milton Terry's, *Biblical Hermeneutics, A Treatise on the Interpretation of the Old and New Testaments;* Zondervan Publishing House; Grand Rapids, Mi. (1883); and of course, my Master Study Bible (NASB); Holman Bible Publishers; Nashville, Tn. (1981)–all formed the kernel of my learning about eschatology. There are, of course, many other books which I have read on this subject.

Thank you, Ted Rivera and Gary Valine, elders; Tom and Gail Davis, deacons; and special thanks to Michelle Bowsher. Michelle – what a sweet girl she was; she brought me to Grace Alliance, my first church, and she was my rock when I was a baby Christian. Art Bergquist and Vinnie Cacciola, both of whom I became good friends with, along with the others mentioned and many others besides, were all instrumental in my early growth as a Christian.

Thank you also, Tim Bench, who compiled a collection of writings about Nero and Christianity, titled *False Doctrines,* dated 02/19/2015, some of those writings which are included in this book, have helped me immensely. There are many other people who did so much research on the subject of eschatology and compiled so many articles and books which I have read but no longer possess or recall titles and authors – thank you all.

Finally, after relocating to Florida, my good friends Alan and Alicia Rice opened up their home for a couple of years and hosted a Bible study, along with Ken and Angela Berger, and, of course, my lovely wife, Renee, where I had the honor to lead and we embarked on (again) the book of Acts and then 1st and 2^{n} Kings, all of which contributed immensely in my preparation for this book. Special thanks to you all.

Introduction

So, who is the harlot of Revelation?

She is identified in the text as Babylon the Great (Revelation 17:5). But, contrary to what many say, and despite the text stating that the harlot *is* Babylon, it is not–the language is metaphor (see Glossary). Ancient Babylon's claim to fame is that she was used as a tool of God to come in judgment against Judah; just as the Assyrians had been used by God when they captured Israel (Samaria), ending the days of the Divided Kingdom. Rome, too, was used as a tool of God when Titus destroyed the Temple and the city of Jerusalem, overrunning all of Judea in 70AD.

God had told His people, through His prophets, that He was going to bring a strange people against them, to burn Jerusalem and destroy the Temple–and He did so. Babylon, under Nebuchadnezzar in 586BC, destroyed the Temple, burned Jerusalem, and forced the people of Jerusalem and Judah into captivity in Babylon where they remained for seventy years. God also stated that He would judge Babylon, which He eventually did. This does not qualify ancient Babylon as the harlot.

The suggestion of whether or not Babylon is the harlot is not even valid because it does not provide any solutions to the myriad questions about eschatology; it only provokes more. It is part of a futurist view which is, incorrectly and unfortunately, the prevailing view. The futurist view does not even make possible answers to any of the many questions that it provokes because, quite simply, according to that view, those things haven't happened yet.

The futurist view, in creating so many more questions, only provides the opportunity to pervert and manipulate the truth. Under that guise, the questions *could* be, "Is the text talking about ancient Babylon? A future Babylon? Metaphoric Babylon? The Papacy? A resurgent Rome?" etc., etc. That is what happens with the futurist view–no answers; only more questions.

The futurist view has caused an incorrect interpretation of eschatology, which *must,* in some way, hinder the true understanding of the rest of the Scriptures in general. How could it not? Prophecy, which includes Revelation, doesn't even make up ¼ of 1% (.25%, or 0.0025) of all of the written Word, yet it probably has as sizable a collection of books in Christian book stores as any other genre. Revelation makes up ~8.5% of the New Testament (taking the number of chapters of Revelation and dividing by the total number of chapters of the N.T.). The subject of the harlot, the woman, the beast, Babylon the Great, using the number of verses, makes up ~13.3% of Revelation. Everybody has an opinion about eschatology, even non-Christians, such as some other religions and cults, and it all usually has some sort of futurist bent to it.

There have been some incredibly great and wonderful books written about Scripture, and the number of those are legion, written with much depth and knowledge and tender loving. But, somehow, eschatology is not one of those topics in which the writings are considered great and wonderful. Opinions are way out there. In fact, some have suggested that God actually puts words about the end times in the middle of passages which are speaking about something completely different, such as in Isaiah 13. He does not.

While searching the Scriptures and researching other books for this book, it became clear that even some of the earliest church historians were confused about Revelation (we will discuss that in Part IV). The entire Irenaeus argument (he was one of the earliest,

INTRODUCTION

if not *the* earliest of the Christian church fathers often cited and quoted when doing any research about Revelation) was about the *identity* of the Antichrist. That is what he was writing about. That is the context in which a statement he made about John was misconstrued into being a statement about the apocalypse itself, which shifted the emphasis to the *date* the Revelation was seen, not the number of the beast. That shift created the futurist view.

The Scriptures do not talk about *the* Antichrist. Nevertheless, those early church historians that read the Revelation (especially those who quote Irenaeus as their source–and who doesn't?) assumed "the Antichrist" was coming. The Scriptures say no such thing. In fact, they talk of just who or what antichrist is, and it is not what the futurist view has put forward. Nowhere is it about *the* Antichrist; it is about a spirit of antichrist, or of many antichrists. That is a big difference.

So, why would the early historians be confused? Just because they lived back in the day doesn't mean that they knew everything about everything, let alone something as difficult as the Revelation, eschatology, or prophecy. Was the Antichrist the beast? There are many who think so. If so, which beast? The beast of the sea? Or the beast of the land? Or is he, or it, *an* Antichrist, a man, so horrendous that he is "the recapitulation of the apostasy?"

Why was the harlot riding on a beast – and which beast? Is the Antichrist the abomination of desolation? Errors of interpretation begin to compound over time. There are too many questions. God's word is not that confusing. It has all become a house of cards – a ziggurat.

There have also been mistranslations and re-definitions, as we will see, of certain words, all in order to fit the futurist view. These are the types of things that blur lines and mix-up opinions, and that is what has prevented us from understanding eschatology. Those are not sound principles of interpretation. That is not sound Biblical hermeneutics. (See Acknowledgements, for the 19th-century masterpiece, by Milton Terry, *Biblical Hermeneutics*). A person once asked me when discussing such things, and the subject of hermeneutics was brought up, "Whose hermeneutics?" A wise adage: "the best answer is most times the simplest," also known as Occam's Razor.[1]

It was God who gave us the Revelation. It was given by Him *to* Jesus Christ and it was *about* Jesus, who then sent and communicated it by His angel, *to* John (Revelation 1:1). The angel says, "Therefore, **write** the things which you have seen, and the things which are, and the things which will take place after these things (1:19)." John was told, ten times, to write–and he wrote (1:11,19; 2:8,12,18; 3:7,14; 14:13; 19:9 and 21:5). And what he wrote was the last book of the Bible–the Revelation of Jesus Christ. Thirteen percent of the Revelation is about the harlot. That is what we will be discussing. If you get that concept, you're on the way to understanding Revelation.

The voice John heard and the person he saw in Revelation 1:9-20 was none other than the risen Lord Jesus Christ. John, ordered to *come up here*, was immediately in the spirit and *up there* (4:1-2). Some actually believe that those verses are the rapture – incredible!

It was the Lord Jesus who broke the seals of the book (6:1,3,5,7,9,12, and 8:1); from which the trumpets came (8:1-2), and from whence they sounded (8:7,8,10,12; 9:1,13, and 11:15); and it was Jesus who spoke in 22:16 and said that He had sent His angel to testify of these things for the churches (which are the seven churches we see in chapters two and three). It is the Revelation of Jesus Christ – it all points to Christ.

John said, "I saw…" thirty-eight times; "I heard…" twenty-six times; and "I looked…" eleven times; and he wrote those things down; he wrote as he saw, heard, and looked. The vision that he saw

---

[1] The principle (attributed to William of Occam) that in explaining a thing, no more assumptions should be made than are necessary–Wikipedia

and the things he heard were God's plan of redemption, played out from different aspects, again and again. It is the same story that we learn from the rest of the Scriptures. The entire book of Revelation is God's plan of redemption, repeated in different ways. The fact that there are ecstatic scenes and apocalyptic language in no way changes the fact that the entire revelation is *of*, and *about*, Jesus Christ. That is why we see Jesus throughout. "The Revelation of Jesus Christ..." is what the text says (1:1). It is not about the end of the world.

The core of the futurist view is not even credible on its face because it implies that nobody really knows what will happen because it hasn't happened yet. Under that premise, how can a person establish a theology of the end which is consistent with the rest of Scripture when it is based on supposition? What makes it even more unbelievable is that the futurist view implies that those who believe that particular view can rightly interpret all, or even some, of the difficult language in Revelation. Their record on that is horrible. The futurist view has created a platform whereby books of fiction are written as sound Biblical theology.

In reality, what has happened is that man has been duped and has usurped God, and as a result, the church has grown cold and weak. Far too many believe that we are living in the end times. In other words, this is it, it's all about us, look at us! Look at me! And blah, blah, blah. Many are waiting, hoping, and praying for Jesus to come back and rescue them from this mean and nasty world, to end it all in bliss. Don't the Scriptures teach that it *will* be bliss for believers anyway when they die? We have eternal life in Christ.

Why must Jesus come back? For those who have died and gone to heaven, have they missed out, or will they miss out, on something better? Will we be in a better place once Jesus does come back? Better than heaven? Absurd! That is futurism. Eschatology has become a white flag of surrender and a call to Jesus to "save us" and "rescue us." It is not an eschatology of victory.[2]

A book can be either fiction or non-fiction. In the futurist view, what the Scriptures say about things of the end has been abused. They have been taken out of context, based on flawed thinking, then replicated and perpetuated, wittingly and unwittingly. And, since it is supposedly all in the future, it is really unknown. So, from that point onward, it is no longer reality; it is all conjecture or opinion – fantasy. How then, can it be anything but fiction?

Think about this – if something as monumental as the supposed end of the world (the end times), the Battle of Armageddon, Christ returning to earth (the Second Coming), ruling from a newly-constructed Temple in Jerusalem (sacrifices?), the Great Tribulation, the great persecution, the time of distress, the Rapture (pre, mid, or post tribulation?), beasts from the earth and sea, the Antichrist, the abomination of desolation – if all that is couched in such symbolic, allegoric, metaphoric, apocalyptic language, driving well-intentioned people to such wild scenarios, how can anybody possibly understand what the text really means and what is expected of us?

Fortunately, there is another explanation – there must be. God is not a God of confusion, but of peace. The text is there to be understood. We will show who the harlot is, who the beast is, that the Great Tribulation has already occurred, the Great Commission has been fulfilled and that the new Jerusalem, which comes down from heaven, actually came down from heaven at the resurrection – which is the defining point of history.

---

[2] For an excellent book by that name: *An Eschatology of Victory*, J. Marcellus Kik; Presbyterian and Reformed Publishing Co.; Phillipsburg, N.J. (1971).

The Harlot

PART I – IN THE OLD TESTAMENT

PREAMBLE

The story of Babylon the Great, the mother of all harlots, is not about ancient Babylon. It is about Jerusalem, and only Jerusalem, which was the capital of Judah (later Judea), and more importantly, it is where the Temple was built. It was the center of God's people. It is *the* story. The reader will see – it was always about Jerusalem, the city God chose to lead His people to.

There is coherence to God's story. Futurist views fall apart. They leave us to our own devices, and hence, with no hope. If Babylon is the harlot, or Rome, or the papacy, or whomever or whatever is the harlot (see all the differences of opinion), then why do we see stories of Paul and the other disciples being confronted by Jews, not Chaldeans or Romans, in Acts? Why did Jesus constantly have to grapple with the religious leaders of Judea–the Jews? When He would be in the Temple teaching the people, it was the Jews of Judea, the religious leaders, who were fussing and arguing with Him. There is a Biblical explanation, of course, regarding the role Babylon was to fill, but it wasn't that of the harlot.

Jeremiah 50:17-20 [17]"**Israel** is a scattered flock; the lions have driven them away. **The first one who devoured him was the king of Assyria, and this last one who has broken his bones is Nebuchadnezzar king of Babylon.** [18]**Therefore thus says the Lord of hosts, the God of Israel: 'Behold, I am going to punish the king of Babylon and his land, just as I punished the king of Assyria.** [19]**And I will bring Israel back to his pasture** and he will graze on Carmel and Bashan, and his desire will be satisfied in the hill country of Ephraim and Gilead. [20]In those days and at that time,' declares the Lord, 'search will be made for the iniquity of Israel, but there will be none; and for the sins of Judah, but they will not be found; **for I will pardon those whom I leave as a remnant.'"**

Romans 13:1-7 [1]Every person is to be in subjection to the governing authorities. **For there is no authority except from God, and those which exist are established by God.** [2]Therefore whoever resists authority has opposed the ordinance of God, and they who have opposed will receive condemnation upon themselves, [3] For rulers are not a cause of fear for good behavior, but for evil. Do you want to have no fear of **authority**? Do what is good and you will have praise from the same; [4] **for it is a minister of God to you for good.** But if you do what is evil, be afraid; for it does not bear the sword for nothing; **for it is a minister of God, an avenger who brings wrath on the one who practices evil.** [5] Therefore it is necessary to be in subjection, not only because of wrath but also for conscience' sake.

> **⁶** For because of this you also pay taxes, **for rulers are servants of God**, devoting themselves to this very thing. **⁷** Render to all what is due them: tax to whom tax is due; custom to whom custom; fear to whom fear; honor to whom honor.

We begin here because we must establish that God is in control of the nations and therefore the above passages relate to each other. Understanding that whoever is reading this undoubtedly has a love for God and an interest in eschatology, there is an abstract way in which we read and comprehend God's Word, and as a result we miss much of what is there. As an example, three of the Gospels record that Jesus was scourged (Matthew 27:26; Mark 15:15; and John 19:1). However, as can be seen, they all give it just one verse. How quickly do we go right-on-by as we continue with the text? Flogging is not a simple matter or a blink-of-the-eye occurrence. Who would want to experience one?[ii] Check out the movie, *The Passion of the Christ,* and read the end-note to see for yourself.

Here is what we do see, according to these two passages: Assyria devoured Israel; Babylon broke the bones of Judah; God punished Assyria; God will punish Babylon; God will bring the Israelites back; the iniquity of Israel will not be found; God will pardon those He will leave as a remnant; there is no authority except *from* God; those authorities which exist are established *by* God; it is a minister *of* God; and rulers are *servants* of God. God was and is in control; it's up to us to understand what it all means.

The facts that Israel and Judah had been made desolate, and that God had judged Assyria are given in the text. The rest had not yet occurred. It is incorrect to say that they *still* have not occurred. The only way to determine that is through context. There are also implied facts, namely those words which are highlighted in **bold** in the Romans passage, which complement what Jeremiah said. What this shows is that the current-events, which may look like just that – current events – are, in reality, all happening within the will of God. We may see it in hindsight, but it could take more than a hundred years to see it. In the meantime, we can only turn our backs on God so much before He turns His face from us.

Jeremiah prophesied to Judah after Assyria had taken Israel, so he was prophesying before and during the time when Babylon came against Judah, as were the prophets Ezekiel and Daniel (see Table of Kings and Prophets). What is striking is that God, even after He had given His people the Law, still had to send prophets. The people just didn't obey. The people of Judah had seen so much happen around themselves, including their brothers in Israel being marauded by a strange people, but even with their rich history, the law, and the prophets, they still did not avoid doing that which would get them judged; namely, they played the harlot by serving other gods.

The timeline for this is the one hundred thirty-six year period between the capture of God's people by Assyria and Babylon, from 722 to 586BC. Think about this – God could have uttered those words through Jeremiah at any time during that span (we don't know exactly when He did it). People of five or six generations would have been around in various stages of their lives during that time. That would be like today, 2019, looking back to the 1880s. We are talking about children, grandchildren and great-grandchildren; parents, grandparents, great-grandparents and greater. Time had passed and the people became complacent and careless.

We have no idea, no clue really, about living under the conditions as they were then. We also have friendly borders. If Canada and Mexico were to ever get taken over by malignant governments, who then set their sights on America, and we lived under those conditions for generation after generation, we would have a different outlook on life. But the Israelites, nevertheless, refused to heed the warning signs, and they refused to obey God.

Preamble

Babylon may have been the great world power at that time but her primary purpose, as far as the Scriptures are concerned, was to be used as a tool of God to punish His unruly people. God then punished the punisher for inflicting His punishment; then He pardoned the accused's sin, establishing His remnant.

How could ancient Babylon be Babylon the Great–the harlot of Revelation–when the story of the harlot of Revelation is a New Testament story? While some will argue that it isn't a New Testament story at all, but a future story, and that somehow we're in it, that is hogwash! Ignition; lift off. Look at it another way, for ancient Babylon to actually be the harlot, it would mean that God was using the harlot to mete out punishment against Judah, the true harlot. In other words, the harlot punished the harlot–nonsense.

That's what happens when man steps in and plays God. The entire story becomes a jumbled mess because of man's insistence on ignoring the truth as laid out in God's word, replacing it with his own interpretation. God neither used ancient Babylon, nor a metaphoric Babylon, to judge the harlot; He used Rome – the fourth kingdom of King Nebuchadnezzar's dream (Daniel 2:40-45); it was also the fourth kingdom of Daniel's dream and visions (7:23-27); as well as the latter period of the goat in Daniel's subsequent dream (8:23-25); and Gabriel's revelation to Daniel (9:24-27); also the end of Daniel's prophecy (12:1-3). These all lead to the same point in history – the time of Messiah and the apostolic age.

Israel had a long history of doing what God told them not to do. They continually interacted and intermarried with the peoples living in all the lands, who then led them to worship and serve their gods. God warned His people about that and told them not to do it, but they did it anyway. The books of Kings and Chronicles show how nearly every king (save for Hezekiah) would not tear down the "high places," and would openly choose to worship at them, which would ultimately be their downfall.

In the Time of the Exodus

Exodus 34:10-17 [10] **Then God said, "Behold, I am going to make a covenant.** Before all your people I will perform miracles, which have not been produced in all the earth nor among any of the nations; and all the people among whom you live will see the working of the Lord, for it is a fearful thing that I am going to perform with you. [11] "Be sure to observe what I am commanding you this day: behold, I am going to drive out the Amorite before you, and the Canaanite, the Hittite, the Perizzite, the Hivite and the Jebusite. [12] **Watch yourself that you make no covenant with the inhabitants of the land** into which you are going, or **it will become a snare in your midst.** [13] But rather, you are to **tear down their altars** and **smash their sacred pillars** and **cut down their Asherim** [14] **—for you shall not worship any other god,** for the Lord, whose name is Jealous, is a jealous God— [15] **otherwise you might make a covenant with the inhabitants of the land and** *they would play the harlot* with their gods and sacrifice to their gods, and someone might invite you to eat of his sacrifice, [16] and you might take some of his daughters for your sons, and *his daughters might play the harlot* with their gods and *cause your sons also to play*

***the harlot* with their gods.¹⁷ You shall make for yourself no molten gods."**

This is a key passage. God was about to lead the Israelites in their conquest of the Promised Land. God said two things about covenants: a) that *He* was going to make a covenant with *them*, and b) for *them* not to enter into any covenants with the peoples of the land. A covenant is not an equitable agreement. It is as a conqueror over the conquered; or, as a landlord to its tenant; i.e., as one in authority over the one under authority. A covenant discloses what the covenant maker will do for the subject; and what the subject must do to satisfy its responsibility. God made a covenant as the one in authority and the Israelites were the subjects.

God also told the people not to make any covenants with the inhabitants of the land. Why? Because *it will become a snare in your midst* (34:12). That should resonate; a snare is something that slows one down or stops one's progress – unexpectedly, it usually comes as a surprise. No matter how well one prepares, he cannot foresee every possibility. Caught in a snare, prey becomes served up to the predator. The people were commanded not to make a covenant with the other people, nor to worship any other god – not to play the harlot – or it would become a snare.

Moses had led the Israelites out of bondage from Egypt, and they were now in Sinai, which was the "wilderness," where they would wander for forty years (Exodus 16:35; Numbers 32:6-13). God made it clear that He did not want the Israelites to worship other gods. The first two of the Ten Commandments are about exactly that (Exodus 20:1-6; Deuteronomy 5:6-10). The tablets containing the commandments were destroyed and had to be replaced for the very reason that those first two commandments stated – the people had made a golden calf – they were already playing the harlot (Exodus 32:1-20; 34:1-28).

Leviticus 17:1-7 ¹Then the LORD spoke to Moses, saying, ²"Speak to Aaron and to his sons and to all the sons of Israel and say to them, "This is what the LORD has commanded, saying, ³Any man from the house of Israel who slaughters an ox or a lamb or a goat in the camp, or who slaughters it outside the camp, ⁴and has not brought it to the doorway of the tent of meeting to present *it* as an offering to the LORD before the tabernacle of the LORD, blood-guiltiness is to be reckoned to that man. He has shed blood and that man shall be cut off from among his people. ⁵**The reason is so that the sons of Israel may bring their sacrifices which they were sacrificing in the open field**, that they may bring them in to the LORD, at the doorway of the tent of meeting to the priest, and sacrifice them as sacrifices of peace offerings to the LORD. ⁶The priest shall sprinkle the blood on the altar of the LORD at the doorway of the tent of meeting, and offer up the fat in smoke as a soothing aroma to the LORD. ⁷**They shall no longer sacrifice their sacrifices to the goat demons with which they play the harlot**. This shall be a permanent statute to them throughout their generations.""

As Moses was leading the people, and as they hadn't yet settled the Promised Land and therefore the Temple had not yet been constructed, God instructed them to build a "portable" Temple–the tabernacle (Exodus 36-40), in its stead. The people had been making sacrifices to false gods in the open field–to the goat-demons–and God wanted them to bring them instead into the tent of meeting–to the priest–to make a peace offering to the Lord. The people were continuing to play the harlot.

Leviticus 20:4-6 ⁴ If the people of the land, however, should ever disregard that man when he gives any of his offspring to Molech, so as not to put him to death, ⁵ then I Myself will set My face against that man and against his family, and I will cut off from among their people both him and all those who **play the harlot** after him, by **playing the harlot after Molech**.⁶ 'As for the person who turns to mediums and to spiritists, **to play the harlot after them**, I will also set My face against that person and will cut him off from among his people.

Molech was a most despicable god,[iii] and spiritism was what would lead to the downfall of King Saul, the Israelites' first king (1 Samuel 28:3-19).

Deuteronomy 31:14-18 ¹⁴ Then the LORD said to Moses, "Behold, the time for you to die is near; call Joshua, and present yourselves at the tent of meeting, that I may commission him." So, Moses and Joshua went and presented themselves at the tent of meeting. ¹⁵ **The LORD appeared in the tent in a pillar of cloud, and the pillar of cloud stood at the doorway of the tent**. ¹⁶ The LORD said to Moses, "Behold, you are about to lie down with your fathers; **and this people will arise and play the harlot with the strange gods of the land,** into the midst of which they are going, and will forsake Me and break My covenant which I have made with them. ¹⁷ Then My anger will be kindled against them in that day, **and I will forsake them and hide My face from them, and they will be consumed, and**

> **many evils and troubles will come upon them**; so that they will say in that day, 'Is it not because our God is not among us that these evils have come upon us?' [18] But **I will surely hide My face in that day** because of all the evil which they will do, **for they will turn to other gods.**

Moses, who had brought the people from Egypt to where they were now, ready to go into the midst of the peoples of the land, was about to die, "to lie down with his fathers," and Joshua was to lead them in. But God said that the people *will* arise and play the harlot with strange gods; *and that He would hide His face from them.*

There is another aspect of this passage which pertains to our subject of eschatology. We will see that God's presence and His judgments are always depicted by clouds, smoke, thunder, lightning, earthquakes, or fire, even trumpets. When God appeared in the mountain, there were all those events (Exodus 19:16-19). As we see here, God appeared in a pillar of cloud. God had appeared in the cloud by day and a pillar of fire by night to lead the people through the wilderness (Exodus 13:21-22; 14:19-20).

When you read those passages, *it is not the physical universe going through convulsions and exploding.* If necessary, put to the side those things which are hardest to understand, then look for and define those things which you are more familiar with. A broader picture will appear, giving the bounds for interpretation and allowing God's plan to be seen.

In the Time of the Judges

Judges 2:11-23 [11] **Then the sons of Israel did evil in the sight of the Lord and served the Baals,** [12] **and they forsook the Lord**, the God of their fathers, who had brought them out of the land of Egypt, **and followed other gods from among the gods of the peoples who were around them, and bowed themselves down to them**; thus, they provoked the Lord to anger. [13] **So they forsook the Lord and served Baal and the Ashtaroth.** [14] The anger of the Lord burned against Israel, **and He gave them into the hands of plunderers who plundered them; and He sold them into the hands of their enemies around them so that they could no longer stand before their enemies.** [15] Wherever they went, the hand of the Lord was against them for evil, as the Lord had spoken and as the Lord had sworn to them, so that they were severely distressed. [16] **Then the Lord raised up judges who delivered them from the hands of those who plundered them.** [17] Yet they did not listen to their judges, for *they played the harlot* after other gods and bowed themselves down to them. They turned aside quickly from the way in which their fathers had walked in obeying the commandments of the Lord; they did not do as their fathers. [18] When the

Lord raised up judges for them, the Lord was with the judge and delivered them from the hand of their enemies all the days of the judge; for the Lord was moved to pity by their groaning because of those who oppressed and afflicted them. **¹⁹ But it came about when the judge died, that they would turn back and act more corruptly than their fathers, in following other gods to serve them and bow down to them; they did not abandon their practices or their stubborn ways.** ²⁰ So the anger of the Lord burned against Israel, **and He said, "Because this nation has transgressed My covenant which I commanded their fathers and has not listened to My voice, ²¹ I also will no longer drive out before them any of the nations which Joshua left when he died,** ²² in order to test Israel by them, whether they will keep the way of the Lord to walk in it as their fathers did, or not." **²³ So the Lord allowed those nations to remain, not driving them out quickly; and He did not give them into the hand of Joshua.**

So, the people were now in the land that they were to occupy, but they were serving the Baals; and, most importantly, they forsook God, who then *gave them into the hands of their plunderers and enemies*. Then, in God's goodness and graciousness, He raised up Judges who delivered them from the hands of their enemies. Yet, they did not listen to their judges, and they again played the harlot with other gods, transgressing the Lord's covenant, *so the Lord allowed the other nations to remain*.

Judges 8:22-35 ²² Then the men of Israel said to Gideon, "Rule over us, both you and your son, also your son's son, for you have delivered us from the hand of Midian." ²³ But Gideon said to them, "I will not rule over you, nor shall my son rule over you; the LORD shall rule over you." ²⁴ Yet Gideon said to them, "I would request of you, that each of you give me an earring from his spoil." (**For they had gold earrings because they were Ishmaelites**.) ²⁵ They said, "We surely give them." So, they spread out a garment, and every one of them threw an earring there from his spoil. ²⁶ The weight of the gold earrings that he requested was 1,700 shekels of gold, besides the crescent ornaments and the pendants and the purple robes which were on the kings of Midian, and besides the neck bands that were on their camels' necks. ²⁷ **Gideon made it into an ephod and placed it in his city, Ophrah, and all Israel played the harlot with it there, so that it became a snare to Gideon and his household.** ²⁸ So Midian was subdued before the sons of Israel, and they did not lift up their heads anymore. And the land was undisturbed for forty years in the days of Gideon. ²⁹ Then Jerubbaal the son of Joash went and lived in his own house. ³⁰ Now Gideon had seventy sons who were his direct descendants, for he had many wives. ³¹ His concubine who was in Shechem also bore him a son, and he named him Abimelech. ³² And Gideon the son of Joash died at a ripe old age and was buried in the tomb of his father Joash, in Ophrah of the Abiezrites. ³³ Then it came about, as soon as Gideon was dead, that **the sons of Israel again played the harlot with the**

> **Baals**, and made Baal-Berith their god. ³⁴ Thus **the sons of Israel did not remember the LORD their God**, who had delivered them from the hands of all their enemies on every side; ³⁵ **nor did they show kindness to the household of Jerubbaal (*that is*, Gideon) in accord with all the good that he had done to Israel.**

The people turned on Gideon, just as they turned on God; they didn't care, that was the snare (8:35). They did what was right in their own eyes. Gideon was a good judge, but he had flaws, as we all do as fallible human beings, sons of fallen Adam and Eve. Gideon collected an earring from all the Ishmaelites and fashioned it into an ephod, just as the Israelites had done when Moses was up on Mt. Sinai collecting the original tablets of the Ten Commandments, **and all Israel played the harlot with it** (8:24-27). When Gideon died, the people turned around and played the harlot again with the Baal's (8:33). Worshipping other gods was an ongoing problem with the Israelites.

In the Time of the Kings

The Bible books of Samuel, Kings, and Chronicles are the history of God's people while they were led by their kings. The books of Samuel are a transition from the people being led by Judges to being led by Kings. The books of Kings swing back and forth between the Kings of Israel to the Kings of Judah, until the plunder of Samaria (Israel) by the Assyrians in 722BC. (Samaria is a city and was the capital of the northern nation of Israel. There was a region in northern Judea called Samaria in the time of Christ).

The Chronicles focus on the history of the people of Judah during the time of the kings. The line of Jesus is through the tribe of Judah, through David, then the rest of the kings of Judah; Jesus is the *Lion of the Tribe of Judah*.[3] After 722BC there was left only Judah until the Babylonians came along one hundred thirty-six years later. The land would become known as Judea sometime after the return of the people from their seventy-year captivity in Babylon.

The people didn't want God to lead them; they rejected Him. They wanted to be led by a king "like all the other peoples" (1 Samuel 8:4-9; 19-22; and 10:17-19), so Saul became their first king (10:20-24). He was a miserable failure and he reigned about forty years, as did David, who followed, and Solomon, David's son. The kingdom was at its greatest under Solomon after David had subdued all of the enemies of Israel. Throughout all of this,

---

[3] See Jesus' genealogy in Matthew 1:1-17 and Revelation 5:5.

the people continued to worship strange gods, and God once again very succinctly stated all of the evil which would fall upon them if they continued to do as they were doing; and all of the good things He would do for them if they would only humble their hearts before Him (2 Chronicles 7:12-22). That brings us to the time of the divided kingdom – and to Jezebel.

Jezebel and Athaliah

The story of Jezebel begins in 1 Kings 18. She was a killer of the prophets of God (18:4,13). The prophet Elijah summoned from King Ahab all the people and the prophets of Baal and Asherah who ate at the table of Jezebel (18:19), the king's wife. Elijah would slay those prophets (18:40). When the king told his wife what happened, she threatened Elijah's life (19:1-2). He got scared and ran to Beersheba, in Judah (19:3). The word of the Lord came to him and told him to go to Mt. Horeb (Mt. Sinai). Once there, the Lord came to him and told him to go to Damascus and to anoint Jehu king over Israel, and Elisha, prophet in his place.

Just before the Lord told him to go, Elijah had been pleading his case as to why he had run away to there, and he said this crucial phrase, *"for the sons of Israel, have forsaken Your covenant, torn down Your altars* **and killed Your prophets** *with the sword"* (19:9-14).

Elijah had just run away from Jezebel, going from Samaria to Beersheba to Mt. Sinai (Horeb, where the Ten Commandments were given). This was at the southern tip of the Sinai Peninsula. He then went north to Damascus, where he was replaced by Elisha (19:19).

When next we see Jezebel, she was inquiring of her husband, King Ahab as to why he was so sullen. When he told her, she devised a scheme and defrauded Naboth, the owner of a vineyard which had been in his family and which he didn't want to sell. But king Ahab had made a proposal for it, for the king coveted it. The defrauding resulted in the murder of Naboth when he was falsely accused of cursing God and the king, and subsequently stoned to death (1 Kings 21).

In the meantime, Elisha had sent his servant to Jehu to anoint him king over Israel, and as the servant was doing so, he said to him, "Thus saith the Lord, the God of Israel, 'I have anointed you king over the people of the Lord, even over Israel. You shall strike the house of Ahab your master, *that I may avenge the blood of my servants the prophets*, and the blood of all the servants of the Lord, *at the hand of Jezebel*'" (2 Kings 9:1-7).

> **2 Kings 9:22** ²² When Joram saw Jehu, he said, "Is it peace, Jehu?" And he answered, "What peace, so long as **the harlotries of your mother Jezebel and her witchcrafts** are so many?"

Up till now, the primary sin of the people had been their worshipping other gods. But now we see that the killing of God's prophets is mentioned, and at the hands of Ahab and Jezebel. Worshipping false gods and the slaying of the prophets are related because the prophets were sent to tell the people to return to the law and to warn them that they were not to serve other gods.

Until the prophets, the given law was the primary guide of the people. Now, we see the prophets calling for the people to obey the law. The prophets were not even mentioned in the Scriptures until King Saul was seen prophesying with some in 1 Samuel 10:9-13. So, the story became, from that point forward, about the law and the prophets–they are the two witnesses which testify of God.

Jezebel was a killer of God's prophets, and that would bring God's judgment upon her. The last of Elisha's charges to Jehu was that the whole house of Ahab would perish and that the dogs would eat Jezebel and that none shall bury her (2 Kings 9:8-10). There appears a rather virulent distaste for the woman.

Joram, now king of Israel, and Ahaziah king of Judah came out to meet Jehu as he was on his way to Jezreel to kill Joram (9:14-16). When King Joram hailed him, Jehu answered as he did, above, stating Jezebel's harlotries and witchcraft (9:21-22), which included her killing of the prophets, in addition to all the other dastardly deeds she committed.

Meanwhile, when Jezebel heard that Jehu was in Jezreel, she painted her eyes and *adorned her head* (pay attention to the word 'adorned,' as we will see it play a part in our story) and looked out the window (9:30). Jehu hollered to throw her down, and some officers who were there did so, her blood spattering on the wall and on the horses. Jehu proceeded to trample her underfoot, then he went inside and ate and drank.

He ordered for her to be buried but there was nothing left of her except her skull, her feet, and the palms of her hands–how fitting. And he said, "This is the word of the Lord, which He spoke by His servant Elijah the Tishbite, saying, 'In the property of Jezreel the dogs shall eat the flesh of Jezebel; and the corpse of Jezebel will be as dung on the face of the field in the property of Jezreel, so they cannot say, "This is Jezebel" ' " (9:33-37). The property was Naboth's former land, which Jezebel had swindled.

Jezebel was now dead, but her evil seed lived on. Her daughter Athaliah became the wife of Jehoram, king of Judah (2 Kings 8:16-18,26; 2 Chronicles 21:5-6). The evil seed was now in position in an attempt to thwart God's plan of the coming of Messiah. Jezebel had already wreaked a lot of havoc, being that she was a killer of God's prophets, but this was a family straight from hell. Ahab, King of Israel – who did evil in the sight of the Lord, more than all who were before him – had married Jezebel, daughter of Ethbaal. Look at that name – Eth baal – as in Baal; and he (Ahab) went to serve Baal and he worshipped him (1 Kings 16:30-31). This was the trifecta of evil – Ahab, Jezebel, and Athaliah.

Athaliah's son, Ahaziah, took the throne of Judah after his father Jehoram (Athaliah's husband) died, and he reigned for only one year before he died. Athaliah took the throne and immediately killed the royal offspring. She died after six years and was succeeded by Ahaziah's son Joash, which was her grandson.

Joash had been hidden away for the six years that she reigned because of her order of the deaths of the royal offspring (2 Kings 11:1-3). Joash was one of the few kings who did right in the sight of the Lord; but he didn't take away the high places (which we will see repeatedly), and he burned incense there (2 Kings 12:1-3). Joash had a son named Amaziah, and he, too, ruled Judah and he, too, did right in the sight of the Lord, but he, too, did not take away the high places, and the people continued to sacrifice and burn incense there (2 Kings 14:1-4).

These last four kings of Judah, starting with the offspring of Athaliah and Jehoram i.e., Ahaziah, then Athaliah, Joash, and Amaziah – are nowhere to be found in the genealogy of Jesus Christ, as written in Matthew 1:8. It lists, beginning from Jehoshaphat…, Jehoram (or Joram, the alternate spelling and whom Athaliah married), then Uzziah. The kings: Ahaziah, Athaliah, Joash, and Amaziah, do not appear between Jehoram and Uzziah!

Look at what God had said in Exodus 20:4-6 and Deuteronomy 5:6-10, when He was giving the Ten Commandments. Commandment number two is, "You shall not make an idol. You shall not worship them or serve them, *for I, God, will visit the iniquity of the fathers on the children* **on the third and fourth generation of those who hate me**." Coincidence? Think about this – four generations are blotted out of Christ's lineage. Why? Jezebel, the reviled Jezebel, weaved Satan's diabolical plot which could have either succeeded in preventing or polluting the advent of Christ, or gained a lasting and abominable presence in His lineage. Her influence was blotted out by God though, and the passage of four generations was sufficient to thin out the gene pool and to erase her vile traits.

2 Chronicles 21:1-15 ¹Then Jehoshaphat slept with his fathers and was buried with his fathers in the city of David, and Jehoram his son became king in his place. ² He had brothers, the sons of Jehoshaphat: Azariah, Jehiel, Zechariah, Azaryahu, Michael and Shephatiah. All these were the sons of Jehoshaphat king of Israel. ³ Their father gave them many gifts of silver, gold and precious things, with fortified cities in Judah, but he gave the kingdom to Jehoram because he was the firstborn. ⁴ Now when Jehoram had taken over the kingdom of his father and made himself secure, he killed all his brothers with the sword, and some of the rulers of Israel also. ⁵ Jehoram was thirty-two years old when he became king, and he reigned eight years in Jerusalem. ⁶ He walked in the way of the kings of Israel, just as the house of Ahab did (**for Ahab's daughter was his wife**), and he did evil in the sight of the LORD. ⁷ **Yet the LORD was not willing to destroy the house of David because of the covenant which He had made with David, and since He had promised to give a lamp to him and his sons forever.** ⁸ In his days Edom revolted against the rule of Judah and set up a king over themselves. ⁹ Then Jehoram crossed over with his commanders and all his chariots with him. And he arose by night and struck down the Edomites who were surrounding him and the commanders of the chariots. ¹⁰ So Edom revolted against Judah to this day. Then Libnah revolted at the same time against his rule, because he had forsaken the LORD God of his fathers. ¹¹ **Moreover, he made high places in the mountains of Judah, and caused the inhabitants of Jerusalem to** *play the*

***harlot* and led Judah astray.** ¹² Then a letter came to him from Elijah the prophet saying, "Thus says the LORD God of your father David, 'Because you have not walked in the ways of Jehoshaphat your father and the ways of Asa king of Judah, ¹³ but have walked in the way of the kings of Israel, and have caused Judah and the inhabitants of Jerusalem to **play the harlot as the house of Ahab played the harlot,** and you have also killed your brothers, your own family, who were better than you, ¹⁴ behold, **the LORD is going to strike your people, your sons, your wives and all your possessions with a great calamity; ¹⁵ and you will suffer severe sickness, a disease of your bowels, until your bowels come out because of the sickness, day by day.'"**

Going back to Jehoshaphat, the father-in-law of Jezebel, and moving our attention away from her and Athaliah, we see that the people and their kings were infected with the sin of idolatry. Jehoshaphat was good and the Lord was with him (2 Chronicles 17:3-6) but his son and his son's son did evil in the sight of the Lord (2 Chronicles 21:4-7; 22:2-4). It wasn't until Joash and Amaziah that we saw kings who did right by God, but they, too, as we saw, had problems with the high places. And, more importantly, they were part of God's diluting and winnowing of the aforementioned evil gene pool. Finally, there was Uzziah, son of Amaziah, and he did right in the sight of the Lord (2 Chronicles 26:3-5), and his name *does* appear in Jesus' genealogy.

What the Prophets Said

Isaiah 1:1-31 ¹The vision of Isaiah the son of Amoz **concerning Judah and Jerusalem**, which he saw during the reigns of Uzziah, Jotham, Ahaz and Hezekiah, kings of Judah. ²Listen, O heavens, and hear, O earth; For the Lord speaks, "Sons I have reared and brought up, But, they have revolted against Me. ³"An ox knows its owner, And, a donkey its master's manger, But Israel does not know, My people do not understand." ⁴Alas, sinful nation, People weighed down with iniquity, Offspring of evildoers, Sons who act corruptly! They have abandoned the Lord. They have despised the Holy One of Israel. They have turned away from Him. ⁵Where will you be stricken again, as you continue in your rebellion? The whole head is sick and the whole heart is faint. **⁶ From the sole of the foot even to the head There is nothing sound in it, only bruises, welts and raw wounds, not pressed out or bandaged, nor softened with oil.** ⁷**Your land is desolate**. Your cities are burned with fire. Your fields—strangers are devouring them in your presence**; It is desolation, as overthrown by strangers.** ⁸The daughter of Zion is left like a shelter in a vineyard, like a watchman's hut in a cucumber field, like a besieged city. ⁹**Unless the Lord of hosts had**

The Harlot *of* Revelation

left us a few survivors, we would be like Sodom, we would be like Gomorrah. [10]Hear the word of the Lord, You rulers of Sodom; Give ear to the instruction of our God, You people of Gomorrah. [11]"What are your multiplied sacrifices to Me?" Says the Lord. "I have had enough of burnt offerings of rams and the fat of fed cattle; And I take no pleasure in the blood of bulls, lambs or goats. [12]"When you come to appear before Me, who requires of you this trampling of My courts? [13]"Bring your worthless offerings no longer, Incense is an abomination to Me. New moon and sabbath, the calling of assemblies— I cannot endure iniquity and the solemn assembly. [14]"I hate your new moon festivals and your appointed feasts. They have become a burden to Me; I am weary of bearing them. [15]"So when you spread out your hands in prayer, **I will hide My eyes from you**; Yes, even though you multiply prayers, **I will not listen**. Your hands are covered with blood. [16]Wash yourselves, make yourselves clean; Remove the evil of your deeds from My sight. Cease to do evil, [17]Learn to do good; Seek justice, Reprove the ruthless, Defend the orphan, Plead for the widow. [18]**"Come now, and let us reason together," Says the Lord, "Though your sins are as scarlet, they will be as white as snow; Though they are red like crimson, they will be like wool.** [19]'If you consent and obey, you will eat the best of the land; [20]"But if you refuse and rebel, you will be devoured by the sword." Truly, the mouth of the Lord has spoken. [21]How **the faithful city has become a harlot**, she who was full of justice! Righteousness once lodged in her, But now murderers. [22]Your silver has become dross, your drink diluted with water. ²³Your rulers are rebels and companions of thieves; Everyone loves a bribe and chases after rewards. They do not defend the orphan, nor does the widow's plea come before them. ²⁴Therefore the Lord God of hosts, The Mighty One of Israel, declares, 'Ah, I will be relieved of My adversaries and avenge Myself on My foes. ²⁵'I will also turn My hand against you and will smelt away your dross as with lye and will remove all your alloy. ²⁶**"Then I will restore your judges as at the first, and your counselors as at the beginning; After that you will be called the city of righteousness, A faithful city."** ²⁷ **Zion will be redeemed with justice and her repentant ones with righteousness.** ²⁸But transgressors and sinners will be crushed together, and those who forsake the Lord will come to an end. ²⁹ Surely you will be ashamed of the oaks which you have desired, and you will be embarrassed at the gardens which you have chosen. ³⁰ For you will be like an oak whose leaf fades away or as a garden that has no water. ³¹ The strong man will become tinder, His work also a spark. Thus, they shall both burn together and there will be none to quench them.

Isaiah is the earliest of the major prophets, prophesying to both Israel and Judah. He saw what had happened when Assyria overran Israel. Surely, the people of Judah would take heed after seeing that. Recall the analogy we made earlier about us, today, looking back to the 1880's. If we had the help of prophets, seeing what had happened then, would we take heed and not do what our forefathers had done? That was the predicament of the Jews–they all had been warned and knew what not to do.

The first chapter of Isaiah must be looked at in its entirety in order to see the complete message that God is trying to show us. He talks about Jerusalem, the city of righteousness, the faithful city – but a faithful city that became a harlot (1:21). He also discusses a number of other issues important in the understanding of eschatology. He states, from the beginning, who is being addressed, in this case, Judah and Jerusalem, and the time frame, in this case, during the reigns of Uzziah, Jotham, Ahaz, and Hezekiah, kings of Judah.

Oftentimes, the words of the prophets will take on apocalyptic overtones, and people will separate those verses from the rest of the text and apply their eschatological interpretations to them. It is here that great error is being done. One must always keep in mind who is speaking, who is being spoken to, when and where it is being spoken, and any other important tidbit of information given, in order to make a sound interpretation. It is uttered within the context of what he is speaking overall, so it cannot and should not be separated. If it doesn't click, move on; nobody will understand it all; at least not this side of heaven.

The Uzziah mentioned is the same as he who came immediately after the four blotted-out generations of Jesus' genealogy as per Matthew 1, so Isaiah was there immediately after, and probably during part of, the Jezebel debacle. Isaiah talks about desolation – *and he gives us the definition of the word and the context in which it is used*: your cities are burned with fire, strangers are devouring your fields in your presence, *it is as overthrown by strangers* (1:7). This is the context we use in this book, otherwise all understanding is lost.

Through it all, the Lord left a few survivors (1:9). "Cease to do evil; learn to do good," he said (1:16,17). "If you consent and obey, you will eat the best of the land; but if you refuse and rebel, you will be devoured by the sword" (1:19-20). That is the essence of the law – blessings for obedience and curses for disobedience. "I will restore your judges ... and your counselors ... you will be called the city of righteousness, a faithful city ... Zion and her repentant ones will be redeemed with justice and righteousness (1:26-27)." Zion is the city of David (2 Samuel 5:1-10), it is Jerusalem, and it is the harlot.

Isaiah was certainly prophesying in a historic era as he witnessed the destruction and desolation of Samaria (Israel) (2 Kings 17). With that as a backdrop, he continued to prophesy in Judah. The people were more obstinate than a donkey or an ox; they were corrupt and did not understand (Isaiah 1:2-4), abandoning the Lord. They had therefore been stricken and would continue to be stricken as they continued in their rebellion: the head is sick, the heart is faint, and there is nothing sound, from head to foot–bruises, welts, and raw wounds (1:6). Ouch!

Going back to one of our all-important words–the text says that their land is *desolate*. This is another term we will see frequently, and it is used in the same context as given above by Isaiah, as in *overthrown by strangers*. The word is consistently misinterpreted as though it means something supernatural, as we will show. Jesus used it in Matthew 23:38 against the religious leaders that He was excoriating; and again in Matthew 24:15 (also Mark 13:14) when He quoted Daniel. Daniel had used the term *abomination of desolation* twice (Daniel 11:31 and 12:11), after he said this in 9:27: "And *he* will make a firm covenant with the many for one week, but in the middle of the week *he* will put a stop to sacrifice and grain offering; **a**nd *on the wing of abominations will come one who makes desolate*, even until a complete destruction, one that is decreed, is poured out *on the one who makes desolate*."

When Jesus referred to Daniel, He was stating that the abomination of desolation will appear again. Remember the context, *as overthrown by strangers*, as opposed to the spectacular definition given it by those who still look to the future. The faithful city had become a harlot (Isaiah 1:21). Who is the faithful city, Babylon? No! Babylon destroyed Jerusalem, as described in the time of the kings; then they profaned and destroyed the Temple. Was the faithful city

Rome? No! They also destroyed Jerusalem and the Temple. Was the faithful city Jerusalem? How could it *not* be? It could only be Jerusalem, the city of righteousness, the faithful city, the city that contained God's Temple, and from where every nation flowed.

Alas, the Lord left a few survivors, a remnant. Zion would be redeemed with justice (Isaiah 1:9,27). Though their sins were as scarlet, they would be as white as snow; though they were red like crimson, they would be like wool (1:18). We saw the same promise in our opening passage of Jeremiah 50:17-20 when God said, "And I will bring Israel back to his pasture ... for I will pardon those whom I leave as a remnant" (50:19-20). Jeremiah prophesied ~60 years after Isaiah; this will be a recurring theme.

> **Isaiah 23:13-17** ¹³ Behold, the land of the Chaldeans—this is the people *which* was not; Assyria appointed it for desert creatures—they erected their siege towers, they stripped its palaces, they made it a ruin. ¹⁴ Wail, O ships of Tarshish, For your stronghold is destroyed. ¹⁵ Now in that day Tyre will be forgotten for **seventy years** like the days of one king. At the end of seventy years it will happen to Tyre as *in* the **song of the harlot**: ¹⁶ Take *your* harp, walk about the city, O forgotten **harlot**; Pluck the strings skillfully, sing many songs, That you may be remembered. ¹⁷ It will come about at the end of seventy years that the LORD will visit Tyre. Then she will go back to her **harlot's wages** and will **play the harlot** with all the kingdoms on the face of the earth.

Tyre was a city in Asher, one of the original twelve tribes of Israel after the Israelites had settled the land under Joshua. During the time of the divided kingdom, it was a city in Phoenicia, neither a part of Israel nor Judah. It was a city of significance though, and she played the harlot in the same way as Israel and Jerusalem. God chose to chastise her with seventy years of captivity, and it was carried out by the Chaldeans (23:13), the same people who would come against Judah.

> **Jeremiah 2:20** ²⁰ For long ago I broke your yoke and tore off your bonds; But you said, 'I will not serve!' For on every high hill and under every green tree You have lain down as a **harlot**.

This is regarding Judah and Jerusalem, and the high places referred to are the high places that Jeroboam had erected and which played a large part in the idolatry of God's people.[4]

> **Jeremiah 3:6-10** ⁶Then the LORD said to me in the days of Josiah the king, 'Have you seen what faithless Israel did? She went up on every high hill and under every green tree, **and she was a harlot there**. ⁷ I thought, 'After she has done all these things, she will return to Me'; but she did not return, and her treacherous sister Judah saw it. ⁸ And I saw that for all the adulteries of faithless Israel, I had sent her away and given her a writ of divorce, yet her treacherous sister Judah did not fear; **but she went and was a harlot also**. ⁹ Because of **the lightness of her harlotry**, she polluted the land and committed adultery with stones and trees. ¹⁰ Yet in spite

---

[4] Read about Jeroboam and the high places in 1 Kings 12:25-33.

of all this her treacherous sister Judah did not return to Me with all her heart, but rather in deception,' declares the LORD.

Here, God is making a juxtaposition between Israel and Judah, and this is the point we were making earlier about Judah not heeding the warnings from the prophets and not learning from the mistakes of her sister Israel. This occurred when Josiah was king of Judah, who was one of the few kings who did right in the sight of the Lord. God was saying to Judah through Jeremiah that Israel had been faithless, and He was calling attention to what she did (3:6). Israel's sister Judah, who He called treacherous (v. 10), saw what had happened but she had no fear and she played the harlot also, and she polluted the land.

Ezekiel 6:1-14 ¹And the word of the LORD came to me saying, ² "Son of man, set your face toward the mountains of Israel, and prophesy against them ³ and say, 'Mountains of Israel, listen to the word of the Lord GOD! Thus, says the Lord GOD to the mountains, the hills, the ravines and the valleys: "Behold, I Myself am going to bring a sword on you, and **I will destroy your high places**. ⁴ So **your altars will become desolate** and your incense altars will be smashed; and I will make your slain fall in front of your idols. ⁵ I will also lay the dead bodies of the sons of Israel in front of their idols; and I will scatter your bones around your altars. ⁶ In all your dwellings, cities will become waste and **the high places will be desolate**, that your altars may become waste and **desolate**, your idols may be broken and brought-to-an-end, your incense altars may be cut down, and your works may be blotted out. ⁷The slain will fall among you, and you will know that I am the Lord. ⁸ "**However, I will leave a remnant**, for you will have those who escaped the sword among the nations when you are scattered among the countries. ⁹ Then those of you who escape will remember Me among the nations to which they will be carried captive, how I have been hurt by their adulterous hearts which turned away from Me, and by **their eyes which played the harlot after their idols**; and they will loathe themselves in their own sight for the evils which they have committed, **for all their abominations.** ¹⁰ Then they will know that I am the Lord; I have not said in vain that I would inflict this disaster on them.'" ¹¹ "Thus says the Lord God, 'Clap your hand, stamp your foot and say, "Alas, because of all **the evil abominations** of the house of Israel, which will fall by sword, famine and plague! ¹² He who is far off will die by the plague, and he who is near will fall by the sword, and he who remains and is besieged will die by the famine. Thus will I spend My wrath on them. ¹³ Then you will know that I am the Lord, when their slain are among their idols around their altars, on every high hill, on all the tops of the mountains, under every green tree and under every leafy oak—the places where they offered soothing aroma to all their idols. ¹⁴ So throughout all their habitations I will stretch out My hand against them **and make the land more desolate and waste than the wilderness** toward Diblah; thus, they will know that I am the Lord."'"

This is a prophecy against "the mountains of Israel" (6:2). This is obviously metaphor (Glossary), for prophesying against mountains appears to be ecstatic, apocalyptic and metaphoric. Ezekiel had prophesied just a handful of years before Jerusalem's desolation. We see some interesting things here: God will destroy their high places (6:3); their altars will become desolate (there's that word again, 6:4, 6, 14); they played the harlot (6:9), their harlotry was an abomination, and God will leave a remnant (6:8). There is a pattern here.

> **Ezekiel 16:1-63** ¹Then the word of the Lord came to me, saying, ²"Son of man, make known to Jerusalem **her abominations** ³ and say, 'Thus says the Lord God to Jerusalem, "Your origin and your birth are from the land of the Canaanite, your father was an Amorite and your mother a Hittite. ⁴As for your birth, on the day you were born your navel cord was not cut, nor were you washed with water for cleansing; you were not rubbed with salt or even wrapped in cloths. ⁵No eye looked with pity on you to do any of these things for you, to have compassion on you. ⁶"When I passed by you and saw you squirming in your blood, I said to you while you were in your blood, 'Live!'… ⁷I made you numerous like plants of the field. Then you grew up, became tall and reached the age for fine ornaments. ⁸"Then I passed by you and saw you…**I also swore to you and entered into a covenant with you so that you became Mine**," declares the Lord God. ¹¹**I adorned you with ornaments**…¹² a beautiful crown on your head. ¹³**Thus you were adorned with gold and silver**…so, you were exceedingly beautiful and advanced to royalty.

¹⁴ Then your fame went forth among the nations on account of your beauty, **for it was perfect because of My splendor which I bestowed on you**," declares the Lord God. ¹⁵ "But you trusted in your beauty and **played the harlot** because of your fame, and you **poured out your harlotries** on every passer-by who might be willing. ¹⁶ You took some of your clothes, **made for yourself high places** of various colors **and played the harlot on them**, which should never come about nor happen. ²⁰ "Moreover, **you took your sons and daughters** whom you had borne to Me **and sacrificed them to idols to be devoured**. ²¹ You slaughtered My children and offered them up to idols by **causing them to pass through the fire**. ²² Besides all **your abominations and harlotries you did not remember the days of your youth…** ²³ ('**Woe, woe to you!**' declares the Lord God), ²⁴ that **you built yourself a shrine and made yourself a high place in every square**. ²⁵ **You built yourself a high place at the top of every street** and made your beauty **abominable**, ²⁷ Behold now, I have stretched out My hand against you and diminished your rations. **And I delivered you up to the desire of those who hate you**…. ⁴¹ Then I will stop you from **playing the harlot**…. ⁴² So **I will calm My fury against you** and **My jealousy will depart from you**, and **I will be pacified and angry no more**. ⁴⁶ Now your older sister is Samaria, who lives north of you with her daughters; and your younger sister, who lives south of you, is Sodom with her daughters. ⁴⁷ …you acted more corruptly in all your conduct than they. ⁴⁸ As I live," declares the Lord God, "Sodom, your sister and her daughters have not done as you and

your daughters have done. **⁴⁹ Behold, this was the guilt of your sister Sodom: she and her daughters had arrogance, abundant food and careless ease, but she did not help the poor and needy. ⁵⁰ Thus they were haughty and committed abominations before Me therefore I removed them when I saw it**. ⁵³ "Nevertheless, I will restore their captivity, the captivity of Sodom and her daughters, the captivity of Samaria and her daughters, and along with them your own captivity. ⁶⁰ "Nevertheless, **I will remember My covenant with** you in the days of your youth, and **I will establish an everlasting covenant with you.** ⁶² Thus **I will establish My covenant with you**, and **you shall know that I am the** LORD.

[Because of the length of chapter sixteen, some of the verses have been omitted. Some were also shortened, as sentences can be rather long in Scripture. No words or verses were changed or paraphrased.]

God was describing, in graphic detail, how He chose the Israelites as a people and that He entered into a covenant with them, whom He would call "Mine" (16:1-10). That people, Jerusalem, whom He depicted as a woman, grew up to be as a beautiful woman whom He *adorned* with ornaments, gold, and silver (16:11-13). There's that word again, which is a second word we are keeping track of as we read the Scriptures, the first being *desolate*. We will see a certain picture appear where those words play a key role.

Then God tells how that beautiful woman played the harlot: she sacrificed to idols and at the high places of Jeroboam, she slaughtered His children and offered them up to idols, making them pass through the fire to be devoured (16:14-21). God then *delivered them up* to the desire of those who hate them (16:27).[5] But then we see God's anger subsiding (16:41-42); God remembered His covenant with them and He established another covenant with them, an everlasting covenant (16:60-62).

The mention of Jerusalem's sisters, her older sister Samaria to the north and her younger sister Sodom to the south, is interesting indeed. We know what Samaria did; we have been trying to hold her up as an example as to why Judah should not follow in her older sister's ways – but Sodom is a different story. Most people, when Sodom is mentioned, will think of Sodom and Gomorrah and the fire and brimstone levied down upon them because of their sexually-deviant behavior. But Ezekiel says that the guilt of Sodom was her *haughty spirit*. She was arrogant; she had abundant food and careless ease, but she did not help the poor and needy (16:46-50). We will see that haughty spirit come into play again, later.

> **Ezekiel 23:1-49** ¹The word of the LORD came to me again, saying, ² "Son of man, there were two women, the daughters of one mother; ³ and **they played the harlot in Egypt. They played the harlot in their youth**... ⁴ Their names were Oholah the elder and Oholibah her sister. And they became Mine, and they bore sons and daughters. And as for their names, **Samaria is Oholah and Jerusalem is Oholibah**. ⁵ "**Oholah played the harlot while she was Mine**; and she lusted after her lovers, after the Assyrians, her neighbors, ⁶ who were clothed in purple, governors and officials, all of them desirable young men, horsemen riding on horses. ⁷ **She**

---

[5] A rather interesting but graphic choice of words. When God gives a people over, or up, it is usually to destruction (Romans 1:24, 26).

bestowed her harlotries on them, all of whom were the choicest men of Assyria; and with all whom she lusted after, **with all their idols she defiled herself**. ⁸ **She did not forsake her harlotries** from the time in Egypt... ⁹ **Therefore, I gave her into the hand of her lovers, into the hand of the Assyrians**, after whom she lusted. ¹⁰ They uncovered her nakedness; they took her sons and her daughters, **but they slew her with the sword**. Thus, she became a byword among women, and they executed judgments on her. ¹¹ "**Now her sister Oholibah saw this, yet she was more corrupt in her lust than she, and her harlotries were more than the harlotries of her sister**. ¹⁴ **So she increased her harlotries**. And she saw men portrayed on the wall, images of the Chaldeans portrayed with vermilion ¹⁵˙˙˙ like the Babylonians in Chaldea, the land of their birth. ¹⁶ When she saw them, she lusted after them and sent messengers to them in Chaldea. ¹⁷ The Babylonians came to her... and defiled her with their **harlotry**....¹⁸ She uncovered her **harlotries...** ¹⁹ **Yet she multiplied her harlotries, remembering the days of her youth when she played the harlot in the land of Egypt.** ²² "Therefore, O Oholibah, thus says the Lord God, 'Behold I will arouse your lovers against you, from whom you were alienated, and I will bring them against you from every side: ²³ the Babylonians and all the Chaldeans.... ²⁴ ˙˙˙ **and I will commit the judgment to them**, and they will judge you according to their customs. ²⁵ **I will set My jealousy against you**, that they may deal with you in wrath... ²⁷ Thus I will make your lewdness and your **harlotry** brought from the land of Egypt to cease from you… ²⁸ For thus says the Lord GOD, 'Behold, **I will give you into the hand of those whom you hate…** ²⁹ They will deal with you in hatred, take all your property, and leave you naked and bare. And the nakedness of **your harlotries will be uncovered**, both your lewdness and your **harlotries**. ³⁰ These things will be done to you because **you have played the harlot with the nations because you have defiled yourself with their idols.** ³¹ **You have walked in the way of your sister; therefore, I will give her cup into your hand.**' ³² Thus says the Lord GOD, '**You will drink your sister's cup**, which is deep and wide… it contains much. ³³ 'You will be filled with drunkenness and sorrow, **The cup of horror and desolation**, The cup of your sister Samaria. ³⁴ 'You will drink it and drain it. Then you will gnaw its fragments… For I have spoken,' declares the Lord GOD. ³⁵ Therefore, thus says the Lord GOD, 'Because you have forgotten Me and cast Me behind your back, bear now the punishment of your lewdness and your harlotries.'" ³⁶ Moreover, the LORD said to me, "Son of man, will you judge Oholah and Oholibah? Then declare to them **their abominations.** ³⁷ For they have committed adultery, and blood is on their hands. Thus, they have committed adultery with their idols and even caused their sons, whom they bore to Me, to pass through the fire to them as food. ³⁸ Again, they have done this to Me: **they have defiled My sanctuary** on the same day **and have profaned My sabbaths.** ³⁹ For **when they had slaughtered their children for their idols, they entered My sanctuary on the same day to profane it; and lo, thus they did within My house.**

⁴⁰ "Furthermore, they have even sent for men who come from afar, to whom a messenger was sent; and lo, they came—**for whom you bathed, painted your eyes and decorated yourselves with ornaments**; ⁴² **And they put bracelets on the hands of the women and beautiful crowns on their heads**. ⁴⁵ But they, righteous men, will judge them with the judgment of adulteresses and with the judgment of women who shed blood because they are adulteresses and blood is on their hands. ⁴⁶ "For thus says the Lord GOD, '**Bring up a company against them and give them over to terror and plunder**. ⁴⁷ The company will stone them with stones and cut them down with their swords; they will slay their sons and their daughters and burn their houses with fire. ⁴⁹ **Your lewdness will be requited upon you, and you will bear the penalty of worshiping your idols**; thus, you will know that I am the Lord GOD.'"

[Like chapter sixteen, chapter twenty-three is lengthy, so some verses have been omitted, and others shortened, but no verses changed or paraphrased.]

There is so much here. Israel and Judah were Oholah and Oholibah, respectively. They both played the harlot while they were in Egypt (23:3), which goes all the way back to the beginning, when the Jews were enslaved there. Although they were not the kingdoms of Samaria and Judah at the time, they would eventually become those entities, hence the titles. As we know, Samaria (Israel) played the harlot with Assyria and would be overrun and taken into captivity by them, as did Judah with the Chaldeans (the Babylonians). Notice, in 23:9, that God *gave Israel into the hands of the Assyrians*, just as He brought the Chaldeans against Judah (23:22, 28).

God is in control; He committed the judgment to them (23:24). Notice also (23:25) that God set His jealousy against them.[6] Notice again, the cup (23:31-33); the cup of horror and desolation (that word again). We will see God's cup of wrath later. The people defiled His sanctuary, profaned His sabbaths, and slaughtered their children for their idols (23:38-39). They bathed, painted their eyes, decorated themselves with ornaments, and put bracelets on the hands of the women and beautiful crowns on their heads (23:40, 42) (dare we say they were *adorned*?). They would bear the penalty for worshiping idols and would know that God was the Lord God (23:49). They were the harlot.

> **Hosea 4:1,6,10-19** [1]Listen to the word of the Lord, O sons of Israel, For the Lord has a case against the inhabitants of the land. Because **there is no faithfulness or kindness or knowledge of God in the land**. [6] **My people are destroyed for lack of knowledge**. Because you have rejected knowledge, I also will reject you from being My priest. Since you have forgotten the law of your God, I also will forget your children. [10] They will eat, but not have enough; **They will play the harlot**, but not increase, because they have stopped giving heed to the Lord. [11] Harlotry, wine, and new wine take away the understanding. [12] My people consult their wooden idol, and their diviner's wand informs them; For **a spirit of harlotry has led them astray, and they have played the harlot, departing from their God**. [13] They offer sacrifices on the tops of the mountains and burn incense on the hills...

---

[6] In the 2nd Commandment, God said, "For I am a *jealous* God…" and went on to say how He would visit the iniquity of the fathers on the 3rd and 4th generation of those who hate Him (Exodus 20:3-6; Deuteronomy 5:6-10).

> Therefore, **your daughters play the harlot** and your brides commit adultery. ¹⁴ I will not punish your daughters when **they play the harlot** or your brides when they commit adultery, for the men themselves, go apart with **harlots** and offer sacrifices with Temple prostitutes; so, the people without understanding are ruined. ¹⁵ Though **you, Israel, play the harlot**, do not let Judah become guilty…¹⁶ Since Israel is stubborn like a stubborn heifer…¹⁷ Ephraim is joined to idols…¹⁸ **They play the harlot continually**; Their rulers dearly love shame. ¹⁹ The wind wraps them in its wings, and they will be ashamed because of their sacrifices.

Hosea is one of the "minor" prophets, unlike Isaiah, Jeremiah, Ezekiel, and Daniel, who are considered the "major" prophets. Hosea prophesied to Israel and ended his ministry before the Assyrian invasion. Proverbs 1:7 says, "The fear of the Lord is the beginning of knowledge…" but Hosea 4:1 says that there was no knowledge of God in the land, and 4:6 says that His people were destroyed for lack of knowledge and that they had rejected knowledge; they had forgotten the law of their God. The people played the harlot and a spirit of harlotry had led them astray (4:12). They sacrificed on the high places (4:13) and with the Temple prostitutes (4:14). Thus, the warning to Israel, *do not let Judah become guilty*; but we know that they did just that. They will be ashamed because of their sacrifices (4:19).

> **Micah 1:1-16** ¹The word of the LORD which came to Micah of Moresheth in the days of Jotham, Ahaz and Hezekiah, kings of Judah, which he saw concerning Samaria and Jerusalem. ² Hear, O peoples, all of you; Listen, O earth and all it contains, and let the Lord

GOD be a witness against you, The Lord from His holy Temple. **³ For behold, the LORD is coming forth from His place. He will come down and tread on the high places of the earth. ⁴ The mountains will melt under Him and the valleys will be split, like wax before the fire. Like water poured down a steep place.** ⁵ All this is for the rebellion of Jacob and for the sins of the house of Israel. What is the rebellion of Jacob? Is it not Samaria? What is the high place of Judah? Is it not Jerusalem? ⁶ For I will make Samaria a heap of ruins in the open country, Planting places for a vineyard. I will pour her stones down into the valley and will lay bare her foundations. ⁷ All of her idols will be smashed. All of her earnings will be burned with fire and all of her images I will make **desolate**, for she collected them from **a harlot's earnings**, and **to the earnings of a harlot they will return**. ⁸ Because of this I must lament and wail, I must go barefoot and naked; I must make a lament like the jackals and a mourning like the ostriches. **⁹ For her wound is incurable, for it has come to Judah**; It has reached the gate of my people, Even to Jerusalem. ¹⁰ Tell it not in Gath, Weep not at all. at Beth-le-aphrah roll yourself in the dust. ¹¹ Go on your way, inhabitant of Shaphir, in shameful nakedness. The inhabitant of Zaanan does not escape. The lamentation of Beth-ezel: "He will take from you its support." ¹² For the inhabitant of Maroth becomes weak waiting for good, **because a calamity has come down from the LORD TO the gate of Jerusalem**. ¹³ Harness the chariot to the team of horses, O inhabitant of Lachish— She was the beginning of sin to the daughter of Zion— Because **in you were found the rebellious acts of Israel**. ¹⁴ Therefore you will give parting gifts on behalf of Moresheth-gath; The houses of Achzib will become a deception to the kings of Israel. [15] Moreover, I will bring on you the one who takes possession, O inhabitant of Mareshah. The glory of Israel will enter Adullam. [16] Make yourself bald and cut off your hair, Because of the children of your delight; Extend your baldness like the eagle, **or they will go from you into exile.**

This is a fitting passage to end this section. The prophecy occurred toward the end of the days of Israel, through the Assyrian invasion and beyond, so Micah's prophecy was to Israel and Judah (1:1). God would make Samaria a heap of ruins. All of her idols would be smashed. Her images would be made *desolate*. Its earnings are those of a harlot; her wound is incurable (1:6-9). Her incurable wound had come to Judah, to Jerusalem; calamity had come down from the Lord to the gate of Jerusalem (1:9,12), and her children would go into exile (1:16).

Within this prophecy against Israel and Judah is the apocalyptic rant about the Lord coming forth from His place and treading on the high places of the earth when the mountains will melt under Him and the valleys will be split like wax before a fire (1:3-4). Is this literal, or is this metaphor? Does God just sprinkle these kinds of words in the middle of something which have nothing to do with the overall message?

As we noted before, it is language like this that is separated from its context and put into the "end times" bucket and cobbled together with like verses, and the futurist end times scenario is perpetrated. Rubbish. This cannot be taken literally. We know who this is addressed to and we know when it was said. We also know what happened after these things were said. The text actually tells you why it was said: *all this is for the rebellion of Jacob and the sins of Israel* (1:5).

Summary

The message of harlotry as it relates to idolatry is pervasive and unmistakable throughout Scripture. God's people were behaving as a harlot by worshipping other gods instead of Him. Seeing this and understanding its implications will make understanding eschatology so much easier because so much of Scripture is predicated on those grounds. Why is that so hard to accept? A person's life would go so much easier if he did. He wouldn't have to contend to be perfect because he never could be. Accept that. Then go on and be the best you can be. Nobody is as God.

Studying the concept of the harlot throughout the history of the Israelites reveals much of what God had been trying to impress upon them. If God did not choose them to be a people unto Him, the Israelites would have been no different than all the peoples of the lands. The fact that He did choose them is cause for rejoicing.

The Scriptures are relentless in their message. That message is, "I am God. I chose you. You are Mine. You will worship Me. You will not turn to other gods." That message is a bitter pill for man, for he bristles at the thought of humbling himself before God. That can be traced back to the Garden, when the serpent told Eve that if she ate of the fruit of the Tree of the Knowledge of Good and Evil that she would be like God–and that has been man's problem ever since.

It has been suggested by some, and used as an excuse by others, that God is an angry God who is Himself guilty of genocide and so on and so forth. What they fail to remember is that we are created in His image, so that what they are rejecting are their own attributes

– self-loathing. Looking at society will show anger, hatred, warfare, and subjugation – the very things they attribute to God as reasons for rejecting Him while neglecting His blessings and risking the consequences. For those who puff themselves up and want to hold themselves up as God, they do so at their own peril.

God gave His people the law through Moses as they wandered through the wilderness. It strictly forbade idol worship. It also spelled out God's blessings if the people would keep His law and, alternately, the consequences if they didn't. They had free will and they chose to do evil in the sight of the Lord. After Moses "went to his fathers" and the people settled the land, they were ruled by judges whom God had raised up, but the people rebelled and rejected God as their king as they wanted to choose their own king like all the other nations.

God, forever longsuffering, allowed them to do so and Saul was selected as their first king. He was a failure and was succeeded by King David, who was a man after God's own heart (1 Samuel 13:14; Acts 13:22). He was a warrior, but he shed much blood in subduing the surrounding nations so God told him that he would not be the one to build His Temple, but that his son Solomon would do it. Solomon did, and he was a man of much wisdom. He is the author of many of the Proverbs, a few of the Psalms, the book of Ecclesiastes, and the Song of Solomon. But King Solomon had too many wives and too many concubines who eventually led him astray and into idolatry. God tore the kingdom from him, giving two tribes (Judah and Benjamin) to his son Rehoboam, and the other ten to Jeroboam, and thus began the divided kingdom of Judah and Israel. (Actually, the tribe of Benjamin was given to Rehoboam, with Judah following later - Joshua 18:28; Judges 1:21; 1 Kings 11:9-13, 29-36; 12:20).

As the people continued in their idolatrous ways, God had to send His prophets to chastise them and warn them not to continue doing as they were doing. The people, sinking further into

Summary

debauchery, started killing the prophets, with Jezebel being foremost in that regard. Eventually, God brought the Assyrians against Israel.

Not learning from the mistakes of her sister, Judah fell to the same fate, this time from King Nebuchadnezzar and the Babylonians. The date of the Temple's destruction is 586BC. All this is documented in the books of Kings and Chronicles, with the prophets appearing in the latter half of that period. As the people began coming out from their captivity, a new Temple was eventually built and dedicated in 516BC – seventy years after being taken into captivity. The Biblical books of Ezra, Nehemiah, and Esther are about that period and onward. Though God's people continued intermarrying with the peoples of the lands, there is no account of such idolatry (playing the harlot) during that time.

The Harlot

PART II–IN THE TIME OF OUR LORD

"THIS GENERATION" AND THE END OF THE AGE
(FROM MATTHEW 23)

During the time when Jesus walked the earth and was preaching and teaching, healing and casting out demons, and performing many other wonderful miracles, there was constant tension and conflict between He and the religious leaders (the Pharisees, Sadducees and scribes). All four of the Gospels record instances when Jesus was asked "loaded questions" by those leaders. When He answered, it was His wisdom and the Spirit by which He spoke that confounded them and enraged them. They didn't like His answers! They would argue with Him, or they would try to grab Him and He would slip through their midst, but when they finally did arrest Him, they had him crucified.

Just before being arrested though, there was that day in the Temple when Jesus was speaking to the crowds as He usually did, and while the scribes and Pharisees were present, Jesus talked about them right in front of them–He challenged them. Picture this: You're in a marketplace somewhere, with people milling and walking about and you're talking to a crowd of people.

> **Matthew 23:1-39** ¹Then Jesus spoke to the crowds and to His disciples, ²saying**: "The scribes and the Pharisees have seated themselves in the chair of Moses, ³therefore, all that they tell you, do and observe, but do not do according to their deeds; for they say things and do not do them**. ⁴They tie up heavy burdens and lay them on men's shoulders, but they themselves are unwilling to move them with so much as a finger. ⁵But they do all their deeds to be noticed by men; for they broaden their phylacteries and lengthen the tassels of their garments. ⁶They love the place of honor at banquets and the chief seats in the synagogues, ⁷and respectful greetings in the market places, and being called Rabbi by men. ⁸But do not be called Rabbi; for One is your Teacher, and you are all brothers. ⁹Do not call anyone on earth your father; for One is your Father, He who is in heaven. ¹⁰Do not be called leaders; for One is your Leader, that is, Christ. ¹¹But the greatest among you shall be your servant. ¹²**Whoever exalts himself shall be humbled, and whoever humbles himself shall be exalted**.

Continuing the visualization: there is also another group of people across the way, and they're looking your way, motioning and talking as though they're talking about you. You lift your voice and address your crowd, but you start talking about the other group loud enough so that they can hear you (23:1-12). And then, you turn to them and you start saying, "Woe to you," calling them hypocrites–not once, not twice, but seven times – seven woes.

¹³ "But woe to you, scribes and Pharisees, hypocrites, because you shut off the kingdom of heaven from people; for you do not enter in yourselves, nor do you allow those who are entering to go in. ¹⁴ [Woe to you, scribes and Pharisees, hypocrites, because you devour widows' houses, and for a pretense, you make long prayers; therefore you will receive greater condemnation.]⁷

¹⁵ **"Woe to you, scribes and Pharisees, hypocrites,** because you travel around on sea and land to make one proselyte; and when he becomes one, **you make him twice as much a son of hell as yourselves.**

¹⁶ **"Woe to you, blind guides**, who say, 'Whoever swears by the Temple, that is nothing; but whoever swears by the gold of the Temple is obligated.' ¹⁷You fools and blind men! Which is more important, the gold or the Temple that sanctified the gold? ¹⁸And, 'Whoever swears by the altar, that is nothing, but whoever swears by the offering on it, he is obligated.' ¹⁹ You blind men, which is more important, the offering, or the altar that sanctifies the offering? ²⁰ Therefore, whoever swears by the altar, swears both by the altar and by everything on it. ²¹ And whoever swears by the Temple, swears both by the Temple and by Him who dwells within

---

7   For those unfamiliar with the NASB version: "in text, brackets [] indicate words probably not in the original writings." This is very important as we will see this later in the writings of Irenaeus about the number of the beast. – author

it. ²² And whoever swears by heaven, swears both by the throne of God and by Him who sits upon it.

²³ **"Woe to you, scribes and Pharisees, hypocrites!** For you tithe mint and dill and cumin **and have neglected the weightier provisions of the law: justice and mercy and faithfulness; but these are the things you should have done without neglecting the others**[8]. ²⁴ You blind guides, who strain out a gnat and swallow a camel!

²⁵ **"Woe to you, scribes and Pharisees, hypocrites!** For you clean the outside of the cup and of the dish, but inside they are full of robbery and self-indulgence. ²⁶ You blind Pharisee, first clean the inside of the cup and of the dish, so that the outside of it may become clean also.

²⁷ **"Woe to you, scribes and Pharisees, hypocrites!** For you are like whitewashed tombs which on the outside appear beautiful, but inside they are full of dead men's bones and all uncleanness. ²⁸ So you, too, outwardly appear righteous to men, but inwardly you are full of hypocrisy and lawlessness.

In order to understand the point being made here, think about how long it would take a person to even read these words aloud from his or her favorite Bible, standing in front of a mirror, as though one was practicing for a speech. Go ahead and time it–it would take between five and ten minutes. Now, in the case of Jesus, He was addressing people in real time, talking about–and to, a

---

[8] We will see this later, with the haughty harlot.

hostile crowd. He went from one woe to the next, and as that hostile crowd would have realized what was happening, would they have started to come nearer and possibly tried intimidation tactics or actually gotten physical?

There are myriad things that could have taken place before Jesus was done with the seventh woe. This was an incredible occurrence. If it were anyone else saying what Jesus said, he most likely never would have finished before he was physically stopped. But Jesus spoke with such authority that He was able to complete His charges against them unscathed.

The closest definition for the word "woe" in the Bible is from Isaiah 3:11 where that prophet said: *Woe to the wicked! It will go badly with him, for what he deserves will be done to him.* That, is divine justice. So, woe to the scribes and Pharisees – it would go badly for them, for they would get what they deserved – they were, after all, hypocrites.

We are concerned primarily with the seventh woe (23:29-39), but we will also make note of 23:15, the second woe, when Jesus called them "sons of hell." We will see why, shortly.

> [29] **"Woe to you, scribes and Pharisees, hypocrites!** For you build the tombs of the prophets and **adorn the monuments of the righteous** [30] **and say, 'If we had been living in the days of our fathers, we would not have been partners with them in shedding the blood of the prophets.'** [31] **So you testify against yourselves, that you are sons of those who murdered the prophets.** [32] **Fill up, then, the measure of the guilt of your fathers.** [33] **You serpents, you brood of vipers, how will you escape the sentence of hell?**

Jesus was confronting them, throwing back at them what they had said, that if they had been living back in those days, they wouldn't have been partners with their forefathers in the killing of the prophets. That didn't mean much to Jesus, for He knew they were hypocrites; and we will see just how important that hypocritical statement that they made–is.

Other than Jezebel who we saw earlier had *adorned* herself for Jehu just before he had her tossed out of that upper window (2 Kings 9:30-33 – Part I), that was always a word used to describe God's people – Jerusalem – and how *He* adorned *them* (Ezekiel 16:11-12 – Part I). We will continue to see that word and determine its meaning; but here, Jesus scorns the religious leaders in the sense that they, being so "pious," would traditionally lavish costly stones and luxurious cloths of purple and such on the Temple buildings. The Temple had become as an idol to them and they became haughty about it – they would *adorn* the buildings.

Jesus used their own words against them to condemn them, telling them that they testified against themselves because they admitted that they were the sons of those who had actually murdered the prophets. But even though they weren't the ones who were personally the murderers of the prophets, Jesus told them that they were not simply "innocent sons of their guilty fathers." Shedding the blood of the prophets and playing the harlot with other gods were the primary reasons for which the people had been judged by God in the past, just as they would be the reasons for which they would eventually be judged again in the near future.

The word, "testify" is a legal term, used broadly for making a sworn statement. To testify *against* someone is to make an accusation, usually under oath and/or in a court of law; to testify *to* something is similar to an affidavit, which becomes a legal document. This was not to be taken lightly. In 23:16-22, Jesus made a point about swearing to things, as in this case they had made a sworn statement to God—and Jesus was holding them accountable for their actions as well as their words.

They, too, were complicit in all that their fathers were guilty of, having been idolaters and covenant breakers from the beginning. These religious leaders were no different than those in the past. In telling them to fill up the measure of the guilt of their fathers, Jesus was telling them they would bear the burden of the guilt of their fathers in addition to their own. This was a scathing indictment of them.

Calling them a brood of vipers – snakes – Jesus, the Righteous Judge, was condemning them and pronouncing sentence on them. They could not escape the sentence of hell because they were sons of hell (23:15); indicating that that's where they were bound.

> ³⁴ "Therefore, behold, **I am sending you prophets and wise men and scribes; some** of them **you will kill and crucify,** and **some** of them **you will scourge in your synagogues, and persecute from city to city,** ³⁵ **so that upon you may fall the guilt of all the righteous blood shed on earth**, from the blood of righteous Abel to the blood of Zechariah, the son of Berechiah, whom you murdered between the Temple and the altar. ³⁶ **Truly I say to you all these things will come upon this generation.**

Now we come to the heart of this section. As if to ask and then answer His own rhetorical question, He says, "Okay, you say you wouldn't have killed the prophets if you lived back then? Fine! I'm sending you more, and we'll see." And He told them just what they would do, and which ultimately they did do, that is, that they would be killers of prophets too, proving that they were no different than their fathers, and so they would bear the full penalty for that sin; and we will see exactly that, shortly.

Though their fathers had been judged by God through the Assyrians and Babylonians, the guilt of those fathers was to be credited to *their* account – the people Jesus was talking to, God *imputed* it to them. And not only that, they were also being held responsible for *all* the righteous blood shed on earth, from Abel to Zechariah – from A to Z. Jesus said, "I am the Alpha and the Omega, the first and the last, the beginning and the end" (Revelation 21:6; 22:13). That is completion. and in this case, Jesus held them in complete guiltiness and accountability. It was *all* coming upon *that* generation.

Here is one of those places where eschatology gets misunderstood and abused, and where the true meaning of what the Scriptures say about it gets twisted, or worse – lost. One of the ways this misunderstanding has happened is by the redefining of words–in this case, the word 'generation.' The text must mean what the text says – in context, for text without contest is pretext. Those people whom Jesus was addressing – those religious leaders – *were that* generation, and it was *that* generation upon whom *all those things* would come.

The word 'generation' must mean the same as elsewhere in Scripture when used in that context. It is the period of time between one group of people to their offspring; or, more broadly, those people living at that time. It cannot mean future generations because Jesus was talking to *them* and he said *this* generation, meaning *them*. Jesus may know the future, but people do not. There is no way *they* would interpret what He said to mean future generations, and there is no grammatical or hermeneutical principle that could allow those words to have any other meaning to them (or to us) other than to mean *themselves*. That's why they were so opposed to Him. AD70 was less than forty years away – within that generation.

With that definition, the futurist explanation dies on the vine. So instead, what the futurists have done is redefine the word

"THIS GENERATION" AND THE END OF THE AGE

'generation,' giving it an additional definition making it an indefinite period of time, encompassing whatever time period fits their fanciful interpretation. And, naturally, since most people interpret Jesus' words as futuristic, the redefinition erroneously includes them – they all think they're living in the end times. Context is everything.

This is very important. Matthew 23 is fundamental to understanding chapter 24 (known as the Olivet Discourse, for it was spoken from Mount Olivet, which is also known as the Mount of Olives). Chapter 23 is separate from, but equal to, chapter 24 in that it is the introduction to the Discourse. A correct interpretation of what Jesus said in chapter 24 cannot be attained without first understanding what transpired in chapter 23. They may be separate, but they are separated by, only a short stroll and mere minutes of time. Chapter 23, spoken from *within* the Temple, sets up, and is the prelude to, chapter 24, spoken from *without*.

It might appear as though we're going off on a tangent, or "beating a dead horse," but we are entering into one of those critical areas where man has diverted from God. Our task is to identify those areas and remain faithful to God's Word – God's story, for it is His story – History.

The story of the harlot is immersed in Biblical eschatology, and the Olivet Discourse is the foremost Gospel eschatological utterance, spoken by none other than the Lord Jesus Christ Himself; which is why we must get this right or else we *will* truly go off on a tangent. Matthew 23 *ends* with one very controversial statement containing a very controversial word – *generation*–and chapter 24 *begins* with another very controversial statement containing another very controversial word – *world* (translated from *aión*).

After Jesus had finished His harangue at the religious leaders and He came out of the Temple, He was going away when His disciples came up to Him and pointed out the Temple buildings (24:1), that they were *adorned* (there's that word again) with beautiful stones and votive gifts (Luke 21:5). To this, He said, *"Do you not see all these things? Truly I say to you, not one stone here will be left upon another, which will not be torn down"* (Matthew 24:2). And to that, they asked, *"Tell us, when will these things happen, and what will be the sign of Your coming, and of the end of the age"* (24: 3)?

Now, that may not appear to be an earth-shattering question in and of itself, but the problem is, in earlier translations, the last word of that question (the Greek word *aión*) was mistranslated *world*, instead of *age*. So, the question the disciples asked became, *"Tell us, when will these things happen, and what will be the sign of Your coming, and of the end of the* **world***?"* Repeat–***the end of the world***.

That is a pretty significant error. The end of the *age* would put it at just about the year 70, which *was* the end of an age, or era – the Temple-sacrifice era–the Old Covenant era. The end of the *world* is quite something else. Here then, is the translation problem: the fact is that at least from the year 1611, when the first major English translation became available, the King James Version (KJV), it became the primary English Bible until the twentieth century *and it bore that error*! So, for more than 300 years, we were all reading Matthew 24 as though Jesus was talking about the end of the physical world!

If Jesus meant *world,* He would have used the Greek word *kosmos*, which translates to *world* or *universe*. There is also the Greek word *oikonomía* which is where we get the word *economy*. In that respect Jesus could have used that word, for the Roman *economy* would have encompassed the Roman Empire, which was, at that time, the known world. But He chose *aión*, which translates to *age*, or *era*–not *world*.

This is inspired writing, so it must be correct–and it is our responsibility to correctly translate and interpret it. But that's not the entirety of the problem. If, prior to the twentieth century, nearly 100% of the English-speaking world was reading the misbegotten

"THIS GENERATION" AND THE END OF THE AGE

KJV translation of *aión* into *world* in 24:3, then, from the twentieth century onward, there appeared a plethora of versions, some of which used *age*; some, *world*; and still others, a 'vanilla' translation so that those with very limited Bible acumen would be able to understand their Bible.

In addition to all of that, with the many English translations, some were (and still are), translated more literally, while others are more on the paraphrasing side. Some were translated from the then-earliest manuscripts, while others from those manuscripts dated later. The earlier are considered more reliable because they are closer in time to the source (the autograph), but that's another discussion for another book.

The original language of the written New Testament was Koine (common) Greek, which had no chapter breaks or verse numbers, nor did they have punctuation (we put those in). All of that makes it imperative to read the various English translations carefully and discriminately. Yes! The Bible is inerrant – but in its original form. Translations are only as good as the translators' intent.

The farther one strays from a literal translation, the further from the true meaning it becomes, because, in striving to make it more easily-readable, translators inject their own opinion and bias, intentionally or otherwise. There are so many versions! Understanding has become jumbled, and the original meaning of the story has faded. The story we are concerned with is what happened up to and including the destruction of 70AD.

So then, unless one has a good understanding of chapter 23, a person ending a reading session at the end of 23, and opening another at the beginning of chapter 24, or, arbitrarily starting at 24 without even reading chapter 23, it will be much harder, or even next to impossible, to understand the eschatology of the Discourse. So then, again, we have come to a critical juncture.

We had gotten as far as 23:36 where we ran into the word *generation,* which triggered this entire discussion about its true meaning. Then, because that verse is just four verses prior to the pivotal clause of 24:1-3 where we ran into the second error, the mistranslation of *aión*, which, in turn, triggered another discussion about *it*–both of those errors were exacerbated by the lengthy period of time that the KJV carried them unchallenged. Finally, we have since been inundated with a slew of feel-good and self-help translations, many of which may or may not be helpful to some, but they surely don't help much in the understanding of eschatology.

Back to 23:36, where we look again at the word *generation*. If we read further into the discourse, to 24:34, we see that word again, used in the same context. It says, *Truly I say to you,* **this generation** *will not pass away until all these things take place*. That is nearly identical to, *Truly I say to you all these things will come upon* **this generation** (23:36). There can be no doubt that Jesus meant *that* generation–the generation He was talking to!

Here is another morsel: *that* generation would not pass away until *all those things* took place. We discussed what *all those things* were in chapter 23, but we don't yet know what they are in chapter 24. What we do know is that the Olivet Discourse was one of the loftiest speeches that Jesus ever made about the most difficult content in the Bible.

He talked about the end (24: 6, 13, 14), the tribulation (24:9, 21), false prophets and false Christs (24:11, 24), Daniel and the abomination of desolation (24:15), heavenly convulsions (24:29), the Second Coming (24:30), the rapture (24:31), and *that* generation (24:34). Those topics, except for 'Daniel and the abomination of desolation,' the tribulation, and that generation, are for future writings and are beyond the scope of this book.

Suffice it to say those other topics *are* for another day, but it is clear from the text that they all would happen soon, *within that generation*. What a difference that makes. They either happened before 70AD or after–before Jerusalem fell, or after. That period of time is the pinnacle of history and the implications are huge because it brings us back to our original argument, which is: if it all happened before 70AD, it is within God's story; but if it happened after, then it becomes man's story. The Bible story is His story, History.

We have connected Matthew 23 to 24 through Jesus' words – those which He spoke to the crowds and religious leaders–and anybody else who might have been interested in hearing what He had to say; and those words which He spoke to His disciples and followers–and anybody else who might have been interested in what He had to say.

Harkening back to 23:29-36, those were momentous words that Jesus had spoken to people who were not in the habit of being spoken to in that manner. They were used to being in authority–except over the Romans, that is. In a similar manner, Jesus had not spoken to them like that before, either. The Lord had a heavy heart, and next we see Jesus weep (lament) over Jerusalem:

> *37* **"Jerusalem, Jerusalem, who kills the prophets and stones those who are sent to her!** How often I wanted to gather your children together, the way a hen gathers her chicks under her wings, and you were unwilling." **38 Behold, your house is being left to you desolate!**

My, my, there is that word yet again – *desolate*. But now, because we know the true meaning of it and the context in which it had been used by the Old Testament prophets, and we have the luxury of looking back at history, we know the context and meaning of how it is being used here. And that context is: *as being overthrown by strangers*. Understanding the context helps in coming to the true definition, not only of the *word:* desolation, but the *phrase:* abomination of desolation, and it takes away a key area of contention for those who claim this is all yet to happen.

We know the importance of the destruction of the city and Temple as it happened prior, and the reasons that it came about, and so it is now too. Jesus was referring to what was coming in 70AD. Jesus lamented over Jerusalem; Daniel had also lamented over Jerusalem in his prayer (Daniel 9), as we will soon see. The city then had been destroyed by Nebuchadnezzar and the people were taken into captivity in Babylon. The similarities of what had happened to Jerusalem then, giving rise to Daniel's lament, and what Jesus saw that which would soon happen, within that generation, to Jerusalem, causing Him to lament, are unmistakable.

> **³⁹ For I say to you, from now on you will not see Me until you say, 'BLESSED IS HE WHO COMES IN THE NAME OF THE LORD!'"**

Amen to that. These blind guides will see Him when they stand before Him to give an account of their lives. Then, they will see Him for who He is, the King of kings and Lord of lords, and they will say, *"Blessed is He who comes in the name of the Lord."*

Jesus Speaks of Daniel

Since, here in Part II we are discussing the harlot in the Gospel era, one might wonder why we would be talking about the prophet Daniel, especially since we just left the Old Testament era and prophets in Part I. We did not discuss Daniel then, but we just made mention in the last section here in Part II of the similarities of Jesus' and Daniel's laments over Jerusalem, and we need only look at Jesus' reference to "Daniel the Prophet" in Matthew 24:15 to realize that we must understand the significance of why Jesus said that.

Not only that, Jesus and Daniel are inextricably linked–to the point where Daniel is as important to our study of the harlot in the Gospel era as anyone. He mentioned Daniel by name, using him as a source reference for the abomination of desolation. He actually elevated Daniel's words to the highest possible level – equal to His own, for he was highly esteemed (Daniel 9:23). The context will soon become clear.

Actually, the abomination of desolation was something the people would have recognized, for Jesus said, "Therefore when you see the abomination of desolation which was spoken of through Daniel the Prophet, standing in the Holy Place (let the reader understand)" (Matthew 24:15). Jesus had just gone through a litany of things that would happen before the end would come (Matthew 24:4-14) when He made His comment about the abomination of desolation. He began with "Therefore." You've heard the ditty, "When you see the word 'therefore' make sure you know what it's there for."

So, after that litany of events Jesus said would happen, He said "Therefore," which means 'because of' or 'for that reason,' which means, in this case, that because of or for the reasons He had just previously stated, when the people would see the abomination of desolation standing in the Holy Place – then there is a parenthetical phrase – "let the reader understand." That parenthetical phrase wasn't arbitrarily inserted by the translators – it is part of the inspired original Greek text. So, again, "because of" or "for that reason," "let the reader understand." There is no way that the people would *not* understand what the abomination of desolation was!

If the reader is asking himself this question: why would they know what Jesus was talking about?–well, do not forget what the Chaldeans had done when they destroyed the city and the Temple, which, as we said, was the reason of Daniel's prayer (Daniel 9). By the time of Jesus, Antiochus Epiphanes had also destroyed the city and profaned the Temple by sacrificing swine on the altar (1 Maccabees 1:20-64).

So now, since it had already happened twice, and the significance of such a thing was of such importance to the Jews, they would certainly know what Jesus meant when He made that prophecy. And lo, it would happen again in 70AD. It was, also, according to Jesus, one of *those things* that would take place *before that generation passed away* (Matthew 24:15, 34).

We must begin this section with Daniel's prayer:

> **Daniel 9:1-19** [1]**In the first year of Darius** the son of Ahasuerus, of Median descent, who was made king over the kingdom of the Chaldeans— [2]**in the first year of his reign, I, Daniel, observed in the books the number of the years** which was revealed as the word of the Lord to Jeremiah the prophet **for the completion of the desolations of Jerusalem**, namely, **seventy years**. [3] So I gave my attention to

the Lord God to seek Him by prayer and supplications, with fasting, sackcloth and ashes. ⁴ I prayed to the LORD my God and confessed and said, "Alas, O Lord, the great and awesome **God, who keeps His covenant** and lovingkindness for those who love Him and keep His commandments, ⁵ we have sinned, committed iniquity, acted wickedly and rebelled, even turning aside from Your commandments and ordinances. ⁶ Moreover, **we have not listened to Your servants the prophets, who spoke in Your name to our kings, our princes, our fathers and all the people of the land.** ⁷ "Righteousness belongs to You, O Lord, but to us open shame, as it is this day—to the men of Judah, the inhabitants of Jerusalem and all Israel, those who are nearby and those who are far away in all the countries to which You have driven them, because of their unfaithful deeds which they have committed against You. ⁸ Open shame belongs to us, O Lord, to our kings, our princes and our fathers, because we have sinned against You. ⁹ To the Lord our God belong compassion and forgiveness, for we have rebelled against Him; ¹⁰ nor have we obeyed the voice of the LORD our God, to walk in His teachings which He set before us through His servants the prophets. ¹¹ Indeed all Israel has transgressed Your law and turned aside, not obeying Your voice; so, **the curse has been poured out on us, along with the oath which is written in the law of Moses the servant of God**, for we have sinned against Him. ¹² Thus He has confirmed His words which He had spoken against us and against our rulers who ruled us, to bring on us great calamity; **for under the whole heaven there**

has not been done anything like what was done to Jerusalem. ¹³ As it is written in the law of Moses, all this calamity has come on us; yet we have not sought the favor of the LORD our God by turning from our iniquity and giving attention to Your truth. ¹⁴ Therefore **the LORD had kept the calamity in store and brought it on us;** for the LORD our God is righteous with respect to all His deeds which He has done, but we have not obeyed His voice. ¹⁵ "And now, O Lord our God, who have brought Your people out of the land of Egypt with a mighty hand and have made a name for Yourself, as it is this day— we have sinned, we have been wicked. ¹⁶ O Lord, in accordance with all Your righteous acts, let now Your anger and Your wrath turn away from **Your city Jerusalem;** Your holy mountain; for because of our sins and the iniquities of our fathers, **Jerusalem** and Your people have become a reproach to all those around us. ¹⁷ So now, our God, listen to the prayer of Your servant and to his supplications, and for Your sake, O Lord, let Your face shine on **Your desolate sanctuary.** ¹⁸ O my God, incline Your ear and hear! Open Your eyes and see **our desolations, and the city which is called by Your name**; for we are not presenting our supplications before You on account of any merits of our own, but on account of Your great compassion. ¹⁹ O Lord, hear! O Lord, forgive! O Lord, listen and take-action!

Reading just the words in bold in the above passage (for simplicity, while leaving the entire text for context), one can see what God is saying regarding Jerusalem, its desolation, and all that that entails. This prayer took place during the reign of Darius the Mede

(9:1), who ruled under Cyrus, King of Persia. Medo-Persia had succeeded Babylon, Belshazzar being the last of the Babylonian kings (Daniel 8:1,20), and Medo-Persia preceding Greece (8:21). This was also still within the seventy-year captivity time frame which had been prophesied by Jeremiah (Jeremiah 25:8-12).

The Jews of Judah, when Daniel was offering up his prayer, were, as we just said, still in captivity in Babylon. Daniel, who had been reading in the books of the prophet Jeremiah about their return (Daniel 9:2; see also Jeremiah 29:10-14), *observed in the books... the number of the years for the completion of the desolations of Jerusalem – seventy*. Notice that he used the word *desolation*, which we defined by Isaiah 1:7. The city and the Temple had been turned into rubble, which is why Daniel began to pray in the first place.

Jerusalem was God's city, which was supposed to have been a sweet offering to Him, but had instead been turned into a smoldering ruin. God earlier had dealt harshly with Sodom and Gomorrah with fire and brimstone (Genesis 19:1-29), and still earlier, in the days of Noah when He sent the flood (Genesis 6:11-7:24). But here, in the days of Daniel, the Temple was destroyed and Jerusalem had been overrun by strangers. And now, as per Jesus' prophecy, it was about to be made desolate yet again–in the time of *that* generation.

Remember, Jesus felt compelled to refer to Daniel, and what He referred to was the abomination of desolation: "which was spoken of by Daniel the prophet" (Matthew 24:15), which phrase Daniel had uttered just after his prayer for Jerusalem (Daniel 9:24-27; see also 11:31; 12:11). The "seventy weeks" were the answer to that prayer, brought by "the man (angel) Gabriel" (9:20-23). So, Matthew 24:15 and Daniel 9:27 are describing the same thing – the destruction of Jerusalem, the profaning of the Temple, and its utter desolation – the abomination of desolation! That is why the people would recognize it. Daniel saw what had happened when the Chaldeans did it, and Jesus was foretelling what would happen in 70AD.

Now comes the focal point of this entire segment: *for under the whole heaven, there had not been done anything like what was done to Jerusalem* (Daniel 9:12). What exactly happened to Jerusalem? It was overrun by strangers, as the Babylonians destroyed the city and Temple and the people were forced into captivity. But, so what! Doesn't that always happen in war? "Great" cities have always gotten destroyed along with their sacred buildings, and the people subjected to slavery during warfare. What was so significant about it this time? What was done to Jerusalem that led Daniel to utter something so momentous?

He said, under inspiration, *...for under the whole heaven....* Are there any larger parameters than "under the whole heaven?" Continuing, "...*there has not been done **anything** like what was done to Jerusalem.*" There has not been done anything so momentous? There is nothing in comparison? We will see shortly why there wasn't and still isn't. But then, how destroyed can an army make a city? Is it even to be measured in human terms of destruction? Or, is it the fact that it was the city of God which had been destroyed, along with His Temple, His Holy Place, and His Holy of Holies?

God kept His covenant (Daniel 9:4); the people did not listen to His prophets (9:6); the curse had been poured out on them, along with the oath which is written in the law of Moses (9:11) – [the curses for disobedience, see Deuteronomy 28:15-68 and Leviticus 26:14-39] the LORD had kept the calamity in store and brought it on them (Daniel 9:14). That – is desolation.

Jerusalem was God's city, the city to which He brought His people from the time of Abraham, and from the time of the Exodus. It was where He had King Solomon build His Temple, where the people brought all their sacrifices and offerings for their sin. Now it was destroyed and desolate–overrun by strangers. How much more significant could anything be than that?

Daniel Points to Jesus

Daniel 9:24-27 [24] "**Seventy weeks have been decreed for your people and your holy city, to finish the transgression, to make an end of sin, to make atonement for iniquity, to bring in everlasting righteousness, to seal up vision and prophecy and to anoint the most holy place**. [25] So you are to know and discern that from the issuing of a decree to restore and rebuild Jerusalem until Messiah the Prince there will be seven weeks and sixty-two weeks; it will be built again, with plaza and moat, even in times of distress. [26] Then after the sixty-two weeks the Messiah will be cut off and have nothing, and **the people of the prince who is to come will destroy the city and the sanctuary**. And its end will come with a flood; even to the end there will be war; **desolations** are determined. [27] And he will make a firm covenant with the many for one week, but in the middle of the week he will put a stop to sacrifice and grain offering; **and on the wing of abominations will come one who makes desolate**, even until a complete destruction, one that is decreed, is poured out on the one who makes **desolate**."

> **Daniel 12:1-4** ¹"Now at that time Michael, the great prince who stands guard over the sons of your people, will arise. **And there will be a time of distress such as never occurred since there was a nation until that time; and at that time your people, everyone who is found written in the book, will be rescued. ² Many of those who sleep in the dust of the ground will awake, these to everlasting life, but the others to disgrace and everlasting contemp**t. ³ Those who have insight will shine brightly like the brightness of the expanse of heaven, and those who lead the many to righteousness, like the stars forever and ever. ⁴ But as for you, Daniel, **conceal these words and seal up the book until the end of time**; many will go back and forth, and knowledge will increase."

There is much to understand in the relationship of the prophecies of Daniel and Jesus. As we noted, they refer to each other, with Jesus speaking of "Daniel the prophet" by name while mentioning the "abomination of desolation" (Matthew 24:15), and Daniel prophesying of: finishing the transgression, making an end of sin, making atonement for iniquity, bringing in everlasting righteousness, sealing up vision and prophecy, and anointing the most holy place (Daniel 9:24). Nothing but Jesus' resurrection can satisfy those events.

Some say that a case can be made that Daniel 9:24-27 was prophesying about Antiochus Epiphanes, the Greek general and king, who was soon to come. They say that he actually *was,* or that he actually *committed,* the abomination of desolation by sacrificing a pig on the altar. The abomination of desolation need not be a one-time event. It was satisfied by the Babylonians, then by Antiochus who destroyed the city and profaned the Temple but left it intact (~168BC), and would be satisfied later by the Romans.

So, whether Antiochus himself was the abomination of desolation for doing what he did is really a moot point–but that does not change the facts of history. Those facts, as set forth by God, are: that Jerusalem was the holy mountain of God (Daniel 9:16); it was to where He had brought His people; and it was where God had His holy Temple built, whereupon the altar the sacrifices to Him were performed for the sin of the people. What happened to Jerusalem and the Temple was profound, and that is what matters.

And so it was, the altar and Temple were profaned and defiled by the Chaldeans. Jerusalem had become an abomination–it *was* an abomination, and it was made desolate – therefore, it was the abomination of desolation.

Jesus, on the other hand, by mentioning Daniel by name *and* the abomination of desolation, was prophesying what would happen in 70AD. The facts are that the Roman general Titus entered the Temple and planted the Roman "standard" (a pennant or flag attached to a pole or staff identifying a particular Roman legion, or bearing the likeness of the Roman Emperor) in the Holy of Holies before they, too, destroyed it, the Temple, and the city.

There is no need for any other explanation because the story is not about us in the here and now, or the future–our eternity is sealed if we are in Christ. The story is about God and Christ, and His people, which *are* us – but in that order.

Not only did Daniel point to Christ in 9:24-27, but also in 12:1-3. The last sentence of 12:1 says this: *And there will be a time of distress such as never occurred since there was a nation until that time; and at that time your people, everyone who is found written in the book, will be rescued.*

What time of distress? What book? Rescued? What could possibly happen to fit the bill? Answer: the time of distress is the great persecution of the early Christians by the Jews and Romans as described in Acts. The book is the Book of Life: "For everyone whose name is written in the Lamb's Book of Life from the foundation of the world will be saved (rescued)," according to Revelation 13:8 and 17:8, paraphrased. Daniel was prophesying about the Resurrection of Jesus Christ.

Only the resurrection could fulfill what those verses call for. Daniel was pointing to the cross–everything points to the cross. So, we now know the timeframe and the framework of some of the most difficult passages of Scripture and eschatology. Daniel is the epitome of eschatology, for a discussion of eschatology cannot be had without a discussion of Daniel and his prophecies. And he is, as we said, inextricably linked with Jesus. We now know the bounds of eschatology, the mystery therefore vaporizes, and thus, we've planted the anchor of understanding. Wisdom, knowledge, and understanding – that, with logic and context – will never get you lost.

Consider: Jesus and Daniel, in Matthew 23:37-39 and Daniel 9:1-19, respectively, were both weeping over Jerusalem.

Consider: Mathew 24:15 and Daniel 9:27 both mentioned the abomination of desolation.

Consider: the nexus between Jesus and Daniel in Matthew 24:21 and Daniel 12:1, respectively, with Jesus referring to a great tribulation and Daniel to a time of great distress.

This brings us squarely back to the point Jesus was making in addressing the scribes and Pharisees in Matthew 23:34, telling them that *they* would actually be the ones to bring about the start of the great tribulation when He said: "Therefore, behold, I am sending you prophets and wise men and scribes; some of them you will kill and crucify, and some of them you will scourge in your synagogues, and persecute from city to city."

Here we see Jesus telling the scribes and Pharisees that He will do exactly what He and the Father had done since the beginning of time–and that was to give them the law, then send them more prophets, wise men, and scribes. And those scribes and Pharisees would do exactly what their fathers had done since the beginning of time–and that was to be the harlot by turning from the law, and kill those prophets and wise men. The great tribulation was on.

DANIEL'S FOURTH KINGDOM FIRST CENTURY ROME

We have been talking about the prophet Daniel and the relationship of what he prophesied, to the prophecies of Jesus, and the fact that He mentioned Daniel in the Olivet Discourse. Let us look more closely at his other prophecies and see whether they too are in any way related to what we have been addressing.

The first of his prophecies was his interpretation of King Nebuchadnezzar's dream in his chapter 2. At 2:31-33 he saw a statue with a head of gold, its chest and arms of silver, its belly and thighs of bronze, its legs of iron, and its feet partly of iron and partly of fired clay. In Daniel's interpretation, he identifies the king (Babylon) as the head of gold (Daniel 2:38), and mentions three other kingdoms without identifying any of them (2:39-40).

When Daniel interpreted the handwriting on the wall (5:28) for King Belshazzar, the last king of the Babylonian Empire, he told the king that he had been weighed and found wanting and that his kingdom had been divided and given over to the Medes and Persians. So now we have Babylon and Medo-Persia.

Still during the reign of the Babylonian king Belshazzar, Daniel himself had a dream and visions (7:1). What he saw was four beasts: the first was like a lion and had wings of an eagle. The second resembled a bear raised up on one side with three ribs in its mouth between its teeth. The third was like a leopard, which had on its back four wings of a bird, it had four heads, and dominion was given to it. The fourth was dreadful and terrifying and extremely strong, having large iron teeth and ten horns from which came a little horn possessing eyes like a man and a mouth uttering great boasts (7:3-8).

In desiring to know the identity of the fourth beast, we see that the little horn was waging war against the saints of the Highest One and overpowering them until the Ancient of Days came and judgment was passed in favor of them and they took possession of the kingdom (7:19-22). We see that this little horn will speak out against the Most High and wear down the saints of the Highest One, but that his dominion will be taken away and that dominion will be given to the people of the saints of the Highest One, and that His kingdom will be an everlasting kingdom, and that all the dominions will serve and obey Him (7:24-27). While none of these kingdoms are identified by name, many of the traits of this fourth beast should ring familiar to the reader.

Still in the reign of Belshazzar (8:1), Daniel had another vision, this time of a ram with two horns, butting westward, northward, and southward. No other beasts could stand before him, he did as he pleased, and magnified himself (8:3-4). Daniel also saw a male goat coming from the west with a conspicuous (large) horn between his eyes. This goat came up to the ram, rushed at him in his mighty wrath, striking him and shattering his two horns, hurling him to the ground and trampling him. Then he magnified himself exceedingly, after which the large horn was broken, and in its place four other horns came up toward the four winds of heaven, and out of one of them came a rather small horn (another little horn?), and so on (8:5-9).

The ram with the two horns is identified as the kings of Media and Persia (8:20), and the goat as the kingdom of Greece (8:21). The large horn can safely be said to be Alexander the Great and the little horn as Antiochus Epiphanes. So, now we have identified Nebuchadnezzar (Babylon), Medo-Persia, and Greece definitively as the first three kingdoms. The fourth should not be too hard to identify – unless one is in the futurist camp.

The fourth kingdom of King Nebuchadnezzar's dream is the fourth kingdom of chapter 7, which, as we said, is unidentified. But, as we also said, there are a number of entities that can be safely determined.

As Daniel kept looking, he saw with the clouds of heaven, one like a Son of Man (Christ) coming and He was presented before the Ancient of Days (the Lord God Almighty) and was given dominion, glory, and a kingdom (7:13-14). So, as we see, and as we so noted, the saints of the Highest One (Christ) took possession of the kingdom (7:22); and His kingdom will be an everlasting kingdom (7:27).

Also, the vision of Daniel seeing the Son of Man coming on the clouds of heaven cannot be different from the prophecy of Jesus when He addressed His audience in saying that *they–that generation*–would see the Son of Man coming on the clouds of the sky (Matthew 24:30) – or else that would produce the conundrum of being two separate events, which is untenable. The problem that exists as things stand today is that the majority futurist view puts them both, as one (possibly) event, still in our future. Remember, God comes in judgment against His people. Why could that not be what Daniel and Jesus were both prophesying?

Now we will examine one of the most abused of Daniel's prophecies–one of which we have already touched on. In 9:24-27, also known as the seventy weeks, we noted that that was an answer, by the angel Gabriel, to Daniel's prayer of 9:1-19. Verse 9:24 lays it all out: a. to finish the transgression, b. to make an end of sin, c. to make atonement for inequity, d. to bring in everlasting righteousness, e. to seal up vision and prophecy, and f. to anoint the most holy place. How could anything other than the resurrection satisfy those events?

Here, then: a. the finish of transgression was the point at which God chose to punish the people for the transgression of playing the harlot by worshiping other gods and killing His prophets; b. the end of sin occurred at the cross (Isaiah 1:18; 43:25; 44:22)–aren't our sins forgiven: past, present, and future – if we are in Christ? c. Jesus made the final atonement (Hebrews 7:27; 9:11-12,15,28; 10:12,14); d. the saved have everlasting righteousness (Romans 3:21-22; 4:5; 5:15-21); e. the Scriptures are complete – there is no more inspired vision and prophecy; and f. the Temple is no more – it is now our hearts, where Christ dwells (it is anointed in the Person of the Holy Spirit). This may not be the perfect analogy, and it surely will not satisfy many, but placing another mythical and incomprehensible meaning to those words does violence to them.

As we look at 10:1 and 11:1, we see Daniel identifying this as the time of Cyrus king of Persia, and Darius the Mede, respectively. In other words–Medo-Persia; and 10:20 talks of the prince of Persia and the prince of Greece. Verse 11:3 also mentions the realm of Greece. This has all been covered in the vision of the ram and goat in chapter 8. The rest of chapter 11 talks about the kings of the north and south.

Finally, as part of the vision of chapters 10 and 11, we come to the beginning of chapter 12. We have already discussed this, but the unmistakable fact is this: the time of distress we already alluded to (12:1) cannot be different than the great tribulation of Matthew 24:21, for then the conundrum of having to satisfy two separate events again presents itself, on the one hand. On the other, they would pertain to the same event, but the futurists refuse to accept the Scriptures at face value. This is no different than what they do regarding the Son of Man coming on the clouds, which we previously discussed.

Those in the futurist camp are enamored with expressions of "the end" such as: "the time of the end" (Daniel 8:17,19), or, the "end time" (11:35,40), or, conceal these words and seal up the book until "the end of time" (12:4), or, "the end of the world": [Matthew 13:39,40,49; 24:3; 28:20 (KJV)]; and finally, "the end" (Matthew 24:6,13,14) – these are "the end times!" The futurists put everything way out there in some far away time and they try to shape events to fit whatever scenario that they devise.

The dreams, visions, and interpretations of Daniel identify, as we said, the kingdoms of Nebuchadnezzar (Babylon), Medo-Persia, and Greece, while remaining silent on the identity of a fourth kingdom which was yet to come. Daniel wasn't describing an imaginary kingdom thousands of years hence. Jerusalem had been captured in 586BC, and the seventy-year captivity took the date to 516. This was the time in which Daniel had his dreams, visions, and interpretations, and this was the time in which he was praying.

The *Roman Republic* came into being shortly thereafter, in 510BC, and, in 27BC the *Roman Empire* was declared, lasting to 483AD, thus totaling 993 years; but that is just the half of it. The *Roman Kingdom,* also called the *Byzantine Empire*, or, the *Eastern Roman Empire*, whose capital was Constantinople (formerly Smyrna, now modern-day Izmir, Turkey) and was named after the Roman Emperor Constantine, continued until 1453AD, for a grand total of 1,963 years! Rome was surely Daniel's fourth beast.

A library could be filled with books written on what Daniel's fourth kingdom is or might be, and it would be filled with books which would portray that fourth kingdom almost exclusively as a kingdom still in the future. It is established in history that Babylon was followed by Medo-Persia, then Greece, and then Rome.

It was during the time of the Greece-to-Rome transition that Judea was Hellenized,[9] which is why the New Testament manu-

---

[9] Hellenization (or Hellenisation) is the historical spread of ancient Greek culture, religion and, to a lesser extent, language, over foreign peoples conquered by Greeks or brought into their sphere of influence, particularly during the Hellenistic period following the campaigns of Alexander the Great in the fourth century BC–Wikipedia.

scripts are written in Koine Greek.[10] It was also the time of the virgin birth, the crucifixion, and the resurrection (which gave birth to Christianity and the church), the great persecution of Christianity and the church, the destruction and desolation of Jerusalem and the Temple, and the scattering–all of which changed the world and all of which happened with seventy years.

For some reason, scholars gloss over the significance of that seventy-year period in time during the Roman Empire, and instead put all the emphasis on our future, when it comes to eschatology. The fourth kingdom was Rome, and what happened at the Cross is the pinnacle of history. Rome was in charge–they were "the world." The futurists have anointed themselves, ourselves, and all of mankind from the first century *onward*, as the center of history–instead of recognizing the events *of* the first century as such.

Why would the inspired writers go through such painstaking lengths in identifying three kingdoms to Daniel, the first of which was, at that time, the present kingdom of Babylon; then correctly identify the next two (Medo-Persia and Greece); and then just arbitrarily skip the next, Rome – which was not only the greatest and strongest kingdom ever, even to this day – but it included, without question, the unparalleled events which God brought into existence, such as, to repeat: the long-prophesied Messiah, His virgin birth and His resurrection; the church and the ensuing great persecution; the destruction of Jerusalem and the Temple, ending the old covenant; and the fulfilling of the Great Commission?

---

[10] Koine Greek, also known as Alexandrian dialect, common Attic, Hellenistic, or Biblical Greek, was the common supra-regional form of Greek spoken and written during the Hellenistic period, the Roman Empire, and the early Byzantine Empire, or late antiquity. It evolved from the spread of Greek following the conquests of Alexander the Great in the fourth century BC–Wikipedia

Summary

It is plain to see that the Pharisees, the Sadducees, and the scribes – the religious leaders during the time of the Gospels – were no different than their "fathers" had been in the Old Testament (Part I); and why would they be? They were the sons and grandsons of those Old Testament fathers.

Consider, God had chosen the Israelites from among all the peoples of the land to be His. Those Israelites, the twelve tribes, which were then led by Judges and Kings, were a united Kingdom of Israel through the time of King David and his son King Solomon, at which time ten tribes were taken from him and given to Jeroboam, king of Israel, with the remaining two, Judah going to, and Benjamin given to Solomon's son Rehoboam, which began the kingdom of Judah, thus beginning the Divided Kingdom of Israel and Judah.

Now, in Jesus' time, the land was called Judea, and Jesus was colliding with the descendants of those same fathers of Part I, who were such sticklers to detail in things of minor importance, but neglected the weightier provisions of the law. They continued to kill the prophets and they killed Jesus – they continued to play the harlot.

The Harlot

Part III – In the Revelation

Introduction

By now, readers should be weary of hearing the incessant drumbeat of God's people playing the harlot. So, now we come to Revelation, where the heart of the matter *is* the harlot–as it has been from the beginning, and as it will be to the end. God's people became the harlot because of what they did – they forsook God and worshipped other gods. They played the harlot and became as God. That has always been man's sin.

With the exception of one verse in chapter fourteen, the entirety of the subject of the harlot in the Revelation is in the last part of chapter sixteen, all of chapters seventeen and eighteen, and the first part of chapter nineteen. There are also analogies to chapters twelve and thirteen. They will all be our subject matter. Keeping in mind what was covered in Parts I and II, grasping the concept of the harlot will enable the reader to better understand a sizable chunk of Revelation and see as it relates to all of prophecy in the process–and also offer a look into what God expects of us and how we can go about fulfilling His promise in our lives. This is an important step in understanding all of prophecy.

The prophets came to Israel and Judah to tell the people to stop what they had been doing and turn back to God. This is a thread that has run throughout. God will visit judgment, He will visit the iniquity of the fathers onto the children of those who hate Him–to the third and fourth generation! A God-hater will be inflicting punishment, not only upon himself, but upon his children, their children, and their children. Those are the curses. But more importantly, God is longsuffering and shows lovingkindness, offering His blessings to all those who love Him. The people had the law, and therefore the blessings for obedience, as well as the curses for disobedience, which are stated in Leviticus 26 and Deuteronomy 28.

When it comes to Revelation, many learned people, errantly or otherwise, literally create something out of nothing. Let's face it – we still don't understand what it all means. It has become such a jumbled mess and a tangle of conjecture that none of it makes sense. The end result is this: any way other than God's way is the wrong way, for it becomes a ziggurat, and that is idolatry. Man gets carried away by the lust of his own way, which gives way to the sin of idolatry, for man thinks he is God and contends with God, and tries to supplant God. But man's way is folly. God's Word is the way. God's Word is good. So, whether figuratively, literally, spiritually, in a worldly, earthly, humanly-manner, or however you approach and look at Revelation and eschatology, and every one of those ways will be needed at one time or another, these passages are hard to understand. That makes the interpretation of them susceptible to manipulation, and wherever confusion reigns, there is not God.

That John received the Revelation is not in dispute. The date, however, is. When he received it is one of those areas where some have twisted facts and taken advantage of a general lack of knowledge and understanding of the early, difficult to understand historical writings. As a result, confusion has been sown. The date that the apocalypse was received and written determines what the context will be in interpreting it. If John received and wrote it *before*

INTRODUCTION

70AD, then eschatology can be shown to be about God's people and what happened to them up to the destruction of 70AD, for that is what was looming on the horizon – except they didn't know it.

The implications of that are several: first, the destruction spoken of by the prophets and Jesus was fulfilled, courtesy of Assyria and Babylon in 722 and 586BC, respectively, and then again by Rome in 70AD. That's pretty simple. Those are facts rooted in history. Second, it takes Jesus' beautiful prophecies and parables, and places them into *that* time frame – back *then* – and that allows us to view them and interpret them and analyze them to our heart's content in a much more logical way. Third, it shows that God *imputes* to man the knowledge of interpretation. Without it, man would not be capable of understanding His word. And fourth, it allows us to view the events of those prophecies, and prophecy, in general, as events of history, enabling us to strive to live within God's promise of blessings instead of striving to be God and reaping the curses.

Placing the date *after* 70AD implies that Jesus and Daniel could *possibly* have been talking about 70AD, but, then again, maybe not – maybe it's in the future as the futurists say. It's a choice that creates many other choices – and so much confusion. In reality, know that ignoring the historical facts and not attributing them to God and crediting God is denying God. This sows nothing but confusion, and for the most part, that is what man has done.

"But the rapture and all those things didn't happen yet, so it's still in the future," they say, and so it goes. What that gets us is the hopelessly tangled web of fanciful scenarios and misinformation which have permeated the marketplace of ideas. The entire meaning of the Bible becomes not only in doubt, but in fact, makes it impossible to come to its true and proper meaning at all. It is impossible because those explanations are built on a premise. There is a premise at the beginning of this book, but that doesn't matter in this conversation because this book is only a book, whereas the Bible is God's word. He gave it and gave us the tools so that we would rightly interpret it and understand it. Misinterpreting the Revelation is *our* error and is the root of the error of prophecy and eschatology. Everything which is difficult to interpret is automatically attributed to the end times scenario or to Revelation, and there you have it–the ziggurat bets bigger.

In reality, the fact that prophecy and Revelation are related should make their interpretation somewhat easier. It means that only one explanation is needed for the two. That allows us to *reason* that the great distress that Daniel prophesied in his 12:1, and the Great Tribulation that Jesus prophesied, are the great persecution as described in Acts 8:1, which began at the feet of none other than Saul – Paul! Isn't that fitting? And it then fits into God's story–the same story that we have embarked upon and been studying since page one–His story, History.

Now, taking all which has just been previously stated into consideration, is it fair to ask of the purveyors of the futuristic views that they actually articulate a coherent understanding of Revelation and eschatology? It *is* fair to ask, but they do not have one. They can give you their opinions, theories, and explanations about what all of that symbolism and metaphor means, but it is not coherent or logical. How could it be? If they are not espousing God's story, they are espousing man's story, and everybody has their own opinion of what that story is. Unfortunately, most opinions are in the futurist camp. If you listen closely to what they say, you can pick up the exact spot where they take their leap of faith, and from there, it's "blast off."

Prophecy makes up a significant portion of Scripture, prophecy being defined here as the Revelation, Jesus' Discourse, His other eschatological or prophetic utterances, apostolic utterances, what the prophets themselves said, and any other prophetic utterance by anybody else, as documented in Scripture. But there appears to be a disconnect between prophecy and the rest of Scripture. The futurists have their own explanations about the images and visions

Introduction

in Revelation and prophecy. But what meaning could there be from such a body of Scripture if it is disconnected from the rest?

Their understanding, as the predominant view holds of the events of Revelation, is that the events have not yet occurred. That is why those who espouse those views speak figuratively because nobody really knows. How then, are we to believe that which they tell us, and that which we read, not of the Scriptures themselves, but of that which those learned people have written and spoken of, which supposedly has not yet occurred? There has been much written on this subject by many people since the first century, and they are on the bookshelves and online, available to everybody in the world. And many of the writings of the early church fathers and historians are available also. But it is clear that some of those early learned people were confused by the images of Revelation. Some of them believe that the beast of Revelation is the Antichrist.

Antichrist, depicted as a singular individual who epitomizes or personifies all that is evil in the world, or, as Irenaeus states: the recapitulation of the apostasy–is absurd. The Antichrist is not mentioned in Revelation. It is not even mentioned in Scripture. Only in 1and 2 John does that word even appear, and it is as a *spirit* of antichrist, as mentioned in 1 John 4:3; or *many* antichrists which have appeared, as per 1 John 2:18; and, if you deny that Jesus is the Christ, or if you deny the Father and the Son, *you* are an antichrist, says 1 John 2:22; and finally, 2 John 1:7 says that many deceivers, those that do not acknowledge Jesus Christ, have gone out into the world, denying Him, and *they* are antichrist. So, to repeat: *the* "Antichrist" is not mentioned in Revelation, nor anywhere else in the Bible. It is a figment of man's imagination. Confusing?

But there is a better way. If we can say (and we can) that God's will is to let us know His will, and that He did that by giving us the Scriptures, then why would He confound us with prophecy? There is so much of the Bible that relates to prophecy that it would be a cruel joke on us by God for He to sprinkle, or drop, as some believe, portions of something so incomprehensible, throughout. Well, it is *not* a cruel joke, because He did not sprinkle prophecy throughout in bits and pieces. He *gave* us prophecy. He *wants* us to understand it. Wisdom, knowledge, and understanding are what the Proverbs talk about. And wisdom is something God wants us to have and what He encourages us to seek (James 1:5-8). God is not a God of confusion, but of peace (1 Corinthians 14:33). God is love (1 John 4:8,16). The wild musings that sow confusion are of man.

The better way is to understand that God chose a people, the Israelites, and brought them to His city, Jerusalem, where King Solomon built His Temple. God instituted the sacrifice system to make atonement for our sins. Jesus then came and made the final atonement for sin, and Christianity came into being. God wanted His people to look to Him, and they did, at times, but they ultimately fell away from what God wanted them to do. They put other gods before Him, playing the harlot, so God punished them.

God came in judgment against His people when they rebelled against Him by using the nations as His tools of judgment, then He came in judgment against those nations that He used as the tools to execute His judgment. He came in judgment against His people three times, first by using Assyria over Israel (Samaria) and then Babylon, over Judah and Jerusalem. He later came in judgment against them by using the Roman Empire. God continually told His people throughout – at the beginning with the law and then afterwards with the prophets, i.e. the two witnesses, the Law and the Prophets – not to worship strange gods. Those gods can be anything – fortune, or even fifteen minutes of fame.

When God *comes* in judgment, could that be a *coming*? When the Assyrians came against Israel, and then God used Nebuchadnezzar to come against Judah, forcing the people into captivity, was that the first coming? When the Romans came against Judea, destroying Jerusalem and the Temple again, driving the Jews out (the great persecution and the diaspora), was that the second coming? When

Introduction

Jesus prophesied that He would come again, was He saying that He would physically return to Earth for a second time (chiliasm), or was He saying that He, God, was going to come in judgment against His rebellious people again for playing the harlot by going after strange gods, killing the prophets, and finally killing His Son?

If the latter is chosen as the answer to the last question, God's plan is evident, and all of the events taking place fall within that plan – His story. Jesus even spoke a parable about it (Matthew 21:33-46). That being the case, all we would have to do is to do our part in fulfilling the Great Commission (Matthew 28:19; Mark 16:15; Acts 1:8).

Jerusalem, the city of God,[11] was destroyed three times: by Nebuchadnezzar, Antiochus Epiphanes, and Titus (Rome). All three would qualify as desolations. God's Temple, the building where the people would come to offer sacrifices for the atonement of sin, was profaned thrice and destroyed twice. They were the abominations. Daniel was praying over the desolation of Jerusalem and the Temple in the *past tense*, and Jesus was prophesying the desolation in the *future tense*. But after that final time, the Temple was not rebuilt. It needed not be rebuilt, and it need never be rebuilt. The atonement has been made at the cross.

God gave us the Scriptures to live by. Jesus said to His disciples and to His followers, "To *you,* it has been given to know the mysteries of the kingdom of God" (Matthew 13:11; Mark. 4:11). That did not end with them–for why would it? Aren't we His followers and disciples? Was the promise only to them or to all who profess the name of Jesus? We, therefore–those who believe in Him and love Him, are His disciples and followers, and it is we, too, who have been given to know the mysteries of the kingdom of God.

---

[11] 2 Chronicles 12:13: "…and he reigned seventeen years in **Jerusalem, the city which the LORD had chosen from all the tribes of Israel, to put His name there**… See also Zechariah 3:2

Jesus also said to those disciples, "I will give you the keys of the kingdom of Heaven" (Matthew 16:19). This was said in a somewhat different context than the previous verses, but those keys have also been granted to us. The futurists might say, "Not so." Or maybe they would say there's a double meaning. Then they fabricate. What more are we looking for? Why are there the burning questions: Why am I here? and: Is there more to life than this? God has blessed us with every spiritual blessing in the heavenly places in Christ (Ephesians 1:3), and He has granted to us everything pertaining to life and Godliness (2 Peter 1:3).

Regarding our text itself, first and foremost, we must understand that Jerusalem was the city that God had chosen to put His name; and we must keep in mind that everything must be kept in that context, for we know that text without context is pretext. That is a true statement. Pretext is a reason to hide the truth, so context is of the utmost importance. People say that you must "let the Scriptures speak for themselves," or, to "let Scripture interpret Scripture." But, those excellent words of wisdom appear to have flown the coop when it comes to eschatology. There are so many written works of Biblical wisdom and knowledge about nearly every topic imaginable about the Scriptures–except eschatology. On that topic, there are very few which do not leave reality. Because of man's insistence in believing in the late-date of the Revelation, the true meaning of it, and eschatology, has become lost.

While you must have a healthy skepticism about man's written word, when it comes to Scripture, you must show yourself an approved workman, not ashamed, rightly dividing the word of truth (2 Timothy 2:15, paraphrased). While keeping your feet firmly planted on the ground at all times, there must be no leap of faith concerning what man writes about Scripture. You must keep looking for the bigger picture in all things. That will allow you to temporarily put to the side those harder-to-understand verses, and not become snared by the metaphoric, the symbolic, or the apocalyptic prose.[12]

What we are concerned with here is the identity of the harlot. We saw, in Part I, that Jerusalem was the harlot and the reasons why. We saw, in Part II, that the people who had been leading God's people for over 600 years, from the time of the captivity in 586BC, until the time of Christ's death in ~33AD, were the sons of those very people who led God's people into idolatry and therefore, judgment and captivity. They were the religious leaders, which were the scribes, Pharisees and Sadducees who opposed Jesus. They became the harlot when they killed God's Son and persecuted the church. We will now see that same depiction of the harlot in Revelation, and we will see her demise. It is a continuous story. If you understand the story of the harlot, you will have understood an important part of Scripture.

Revelation 16:17-21

> [17] Then **the seventh angel poured out his bowl upon the air**, and a loud voice came out of the Temple from the throne, saying, **"It is done."** [18] And there were **flashes of lightning** and **sounds and peals of thunder**; and there was **a great earthquake**, such as there had not been since man came to be upon the earth, **so great** an earthquake was it, and **so mighty**. [19] The great city was split into three parts, and the cities of the nations, fell. **Babylon the Great was remembered before God, to give her the cup of the wine of His fierce wrath.** [20] And

---

[12] For a sound interpretation of that metaphoric and symbolic language, please see David Chilton's excellent commentary, *The Days of Vengeance, An Exposition of the Book of Revelation*.

> every island fled away, and the mountains were not found. **²¹** And huge hailstones, about one hundred pounds each, came down from heaven upon men; and men blasphemed God because of the plague of the hail, because its plague was extremely severe.

We begin our study of the harlot in the Revelation with the seventh angel pouring out his bowl upon the air, also known as the seventh bowl of the wrath of God (16:1,17). Notice that God's presence, as well as His judgment, is once again depicted by thunder, lightning, and earthquakes (16:18). Note also that a cursory on-line search would show that the Holy Land does sit on an active tectonic area as the geologic plates of Europe, Asia and Africa are moving, with the Holy Land being the pressure point, or fulcrum. Isn't that fitting? Things could happen there that – well, who knows for sure – for the angel did say the great city was split into three parts (16:19).

The angel said, "It is done (16:17)." What is done? Was it time for judgment? It was the culmination of something. When Jesus said, "It is finished," as He gave up His Spirit on the cross (John 19:30), that was also the culmination of something. He had completed the work He had come here to do–and that was to put an end to the old covenantal practice of bringing sacrifices for the remission of sin. That was accomplished with His crucifixion and resurrection. Here also, we see the harlot having received the cup of the wine of the fierce wrath of God, at the pouring out of the seventh angel's bowl (16:19).

Revelation 17:1-7

> **¹Then one of the seven angels who had the seven bowls came and spoke with me**, saying, "Come here, **I will show you the judgment of the great**

harlot who sits on many waters, [2] with whom **the kings of the earth committed acts of immorality**, and those who dwell on the earth were made **drunk with the wine of her immorality**." [3] And he carried me away in the Spirit into a wilderness; and I saw **a woman sitting on a scarlet beast**, full of blasphemous names, having seven heads and ten horns. [4] **The woman** was clothed in purple and scarlet, and **adorned with gold and precious stones and pearls**, having **in her hand a gold cup full of abominations** and of the unclean things of her immorality, [5] and on her forehead a name was written, a mystery, **"BABYLON THE GREAT, THE MOTHER OF HARLOTS** AND OF THE ABOMINATIONS OF THE EARTH." [6] And I saw **the woman drunk with the blood of the saints**, and with **the blood of the witnesses of Jesus**. When I saw her, I wondered greatly.[7] And the angel said to me, "Why do you wonder? **I will tell you the mystery of the woman and of the beast that carries her**, which has the seven heads and the ten horns.

The angel told John what he was going to do which was to show him the judgment of the harlot (17:1), and he was also going to show him the mystery of the woman and of the beast that carries her (17:7). The Bible usually gives us a lot of information; it is up to us to sort it all out without getting enmeshed in the harder to understand prose. All of that showing and telling for John to write shows (no pun intended) that God wants us to understand His Word. Eschatology is not in the Scriptures to confound us. In 17:1 he says that the great harlot sits on many waters, while 17:3,7 says the woman sits on a beast. It will make sense soon.

The peoples of the earth were made drunk with the wine of the harlot's immorality (17:2). That immorality, as we have seen, is the worship of strange gods and the killing of the prophets. The woman was drunk with the blood of the saints and of the witnesses of Jesus (17:6). She was clothed in purple and scarlet and *adorned* with precious stones and pearls (17:4). This is a vision of Jerusalem and the Temple. Recall how the disciples showed Jesus the Temple buildings, and how *they* were adorned.[13]

The woman also had written on her forehead, "Babylon the Great, the mother of harlots." This is metaphor (see Glossary). The woman, metaphorically called Babylon the Great, the mother of harlots, *was* the harlot–it was Jerusalem–the Temple–the heart of Judea and God's people. It was the epitome of God on earth, if that were possible (for we know that God does not live in structures made with human hands).

We saw, in 16:19, that Babylon the Great was remembered before God, to give her the cup of the wine of His fierce wrath. In 17:4 she had in her hand a gold cup full of abominations and of the unclean things of her immorality. And we saw that the kings and the peoples of the earth were made drunk with the wine of her immorality and that the kings of the earth committed acts of immorality with her (17:2), with whom she played the harlot by worshipping their gods. We also see, in 14:8, the only other place that Babylon the Great is mentioned outside of 16:17–19:6, that she has made all the nations drink of the wine of the passion of her immorality. They were all getting drunk on the wine of her immorality which was the blood of the Old Testament prophets and of the New Testament saints.

The peoples of the lands would revel when the Israelites would worship their false gods and intermarry with them because then they would be able to sap the Israelites' wealth and change their

---

[13] Luke 21:5; Matthew 24:1; Mark 13:1.

way of life – they would be able to influence them. The merchants of the land who did business with her would also share in the wealth and would have influence on them. The surrounding peoples would have known that God was with the Israelites and that they were prosperous. Regardless, Rome was in charge. They ruled north Africa, Egypt, the Holy Land, Turkey, and southern Europe into England – everything around the Mediterranean Sea. Commerce was of Rome. They were the world.

Ultimately, all of this must always be viewed in this context: Satan, who has opposed God from the beginning, had attempted to destroy any chance for Messiah to come by using Pharaoh (Exodus 1:15-16;22), Jezebel and Athaliah (Part I), and Herod (Matthew 2:13,16). Then, upon failing that, we witnessed his efforts to kill Messiah outright (Matthew 4:5-6; see also Revelation 12), and finally, his desire to destroy Messiah's church as we see now with the killing of the saints; and as we will see shortly when we study Paul and the persecution.

The writing on her forehead–*Babylon the Great* – is, as we said, metaphor because it is obvious that it is not Babylon that we are talking about. In spite of this, some misinterpret it and believe that the Babylon named is either ancient Babylon reincarnate, or that "Babylon" is metaphor for a resurgent Rome, or the papacy, and so on.

What is interesting is that those who believe it is a future Rome fail to recognize that the then-present Rome of the first century was the most powerful nation that has ever existed; and, more importantly, it existed in a period that was unprecedented and unduplicable. And then there are those who say that it is metaphor for a future Jerusalem when Antichrist comes and rules from the reconstructed Temple.

To explode those arguments, we must acknowledge that the Babylon of Revelation is pre-70AD Jerusalem, for the internal evidence suggests that it is. John is instructed to "measure" the Temple, the altar, and those who worship in it (Revelation 11:1-2), which would suggest that the Temple was still standing at that time.

Again, why must the futurists explain that away when the choice is either to see it in those terms–God's terms–rather than to construct another hypothesis? We know that the Temple was destroyed in 70AD, and there is no Temple now, so the futurist says it must be a future Temple, and on and on it goes. Some people actually believe that the construction is "ready to go." They ignore the evidence staring them in the face and create their own. Irenaeus actually believed Antichrist will "sit at the Temple." That is an incredibly dubious statement, as we will see.

In the Bible, "measuring" is sometimes used as a way to calculate destruction, as it was when God said He would *measure* Jerusalem with justice and righteousness (2 Kings 21:12-13; Isaiah 28:17), which was before the destruction of 586BC. It is easy to skip over obscure but important words like "measuring" because God's word is packed with so much that no one can absorb it all. But little facts like these are relevant for determining whether John received the Revelation before or after 70AD because, as previously stated, if he received it post-70AD, the Temple that John was told to measure couldn't possibly be the one that was standing pre-70AD; therefore, build another, ignition, blast off.

The simplest choice is oftentimes the most valid when it comes to making a choice, and in this case the simplest choice is that John was told to measure the first-century Temple. We know that *that* Temple was destroyed within *that* generation. God had established that which He would do, first to Samaria, then to Judah – and He did it. And now He was stating once again, to John, what He would do to Jerusalem and the Temple–and He did that, too. Both times it was for the same reason–playing the harlot by worshipping other gods and killing the prophets. This is logical and it is consistent.

The woman–the harlot–Babylon the Great–Jerusalem–was riding on a beast whose identity we are about to discover.

Understand that the relationship between first-century Judea and Rome, which, as previously stated, ruled nearly the entire perimeter of the Mediterranean Sea, was a symbiotic one, which means the two were interrelated in such a way that the relationship was beneficial, as well as detrimental, to both.

Judea became, at one point, a client state of Rome, which, loosely stated, is a "state" which is controlled or influenced by another larger and more powerful state and of which the "client" depends for support and protection. The client, in this case, Judea, was run by Herod the Great who was a builder, and who was the one who repaired and renovated the Temple to its grandeur of the time of Christ. The original Temple had been destroyed by the Babylonians, and was rebuilt when the Jews came out of captivity, as described in the books of Ezra and Nehemiah. This is the Temple that John was instructed to "measure"–more than 600 years afterwards.

The angel has now said that he would tell John the *mystery* of the woman and of the beast (17:7), just as he had told him that he would show him the *judgment* of the harlot (17:1). We have determined the identity of the woman to be Jerusalem. She is sitting on the beast whose identity we will now discover.

Revelation 17:8-18

> **⁸ "The beast that you saw was, and is not, and is about to come up out of the abyss and go to destruction. And those who dwell on the earth, whose name has not been written in the book of life from the foundation of the world, will wonder when they see the beast, that he was and is not and will come. ⁹ Here is the mind which has wisdom.** The seven heads are seven mountains on

which the woman sits, **¹⁰ and they are seven kings**; five have fallen, one is, the other has not yet come; and when he comes, he must remain a little while. **¹¹ The beast which was and is not is himself also** an eighth and is one of the seven, and he goes to destruction. **¹² The ten horns** which you saw **are ten kings** who have not yet received a kingdom, but they receive authority as kings with the beast for one hour. **¹³ These have one purpose, and they give their power and authority to the beast. ¹⁴ These will wage war against the Lamb, and the Lamb will overcome them, because He is Lord of lords and King of kings, and those who are with Him are the called and chosen and faithful."** ¹⁵ And he said to me, "The waters which you saw where the **harlot** sits, are peoples and multitudes and nations and tongues. **¹⁶ And the ten horns which you saw, and the beast, these will hate the harlot and will make her desolate** and naked, and will eat her flesh and will **burn her up with fire**. **¹⁷ For God has put it in their hearts to execute His purpose by having a common purpose**, and by **giving their kingdom to the beast**, until the words of God will be fulfilled. **¹⁸ The woman whom you saw is the great city, which reigns over the kings of the earth."**

Recapping: the spiritual and religious leaders who opposed Jesus and His followers were the descendants of those whom we have been talking about from page one. They are those who had been playing the harlot throughout Part I, and they are those whom Jesus addressed in Matthew 23. They are also the same as those who crucified Him, and the same whom Stephen had to defend himself against in Acts 6 & 7. When they killed him too, it began the great persecution.

There was now a confluence of events taking place which would culminate in total destruction and desolation, and the end of the age. That was first-century Israel, the center of history. Messiah had come! He walked the earth. His wonderful ministry spread the Good News, but they crucified Him after only a little more than a year. Then He arose! He resurrected! That changed everything! And that is the immovable anchor upon which our salvation rests—and it is strong!

Next, there was the time of the apostles—the Apostolic Age—which ended with the destruction of Jerusalem and the Temple. The Christians, who were being mercilessly rooted out, heeded the signs and fled. The Jews were systematically driven out of Judea (the Diaspora), with those remaining being crushed at Masada in 73AD, ending the Jewish War. The Christians dispersed throughout the world, as was the Gospel: from Jerusalem, to Judea and Samaria, and to the uttermost parts of the earth.

Because the Jewish War began in 66AD and lasted seven years, ending with the siege of Masada in 73, some believe that that time span of seven years, and the fact that the desolation of 70 was the *midpoint* of those seven years, that somehow this all has to have something to do with the seventieth week of Daniel 9:24-27. You see, according to 9:25—from the decree of Cyrus to Messiah is sixty-nine weeks (seven weeks plus sixty-two weeks), amongst other things.

Then, 9:26 says that after the total of sixty-nine weeks, in other words – at the *beginning* of the seventieth week – Messiah will be cut off (crucified?)—amongst other things. Following, 9:27 says that in the *middle* of the week the people of the prince who was to come will destroy the city and the sanctuary (70AD), and he will make a firm covenant with many for one week, and that also the abomination of desolation will come. If the Jewish War was the seventieth week, according to one popular scenario, the destruction of 70 was the *middle* of that week – and so it goes.

There has been much written about the seventy weeks, and the seventieth week in particular, with so many elaborate timelines and scenarios. Predictably, the writers of most of those writings are futurists, so they tend to gloss over the importance of the momentous events of that seventy year period from the virgin birth to the desolation. Their thinking is clouded, and their opinions are skewed. They believe it is all still in the future and, by golly, we're in it.

In reality, a God-centered view would see "Messiah being cut off" as being the crucifixion, and the desolation as being, well, the desolation – the destruction of 70AD, period (again, we see that the Scriptures give us some things we can identify). But more importantly, 9:24 lays it all out. It doesn't bother with the seven weeks and the sixty-two weeks, or the final week – it covers the entire seventy weeks. The futurists are all caught-up in 9:25-27. With what we covered in Part II, we showed that only the Resurrection satisfies all of those events.

Also, occurring within that momentous era was Caesar Nero, who ruled the Roman Empire for fourteen long, hard years (54-68AD). So, recalling that the agitation between the religious leaders and Jesus and His followers turned into the great persecution of Acts 8:1 – now comes Nero, the worst of the worst. By the time he died, it had become an orgy of horror, debauchery, and killing. Rome was the center of man's world, and Judea – Jerusalem – was the center of God's. And they were at war with one another.

Opposition to the newly-formed church, as previously shown, came mostly from the Jews, but eventually also from the Romans. There are instances recorded in Acts where the apostles or disciples were confronted, sometimes violently, by various people – mostly Jews. When Jesus was crucified, it was the Jews who had to hand Him over to the Romans because they did not have the legal authority to carry out an execution themselves. They were adamant, though, that they wanted Him crucified, refusing Pilate's offer of His release, and of Pilate even offering to crucify Barabbas in His stead. The religious leaders were playing the harlot to the bitter end by killing the Lord Himself–the Son. The Jews refused Pilate's offer and so the Romans willingly obliged; they routinely had people killed anyway, and they were experts at crucifixion. But the Jews bore the full responsibility, just as Jesus said they would (Matthew 23:35).

Revelation 17:8 says that the beast: was, is not, and *is about to* come. And then it says that it was, is not, and *will* come. Is this important? God said through inspiration, basically the same thing twice in the same sentence, so it *must* be important. And it is important to us in that, as we look at how God interacted with His people, we should act in a way accordingly, which would enable us to avoid the mistakes the Israelites made and thus, avoid God's judgment.

But, putting prophecy and Revelation in our future leaves us in the same vulnerable predicament as the Israelites, and later the Jews of Judea, in that those prophecies and judgments to them would stand as "little more than historical events" with apparently little or no effect; rather than as cause and effect situations, which should be heeded. The result is that 17:8 has blown more minds and caused so much confusion–which is exactly what should not have happened.

The wicked Nero, who committed suicide in 68AD, was thought to have been either dead and was going to come back to life, or that he was not dead at all. Such were the thoughts of the people living under those conditions.[14] We need to understand that the Temple

---

[14] Amazingly, even Nero's death in 68 would not calm the fears of the Roman population. Many believed that reports of Nero's death were untrue, and that the evil despot had simply fled to another nearby nation and would assemble an army in order to once again seize control by force of Rome…In short, the terror that Nero had spawned did not abate with his death, **nor did Christian persecution**, as fears continued **for decades and even centuries** that Nero and all of his horrors and evil would soon reappear…Fears of Nero's return, even from the dead, would continue for decades and even centuries.–Taken from False Doctrines of Man – 2-19-2015. Bench, Abilene, Texas. —-online

was destroyed for a reason, and that reason was *not* that it happened because the Romans did it "strictly as an act of war." They did it because God directed events in such a way that, since the Resurrection, the sacrifice system was no longer needed. A review of the passages of Jeremiah 50 and Romans 13 in the Preamble of Part I, and its pertinence to this subject shows that God is always in control – He is in control of the nations – to fulfill His will.

The entirety of what we've been studying in Parts I and II changed with the Resurrection. Therefore, even the idea of having to make atonement was moot, but the only way to stop the people from continuing to impose the old covenant practice of circumcision and sacrifice, and accept the results of the Resurrection, was to take the old covenant practices out of the way altogether. Hence, the Temple was destroyed and the Jews were driven out of Judea and Samaria (after the Christians had gotten out – to the uttermost parts of the earth).

But, in reality, who could that twice-written statement in 17:8 possibly pertain to, other than those people back then in the period of 30-70AD – those who were being addressed and were literally living the persecution? To the futurist who says that the Revelation was seen after 90AD, it means us and 'everybody and anybody' who comes after us. Just look at all the confusion and conjecture that that has evoked. Think of how much easier many decisions in life would be if you already knew what the outcome would be for many of those profound circumstances and decisions which we all are confronted with from time to time, in which we could just see God's hand and not have to strive to be as God. That is what we have in the Scriptures – everything pertaining to life and Godliness (2 Peter 1:3).

If the student of the Bible looks hard enough, the Scriptures always give you something you can grasp. Verse 17:9 says, "Here is the mind which has wisdom…" Apparently, there is an implication here that we should understand that which came next. The deciphering of the rest of 17:9-12 is beyond the scope of this book–other than what we've already stated. The fact is, that as 17:10 says, "one king is, *and one is to come,*" etc. That vision was a warning – a sign to the Christians – to flee!

So, one may ask: what does "the mind which has wisdom" mean here? The Scriptures say wisdom is something we should all strive to attain (James 1:5); for *the fear of the* LORD *is the beginning of wisdom, and the knowledge of the Holy One is understanding*, says Proverbs 9:10. Wisdom, knowledge, and understanding. If you seek wisdom, knowledge in the understanding of God's word will follow, and you will understand eschatology.

One thing is for certain: man has been obsessed with these kings. The seven heads of the beast are seven kings, and the ten horns are also ten kings – seventeen kings in all. Many scholars have tried to figure out the who's-who of the kings, ignoring the fact that they all have one purpose, and that is to give power and authority to the beast to wage war against the Lamb (Revelation 17:13-14). The Lamb is the Lamb of God – who takes away the sin of the world. It is Jesus Christ – and the Lamb has overcome (1 John 2:13-14; 4:4; and 5:4-5). The Lamb–the Lion of the tribe of Judah – the Root of David–has overcome (Revelation 5:5), which means we have overcome (Revelation 2:7,11,17).

The war that the kings wage even has a name–The Jewish War. It is the war the Jews waged against Rome (66-73), and which the Romans and Jews, in all probability, uncoordinated, were simultaneously waging against the Christians–the great persecution–leading to total destruction and desolation – the end of the old covenant and the fulfillment of the Great Commission.

That the Lamb has overcome is the basic tenet of Christianity. The Lamb could not have overcome had He not been raised from the dead. The Apostle Paul raises that point (no pun intended) in 1 Corinthians 15:12-19, when, in 15:13-14, he states that if there is no resurrection, then not even Christ has been resurrected. He repeats that in 15:16 and then he says, in 15:17 that if that were the case (if there was no resurrection), our faith would be worthless – we would still be dead in our sin.

The "overcoming" occurred at the resurrection, and we have overcome as a *result* of it. We are a by-product of God's work; we are not as God, nor are we a god – period. Jesus is faithful and true (Revelation 3:14 and 19:11), and His words are faithful and true (21:5 and 22:6). That should be an encouragement and an inspiration. We are: called, chosen, and faithful (17:14); but we are not faithful and true, because we are not God. We are imperfect, fallible man – as dust.

Here is another interesting tidbit: how does 17:9 relate "the mind which has wisdom" with the Book of Life which contains those names written in it "from the foundation of the world"–in the middle of our discussion about "the beast which was, and is, and is not?" Not only that, 17:8 does not talk about those whose names *were* written in the Book, it talks of those whose names had *not* been written in the Book since the foundation of the world. And it was *they* who were to wonder when they see the beast.

Here is the reason it is related: the Book of Life contains the names of those who Daniel said, in Daniel 12:1 (see also Part II), would be rescued – rescued! Also: this happens at the same time as the time of distress. So, if God chose those whom He saved and had their names in the Book of life from the foundation of the world, *they* were rescued when they were raised with Christ. And that occurred at the Resurrection. We will see the relationship between Daniel 12:1 and Matthew 24:21, as well as Acts 8:1. It's all related.

So, the Romans hated the Christians. The Romans also hated the Jews. Heck, they pretty much hated everybody. And the Jews likewise, hated the Christians and the Romans. Also at that time, as the persecution intensified, Rome, with a sizable number of Jews *and* Christians, was ready to explode. It is hard to understand how poorly the Christians were considered (in the worst possible way)

– as though they were a plague on humanity. "Persistent rumor held that the Christians were dangerous, 'haters of the human race'" – from Tertullian's *Apology*, by William M. Green-7/11/1968 issue of the Gospel Guardian – Bench, *False Doctrines*.

The Romans had become sunken into debauchery under Nero, who then turned his perverse hatred of the Christians into a full-scale attempt to exterminate them. That hatred had been further fueled by the people of Rome, who accused him of setting the fires which had burned a sizable portion of the city–so he falsely put the blame on the Christians.

> From *"The Bible–Of Divine or Human Origin?"* 9-13-1962 issue of "The Gospel Guardian" – Bench: "The church was often under local and sporadic (though intense) persecution **from the Jews** from her earliest years. But following the burning of Rome in July of 64 A.D., the infamous **Nero, seeking to shift blame** for the fire from himself **accused the Christians** of having fired the city**, and inaugurated an empire-wide effort to exterminate the entire body of Christians in all his domain**. This was the first of ten such imperial persecutions, and many thousands perished in the awful onslaught.

As can be seen from the above, we now come across what are called "imperial persecutions" in which the government had joined in. That may have been the first of many of those imperial persecutions, but there never was a chance at extermination. Jesus changed the world! He changed everything! Nero, to his discredit, was the worst of the worst, and his persecution happened at a time when the Temple still stood and the Jews were still practicing old covenant circumcision (but of the flesh, not of the heart–Romans 2:17-29). But now, with justification by faith (Romans 3:21-31), the old covenant had to go. Man was not going to have his way, God was going to have His, because it is His story – history.

As if that weren't enough, Rome also had been increasing taxes on the Jews of Judea, and it got to the point where the Jews eventually rebelled, and all-out war began (the Jewish War, 66-73AD). Combine that with the great persecution which was already going on from the Jews since the killing of Stephen, and there was now a total conflagration, which culminated in 70AD. There are no greater events that man can create or conjure up that can even come close to that! There is no greater time period in history. Domitian's era has nothing on that, as we will see. How can puny man match that? Why even try? Be still and know that the Lord is God. Be the best that *you* can be. Who could ask for anything more?

> [From: "Clerical Celibacy and God's Word" by Luther W. Martin, 10/10/1957 issue of "The Gospel Guardian." 'Paul is thought to have written his First Corinthians letter about **56-57, and the Neronian persecutions took place between those dates and the end of Nero's reign, which terminated in 68.** He appeared to take personal delight in subjecting Christians to all manner of tortures. It is known that **Nero even brought the torture of Christians to the various provinces of his Empire**, as he went from city to city, engaging in the grossest immoralities… in this series of debaucheries.'

> From: "Preterism, Nero, and Domitian" at www.historicalpreterism.com 'Yet, **this persecution was the first time the government of Rome differentiated Christians from Jews**. Tertullian referred to this as *institutum Neronianum,* which was written describing the persecutions starting with Nero **and**

those who followed in his footsteps.']–Bench, *Doctrines*.

It must be pointed out that the persecution didn't start with Nero. It can be argued that it started with the crucifixion of Jesus, or even at the start of His ministry, as we see all the opposition He endured from the religious leaders. Scripture sets the more accurate origin at the feet of Saul (Paul) in Acts 8:1. Those who followed in Nero's footsteps will soon be discussed.

So, our harlot – the woman – Jerusalem, is riding on the seven-headed ten-horned beast, and all those heads, horns – kings, seventeen in all–had only one purpose, which was to give all their power and authority to the beast. In other words, all the kingdoms – all the kings – all the strength that the Roman Empire could muster, in conjunction with all the hatred of the Jews for the Christians and the Romans, was now turned on the Christians even while those two fought each other. Futurists are still waiting for the great tribulation, which some call the Battle of Armageddon (Revelation 16:16), but the great tribulation was taking place in real time as the war and persecution raged through Judea and Jerusalem–God's city was being burned and leveled, His Holy Place destroyed, and the Christians were being rooted out and killed.

We already saw that the woman – the harlot – Babylon the Great – Jerusalem – was drunk on the blood of the saints and of the witnesses of Jesus (Revelation 17:6). Those were the ones she killed during the great persecution. They, and the saints and followers that she did not kill, are the chosen and faithful (17:14). The harlot, at this point, has been punished. We have overcome. But that does not mean we live persecution-free lives; persecution still comes because man is still sinful, and the spirit of antichrist still exists.

The waters, as we see (17:1,15) are the peoples, multitudes, nations, and tongues of the earth – they are the peoples of the lands. The Roman Empire covered a lot of real estate at that time (the entire perimeter of the Mediterranean Sea), and they held it for about 1,000 years. There has never been another like it. In fact, when you include the Eastern Roman Empire, also known as the Byzantine Empire, Rome had ruled for nearly 2,000 years. It encompassed many peoples, multitudes, and nations–many tongues. It was the *known* world. It was *the* world. It is in *that* context that the word *aión* should be viewed when translated *world*. At that time–that was it! That was the world! Text without context is pretext.

By now we know that the Jews hated the Christians and were literally trying to stomp them out. The problem was that many of their own (Jews) were being converted by the very people (Christians) whose leader (Christ) they (the Jews) had condemned to death for daring to say that He would destroy their Temple and rebuild it in three days (John 2:18-22). He was also someone who claimed to have been resurrected from the dead (Luke 24:44-47). So, the Christians had to go, but so did the Jews (Revelation 17:16).

By the time the Jewish War officially broke out, the Jews *and* Romans were trying to exterminate the Christians, and now the Romans were actually trying to exterminate the Jews, too. The Christians eventually fled, and the Jews were forced out of Judea by the Romans. The city was sacked and burned, the Temple was profaned, and then destroyed. When the Romans planted their standard in the Holy Place, that was the abomination of desolation. "When you see the abomination of desolation, which was spoken of by Daniel," said Jesus. The people had seen this before, they knew what it meant, and they got out. That was desolation, as in overrun by strangers.

["**Nero died two years before the destruction of Jerusalem. The reigning emperor at the time of this event was Vespasian, who basically had an indifferent attitude toward Christianity before**

that event. The destruction of Jerusalem, as previously noted, would change his perception. This is based upon a document cited by Sir William Ramsay describing **Titus, the eldest son of Vespasian and the general completing the siege of the city**, and the observation that **he thought the Christian sect, like a vine, would die with the death of its root, Judaism**. However, as Ramsay notes, that did not happen which, in fact, affected the attitude of the Romans toward the church."–Howard W. Denham, Truth Bible Institute.9 – Bench].

So, Vespasian[15] (69-79AD) followed Nero as Emperor and got his claim to fame from his campaign against Judea before he became Emperor, and now his son Titus would finish the task by destroying the city and the Temple. The attitudes of both are noteworthy. Vespasian was indifferent toward Christians–didn't care if they lived or died, which is bad enough. But his son Titus was even worse. After watching Nero's and his father's failed attempts at extermination, Titus devised an attempt to also exterminate the Jews, surmising *that killing the root would kill the vine*. There it was: a total firestorm.

Scholars don't talk about the fact that the Scriptures *tell you* that the great persecution occurred. Historic events bear that out. Daniel prophesied it, Jesus prophesied it, it began in Acts 8, and history reaffirms it. Man has been lulled to sleep by the siren song of, "We are the ones who will witness the Great Tribulation." Man may yet bring something similar upon himself, and then it will have become a *fait accompli*, but it will not be the Great Tribulation.

---

[15] Vespasian's renown came from his military success; he was legate of Legio II Augusta during the Roman invasion of Britain in 43 and subjugated Judaea during the Jewish rebellion of 66 – Wikipedia

The HARLOT *of* REVELATION

Revelation 18:1-8

¹After these things I saw another angel coming down from heaven, having great authority, and the earth was illumined with his glory. ² And he cried out with a mighty voice, saying, **"Fallen, fallen is Babylon the Great! She has become a dwelling place of demons and a prison of every unclean spirit, and a prison of every unclean and hateful bird. ³ For all the nations have drunk of the wine of the passion of her immorality, and the kings of the earth have committed acts of immorality with her, and the merchants of the earth have become rich by the wealth of her sensuality."** ⁴ I heard another voice from heaven, saying, **"Come out of her, my people, so that you will not participate in her sins and receive of her plagues; ⁵ for her sins have piled up as high as heaven, and God has remembered her iniquities.** ⁶ Pay her back even as she has paid, and give back to her double according to her deeds; in the cup which she has mixed, mix twice as much for her. ⁷ To the degree that she glorified herself and lived sensuously, to the same degree give her torment and mourning; **for she says in her heart, 'I sit as a queen and I am not a widow, and will never see mourning.'** ⁸ **For this reason** in one day her plagues will come, pestilence and mourning and famine, and **she will be burned up with fire; for the Lord God who judges her is strong.**

We have now seen God's judgment on Jerusalem – the harlot– Babylon the Great. She has fallen. This was 70AD. Judea was crushed. Destruction and desolation came upon the Great City. The war had been raging for more than three years and the tribulation had been ongoing for an entire generation. The Romans were pushing the Jews out of Judea and Samaria. The city had been burned. Jerusalem had become a dwelling place for demons and a prison of every unclean spirit, and every unclean and hateful bird (18:2) and her sins had piled up as high as heaven (18:5). That is about as desolate a description as one can make of a city, and it was a description made of Jerusalem. Revelation 16:19 says Babylon the Great was remembered before God, to give her the cup of the wine of His fierce wrath, for God has remembered her iniquities (18:5).

All the nations had drunk the wine of the passion of her immorality, not just the wine of, nor the passion of, but the wine of the passion, of her immorality. We talked about the wine of her immorality in 17:1-7, and we mentioned 14:8, the only other place in Scripture where Babylon the Great is mentioned and which also talks of the wine of the passion of her immorality. We also saw in 17:2 that the peoples, merchants, and kings of the earth had become drunk on the wine of her immorality, while here, in 18:3, the kings of the earth have committed acts of immorality with her and the merchants of the earth have become rich by the wealth of her sensuality.

Finally, we see in 18:7, the epitome of the fall of man: "for she says in her heart, 'I sit as a queen and I am not a widow, and I will never see mourning.'" *She says in her heart these things.* When a person says something in his heart, he believes it with all his being – he is given over. In this case, she developed a haughty spirit; and a haughty spirit goes before a fall (Proverbs 16:18–KJV). That was her sin, just as it had been Judah's (Ezekiel 16:46-50), and it goes directly back to the original temptation in the Garden of Eden–*you will be like God* (Genesis 3:5). That is a haughty spirit. Therefore, Jerusalem was to be burned up with fire, for the Lord God who judges her is strong (Revelation 18:8).

In 18:4, the text says "come out of her my people." There is good reason to believe that the Christians took this as confirmation of a command by Jesus (Matthew 24:15-18) and fled before the destruction. This is certainly another indication that the Revelation was given before Jerusalem fell.[16] Look at the other possibilities – man's answers – they are puny by comparison. For a hearty laugh, ask a futurist for an explanation of the harlot and the great persecution.

Revelation 18:9-24

> [9] "And **the kings of the earth, who committed acts of immorality and lived sensuously with her**, **will weep** and lament over her when they see the smoke of her burning, [10] standing at a distance because of the fear of her torment, saying, 'Woe, woe, the great city, Babylon, the strong city! For in one hour **your judgment has come**.' [11] "**And the merchants of the earth** weep and mourn over her, because no one buys their cargoes anymore— [12] cargoes of gold and silver and precious stones and pearls and fine linen and purple and silk and scarlet, and every kind of citron wood and every article of ivory and every article made from very costly wood and bronze and iron and marble, [13] and cinnamon and spice and incense and perfume and frankincense and wine and olive oil and fine flour and wheat and cattle and sheep, and cargoes of horses and chariots and slaves and human lives. [14] The fruit you long for has gone from you, and all things that

---

[16] https://www.preteristarchive.com/Bibliography/1998_scott_flee-pella.html; also, Gentry.

were luxurious and splendid have passed away from you and men will no longer find them. **¹⁵ The merchants of these things, who became rich from her**, will stand at a distance because of the fear of her torment, weeping and mourning, ¹⁶ saying, 'Woe, woe, the great city, **she who was clothed in fine linen and purple and scarlet, and adorned with gold and precious stones and pearls;** ¹⁷ for **in one hour** such great wealth **has been laid waste**!' And every shipmaster and every passenger and sailor, and as many as make their living by the sea, stood at a distance, ¹⁸ and were crying out as they saw the smoke of her burning, saying, '**What city is like the great city**?' ¹⁹ And they threw dust on their heads and were crying out, weeping and mourning, saying, '**Woe, woe, the great city**, in which all who had ships at sea became rich by her wealth, for **in one hour** she **has been laid waste**!' ²⁰ Rejoice over her, O heaven, and you saints and apostles and prophets, because God has pronounced judgment for you against her." ²¹ Then a strong angel took up a stone like a great millstone and threw it into the sea, saying, "**So will Babylon, the great city, be thrown down with violence, and will not be found any longer**. ²² And the sound of harpists and musicians and flute-players and trumpeters will not be heard in you any longer; and no craftsman of any craft will be found in you any longer; and the sound of a mill will not be heard in you any longer; ²³ and the light of a lamp will not shine in you any longer; and the voice of the bridegroom and bride will not be heard in you any longer; for your merchants were the great men of the earth, because all the nations were deceived by your sorcery. ²⁴ **And in her**

was found the blood of prophets and of saints and of all who have been slain on the earth."

The kings and merchants of the earth lament and mourn and weep over the Great City (18:8), just as Jesus and Daniel wept and lamented over it (Matthew 23:37-39 and Daniel 9:1-19), respectively. The city is *adorned* as a harlot (Revelation 18:16), just as we saw in Part II, where the Temple was adorned as Jesus and His disciples left it, bringing it to His attention as they walked away. "What city is like the great city… (18:18). It was laid waste (18:19), thrown down with violence (18:21), and in her was found the blood of the prophets and of the saints and of *all* who have been slain on the earth (18:24). Jesus had said that upon *them* (the religious leaders of Judea) would fall the guilt of *all* the righteous blood shed on earth (Matthew 23:34-35).

What does "in one hour" mean? It means that it took only a very short period of time for the Mother of Harlots to squander all that God had given her. The futurists will take that "one hour" and point to 2 Peter 3:8 and tell you that it gives justification for their belief that a "generation" can be an endless or indeterminate amount of time, but Revelation 18:17 and 19 are pretty clear in saying that it didn't take long for the harlot to be laid waste.

Rev. 19:1-6

> [1] **After these things** I heard something like a loud voice of a great multitude in heaven, saying, "Hallelujah! Salvation and glory and power belong to our God, [2] BECAUSE HIS JUDGMENTS ARE TRUE AND RIGHTEOUS; for **He has judged the great harlot** who was corrupting the earth with her immorality, and HE HAS AVENGED THE BLOOD OF HIS BOND-SERVANTS

ON HER." ³And a second time they said, "Hallelujah! HER SMOKE RISES UP FOREVER AND EVER." ⁴And the twenty-four elders and the four living creatures fell down and worshiped God who sits on the throne saying, "Amen. Hallelujah!" ⁵And a voice came from the throne, saying, "**Give praise to our God**, all you His bond-servants, you who fear Him, the small and the great." ⁶Then I heard something like the voice of a great multitude and like the sound of many waters and like the sound of mighty **peals of thunder**, saying, **"Hallelujah! For the Lord our God, the Almighty, reigns.**

Heaven is rejoicing (19:1). The harlot has been judged and we know the identities of her and the beast, and the saints and prophets and the followers of Jesus have been avenged (19:2). See the four hallelujahs. Give praise to our Lord, for the Lord God Almighty reigns (19:5-6); and there were peals of thunder. He did it! It is done! It is finished! Give praise to our God; if you believe, you have overcome! You have eternal life! Amen.

Part IV The Early Witness – The Date of the Revelation

Irenaeus – Against Heresies

This author would be remiss if attention was not given to the early eye and ear-witnesses of our Lord and His disciples, and also their friends. Although he was not an eyewitness, nor did he live during the time of Christ and His disciples, Irenaeus was close to some who were their friends. And as Milton Terry said, "It all turns on the testimony of Irenaeus."[17] Sadly, Terry is correct, as we will see. What makes Irenaeus so important for our study was his ability to write, his desire to do so, and what he had to say about the Revelation.

There is no slight intended here toward any of the early fathers, especially Irenaeus, Papias, or Eusebius, but they just didn't get the Revelation right. Eusebius, for his part, had an odd opinion about it which differed from that of Irenaeus, but on the whole, in all of his other writings he was in support of, and in agreement with, Irenaeus. As a result, mankind has suffered as he has struggled with

---

[17] Terry, *Biblical Hermeneutics* pp.237-242.

his understanding of the Revelation and we have, for the most part, been in a stupor ever since about our eschatological roots.

Of all the obstacles to understanding eschatology, the primary one is the words of Irenaeus. He is the earliest and "most reliable" source on the subject, and many of the beliefs that those in the futurist camp hold on the Revelation, nearly two-thousand years hence, trace directly back to him. The date of the book itself is in question because of a "notorious statement" which he made, that we will examine.

There have been other less important impediments to our understanding such as: a) the erroneous translation of the Greek word aión into *world,* b) the loose definition of the word *generation* to mean an indeterminate period of time, and c) the fact that both a and b were exacerbated by the King James Version of the Bible, the first major English translation of the Greek and Hebrew New and Old Testaments, which carried those two errors for more than three-hundred years–virtually unopposed – all of which has been a scenario from hell (we covered a – c in Part II).

The importance of Irenaeus cannot be overstated. He was a prolific writer who lived more than one-hundred ten years after the destruction of 70AD. He didn't know anyone of importance from that era save possibly two – Polycarp, who was more than eighty years old when Irenaeus was a boy of no more than fifteen, and Papias, who was also a futurist, a chiliast, in fact, who died when Irenaeus was approximately twenty-three (see article by Sim, a few pages hence, and the Timeline). These are very important people when it comes to preserving God's word and its teachings, but the connection between them is tenuous because of the age disparities and the nature of the subject.

Irenaeus is highly respected, and his writings are highly regarded, but he did not write under inspiration, therefore his writings should be held up to scrutiny by man in such a way as to refute his futurism. He is revered in his writings, and rightly so, when it comes to most everything else which he wrote about the Scriptures.

The problem is that he is the first futurist who wrote in such abundance on this topic. He is referenced in a rather profuse and tenacious manner by nearly everyone who writes about Revelation. He has been, in fact, *the* source of nearly everybody, ever since.

But neither Irenaeus, nor Papias before him, nor Eusebius after him, nor anyone else for that matter with futurist views, knew anything about which they wrote regarding eschatology–for it is apparent in their writings. How could they, if it was about that which was in their future and supposedly still in ours? Only someone with a view which recognized the events of 70AD as the climax of God's momentous seventy-year period from the virgin birth to the desolation could have a chance at understanding what the message of the Revelation was – and Irenaeus did not share that view. So if we, after nearly two-thousand years, with all the writings in all of that time, still do not understand Revelation, why are we to assume that Irenaeus, after only one-hundred years, did? Furthermore, if we are to assume that he did, why do *we* still not understand it?

The futurist view is man's, not God's, view. Did anyone ever make the point that we have been relying on a futurist as our source about eschatology when that very futurist showed his true colors as a late-date historian, which is what makes him a futurist, when he made his very controversial and notorious statement? That statement is *the* "Irenaean" statement so oft-cited, and it serves as the kernel of man's futurist bent. We will look at that notorious statement, and others, from Irenaeus shortly.

His futurist thought has tainted the entire argument regarding eschatology because his writings have been put forth as the foundational source of nearly everyone after him, such as Eusebius, who was another prolific writer, a very important one at that, and one that we will also look at. As a result, because of the nature of the Revelation, confusion has set in, and where there is confusion it is not of God.

Man has journeyed far afield into the world of the unknown, where science-fiction books have been written and movies have been made on this subject. Man has strayed far from God's word as it relates to Revelation and eschatology. As many as there are who love the Lord, most are confused when it comes to things of the end. Confusion is never good, and as we must accept the fact that confusion has ruled for almost two-thousand years concerning these things, we must also accept that that has hindered our ability to understand. Man has literally been duped.

Could this be a trick from Satan? He does have his ways. Consider: a. the diabolical attempt by Jezebel and Athaliah to destroy or pollute Christ's bloodline. Overall, that effort took approximately one-hundred years before God removed its effects (see Jezebel, Part 1 and Table 1); b. Herod's failed attempt to kill, or to prevent the coming of, the prophesied Messiah when he issued his order to have all first-born males under two years of age murdered (Matthew 2:16); and c. the devil's failure to coax Jesus into throwing Himself off the pinnacle of the Temple (Matthew 4:5-6; Luke 4:9). Taking all of that into account, the two-thousand years of confusion about the date of the Revelation most assuredly had to come from Satan.

Because of man's inability to sort things out, this has become an inadvertent but major besmirching of a large part of the word of God. The result of such flawed thinking is that the church has become weak and cold, always thinking that *their* generation would be *the* generation when Jesus will come back. They view current events as *signs of the end* and *the beginning of birth pangs* (Matthew 24:8); and ultimately, they feel in need of rescue, and thus, their cry for Jesus to come back. Jesus might do that, for no one can say that He can't or won't; but He is more likely to spit us out of His mouth (Revelation 3:15-16). With all of that in mind, know that God always saves a remnant to Himself.

As stated, some of the early church fathers have clearly misunderstood Revelation. As beloved as they were and are considered, they just didn't get it. And why would they? It should be easy for *us* to understand, looking back nearly two-millennia with the luxury of hindsight and written history. But even now it is not easy because we still don't get it either. We all go right back there to that comfort zone and cite Irenaeus and Eusebius, and we end up right back where we started – trying to square Revelation more correctly as the early-date document which it is, when the source of antiquity was a late-dater.[18]

As the reader can see, this article by Sim, in his response to Gundry in his intro, immediately references Papias, somewhat

---

[18] **Here is an example of immediately reverting to the comfort zone,** from: *The Gospel of Matthew, John the elder and the Papias tradition: A response to R H Gundry* by **David C Sim**, Australian Catholic University Melbourne, Australia;–Abstract: As far as the origin of the Gospel of Matthew is concerned, **most modern scholars tend to discount the testimony of Papias**. The major exception in this regard is R H Gundry, who argues that **the tradition transmitted by Papias was delivered to him by John, the Disciple of Jesus**. For Gundry, the apostolic source of **this tradition thereby guarantees its reliability**, in which case we can be confident that Matthew, the Disciple of Jesus, was the author of the Gospel that bears his name. Gundry's arguments are, however, not altogether convincing. **It will be shown that not only is his reading of the Papian tradition questionable, but also that he overstates the reliability of Papias' source**. 1. INTRODUCTION The clear testimony of the ancient Christian church was that the Disciple Matthew wrote the Gospel of Matthew. *The earliest unambiguous statement to this effect was made by Irenaeus around the year 180, who said that Matthew composed a Gospel for the Hebrews in their own dialect while Peter and Paul were preaching in Rome (Against Heresies) 3.1.1; cf too Eusebius, (Church History), 5.8.2). It is generally agreed that Irenaeus' source for this information was Papias, the Bishop of Hierapolis, who wrote about the origins of the Gospels of Mark and Matthew in the early part of the second century* [1] Dr David C Sim (School of Theology, Centre for Early Christian Studies, Australian Catholic University, Melbourne) participates as research associate in the research project "Biblical Theology and Hermeneutics", directed by Prof. Dr Andries G. van Aarde, Department of New Testament Studies, Faculty of Theology, University of Pretoria. An earlier version of this article was presented as a paper at the Western Pacific Rim Patristics Conference in Nagoya, Japan, September 2006. The author thanks the participants for their comments and criticisms. The Gospel of Matthew, John the elder and the Papias tradition 284 HTS 63(1) 2007

disparagingly, then cites Irenaeus, then Eusebius who is quoting Irenaeus, who was in turn using Papias as *his* source. 'It all turns on the unambiguous testimony of Irenaeus.'[19]

This is a prime example of the difficulty in doing research on Revelation. Because Irenaeus is the principal source, who uses Papias, and is then quoted by Eusebius – that is difficult enough, in and of itself. But here we have all that, plus Gundry citing them, then Sim citing him. There should be no doubt in the mind of the reader that a serious undertaking is necessary in rearranging who said what about whom when it comes to things concerning Revelation, and understanding just how convoluted and difficult it is to sort these things out. (Note: cf is used in writing to refer the reader to other material to make a comparison with the topic being discussed – Wikipedia)

In accepting Irenaeus' point of view, look at how far we have strayed in the eighteen-hundred years since his writings. More importantly, the gravity of the events which took place from the birth of Christ until 70AD are unprecedented in history and they scream for acknowledgment, and yet man has managed to ignore their importance. The great persecution started with the killing of Stephen – the Scriptures say so (Acts 8:1). Jesus prophesied it (Matthew 23:34-38; 24:9-12), as did Daniel (12:1), but Irenaeus and the futurists don't even acknowledge it. They are still awaiting the Great Tribulation and Antichrist, who will "destroy all the nations and deceive all the people into believing he is Christ, and who will sit at the Temple." That is incorrect and downright ludicrous.

Consider: a) despite the fact that the persecution was still going full bore in Irenaeus' day–and by the imperial diktat of Rome; b) and despite the fact that Nero was long gone, even though some thought that he was not dead, or that he was coming back to life, according to Revelation 17:8-13 (see footnote 14 Part III); and c)

---

[19] Terry; *Hermeneutics*; p. 237

despite the fact that the desolation of 70 was also long past and, as far as the futurists were concerned, apparently insignificant... despite all of that–the way in which the Gospel was spreading, it had to have made for truly spiritually and emotionally exhilarating, yet very dangerous times.

We have been far too accepting of Irenaeus' view on Revelation. Even today, eighteen-hundred years plus after his passing, the late-daters dominate the argument; and although there is a strong early-date voice, it is a minority view. The early-date view is much more accepting of God's word as events fit, as this author believes he has shown and will continue to show. Things not yet understood will be left uninterpreted and placed aside until more knowledge comes or we go home to the Lord. We need not compete with God.

The Irenaeus argument is also interesting in that he wrote more than one hundred years after the desolation of 70AD, yet he ignores it. He, as a ten or fifteen-year old lad had either 'seen and heard,' or 'sat at the feet of' Polycarp, who knew the Apostle John. So, he actually could have been an apprentice or pupil of Polycarp, or he could have just been present and heard him speak. Polycarp himself was a young man when John died, and Irenaeus was about fifteen when Polycarp died at age eighty-five (see Timeline). Whatever wisdom Polycarp was able to impart upon Irenaeus could have been considerable and valuable, but truncated at best because of the age differential.

Suppose, for the sake of argument, that as a thirty-or-so-year old, Irenaeus was then writing his famous works, *Against Heresies*. The year would be about 170AD, which is 135 or so years after Jesus, and 100 years after the desolation. He would have been writing about the things he learned when he was an early teen from an eighty-five-year old man who might have known John for as many as twenty years at least fifty years prior. It is a complicated and tenuous, but still very possible and plausible, scenario.

And by his own belief in the late date, Irenaeus wrote approximately eighty years after the Revelation was seen. So, after such a period of time, is it reasonable to believe that he somehow understood a writing such as the Revelation? His writings say "no;" and he makes a number of assumptions in the process. Revelation is like no other book in the Bible, and the Bible is like no book ever written by man. Other than Papias and Polycarp, neither of whom have had more than fragments of their writings discovered, who else is available to look to as an authority on the subject–Josephus? He didn't say much on the matter, although his portrayal of the events of the siege, destruction, and desolation of Jerusalem certainly confirms what Jesus prophesied in the Olivet Discourse.

Who is available today who can shed more light on this very difficult subject? Apparently nobody, because everybody uses Irenaeus and Eusebius as their source of choice. Make no mistake, the early historians' writings are learned and useful, and Irenaeus is foremost, but on the subject of eschatology and the apocalypse, they missed the mark. It is guaranteed that at some point in time, Irenaeus, after years of writing, felt pressure to publish, especially in light of the difficulty in fully understanding a subject matter such as the Revelation. If he waited until he understood it fully, he never would have published.

[From an internet search of Irenaeus' *Against Heresies* (Kevin Knight *New Advent* http://www.newadvent,org/fathers/0103.htm), author scanned chapter titles of all the books and determined, for sake of time in not having to read all in their entirety, that Book 5, Chapters 25, 28 and 30 were all that applied to our topic.]

From Irenaeus' *Against Heresies*, **Book V, Chapter 25**–The Fraud, Pride, and Tyrannical Kingdom of Antichrist, as Described by Daniel and Paul:

Paragraph 1: And not only by the particulars already mentioned, but also by means of the events which shall occur in the time of **Antichrist** is it shown that he, being an apostate and a robber, **is anxious to be adored as God**; and that, although a mere slave, he wishes himself to be proclaimed as a king. For he (**Antichrist**) being endued with all the power of the devil, shall come, not as a righteous king, nor as a legitimate king, [i.e., one] in subjection to God, but an impious, unjust, and lawless one; as an apostate, iniquitous and murderous; as a robber, **concentrating in himself [all] satanic apostasy**, and setting aside idols to persuade [men] that he himself is God, raising up himself as the only idol, having in himself the multifarious errors of the other idols. This he does, in order that they who do [now] worship the devil by means of many abominations, may serve himself by this one idol, **of whom the apostle thus speaks in the second Epistle to the Thessalonians: Unless there shall come a failing away first, and the man of sin shall be revealed, the son of perdition, who opposes and exalts himself above all that is called God, or that is worshipped; so that he sits in the Temple of God, showing himself as if he were God.** The apostle therefore clearly points out his apostasy, and that he is lifted up above all that is called God, or that is worshipped — that is, above every idol — for these are indeed so called by men, but are not [really] gods; and that he will endeavour in a tyrannical manner to set himself forth as God.

Let it be clear that the above **emboldened** references to the name "Antichrist" are the first encountered from Irenaeus although contextually, it appears as though he supposes that his readers are familiar with his use of the name. In any event, putting aside for a moment Irenaeus saying: *Antichrist concentrating in himself all satanic apostasy*, comment must be made regarding his reference to 2 Thessalonians 2:3. Here, according to Irenaeus, he is saying that Paul is saying that the man of sin, the son of perdition, *is* the Antichrist and that *he sits in the Temple of God* (this is the first time he makes that statement).

Now keep in mind, Paul's letters to the Thessalonians were written in the early 50's, possibly as early as the year 51–before Nero came to power–while the Temple that Christ and Paul both taught in was still standing! Also keep in mind, as we will show later, Nero himself became the first of the Roman Emperors to officially declare himself to be an enemy of Christianity! That qualifies him to be the personification of the beast.

So, because Irenaeus couldn't figure out what the Scriptures were saying about the so-called Antichrist, he did the best that he could. And, from that supposition, according to him, a new Temple must be built. And that is where *that* hypothesis originates.

Continuing, from *Heresies*:

> Paragraph 2: Moreover, he **(the apostle) has also pointed out** this which I have shown in many ways, **that the Temple in Jerusalem was made by the direction of the true God**. For the apostle himself, speaking in his own person, distinctly called it the Temple of God. Now I have shown in the third book, that no one is termed God by the apostles when speaking for themselves, except Him who

truly is God, the Father of our Lord, by whose directions **the Temple which is at Jerusalem was constructed** for those purposes which I have already mentioned; **in which [Temple] the enemy shall sit, endeavouring to show himself as Christ, as the Lord also declares: But when you shall see the abomination of desolation**, which has been spoken of by Daniel the prophet, standing in the holy place (let him that reads understand), then let those who are in Judea flee into the mountains; and he who is upon the house-top, let him not come down to take anything out of his house: for there shall then be great hardship, such as has not been from the beginning of the world until now, nor ever shall be.

This is rather convoluted, for when Irenaeus says that the Temple in Jerusalem was made by the direction of God, he was correct, but the Temple which he should have been talking about and that which Paul would have been referring to, was the first-century Temple – not a future Temple. Now, Irenaeus published his work in about 180AD; so, in saying that *the Temple which is in Jerusalem... in which Temple the enemy shall sit* (the second time he says that), he appears to be confused. The Temple he is alluding to in which Antichrist will supposedly sit is a Temple which did not and does not exist. And yet that Temple, according to him, is the Temple *made by the direction of the true God*. To add insult to injury, quoting from Matthew 24:15, he equates this enemy, whom he calls the Antichrist, with the abomination of desolation, and he therefore uses Jesus' words in a spurious manner.

Irenaeus, knowing that there is no Temple, believes that a new Temple will be built and that the person known as Antichrist, who is also the abomination of desolation, the son of perdition, and the man of sin, shall sit in it "endeavoring to show that he is

Christ." This, however well-intentioned, is sheer fabrication, and Irenaeus appears as a master builder, for he is constructing a fabulous ziggurat.

> Paragraph 4: **The Lord also spoke as follows to those who did not believe in Him: I have come in my Father's name, and you have not received Me: when another shall come in his own name, him you will receive, calling Antichrist the other, because he is alienated from the Lord.** This is also the unjust judge, whom the Lord mentioned as one who feared not God, neither regarded man, Luke 18:2, etc. to whom the widow fled in her forgetfulness of God – that is, the earthly Jerusalem, – to be avenged of her adversary. Which also he shall do in the time of his kingdom: he shall remove his kingdom into that [city], **and shall sit in the Temple of God**, leading astray those who worship him, as if he were Christ...

It must now be obvious to the point of confirmation that Irenaeus believed, as do many more even today, in a *person* of the Antichrist, when clearly the Scriptures do not state that. They speak, as we noted earlier, in the first two letters from John, of a *spirit* of antichrist, and that *many* antichrists had already come, and that *anyone who denies Jesus* is as antichrist; but nowhere in Scripture is there *the* Antichrist. And yet, here in the very first sentence, Irenaeus, quoting John 5:43, goes on to say: "The Lord also spoke as follows to those who did not believe in Him, '*I have come in my Father's name, and ye have not received Me: when another shall come in his own name, him ye shall receive, calling Antichrist...*'"

Irenaeus is putting words in Jesus' mouth by saying that Christ is saying that Antichrist is, in addition to the other monikers he has already given him, the Unjust Judge of Luke 18:2 and *the other* of John 5:43. Just so the reader understands, it is Irenaeus, not Jesus, who is equating the "other," which is the word Jesus used, with Antichrist. The *other*, as-per Jesus, is simply *another* person so of course, Irenaeus takes Jesus' words out of context. Text without context....

So now, according to Irenaeus, we have Antichrist, who is 1. the son of perdition, 2. the man of sin, 3. the enemy, 4. the abomination of desolation, 5. the unjust judge, and 6. the *other*. Irenaeus, and other futurists, use Antichrist as a mathematician uses the variable 'x'–just plug in a value. That is the problem with futurism. When they can't explain something, they usually have a number of eschatological entities, and they attribute that which they can't explain to one of those other unexplainable entities, in this case Antichrist, and they just go on from there. Most people accept those explanations and so the fallacy is perpetuated and the ziggurat continues to be built.

If only Irenaeus had felt the need to follow John 5:43 with 5:44, he might not have made such an absurd statement. Jesus was not talking about another, such as Antichrist... he was talking about another, such as in 'one another.' In other words, *each other*. Here is 5:44: *"How can you believe, when **you receive glory from one another** and you do not seek the glory that is from the one and only God?"* As the reader can see, they would *receive* another because they *receive glory from* one another, not from God. Jesus was not talking about any particular person, let alone someone such as Antichrist, which, sadly to say, is a figment of Irenaeus' imagination. But that is how it starts, and it builds from there, as we will continue to see.

So, Irenaeus has made a *carte blanche* assumption that the *other* is Antichrist. That is a leap of faith. You can always find the spot where the leap of faith occurs when you listen to futurists. Remember the statement printed at the beginning of this book: text without context is pretext. It is from there, at the place of *no* context, that pretext forms. That is how futurism gets its traction. Irenaeus just assumed that Jesus was talking about a *person* somewhere in our future called the Antichrist, and that he will sit in a Temple which didn't even exist when he wrote (the third time he has said that) but did exist in both Jesus' and Paul's day.

This has become so perplexing and torturous that it is not capable of being understood. How many man-made creations have been made from that leap? a) Antichrist is the *other,* among others, b) he is still in *our* future, c) he will sit in a Temple which didn't exist, therefore, d) we have to build another. That is pretty far-fetched stuff; books have been written and movies made; courses taught and curricula formed; and from there the construction of the ziggurat continues. That simple twist has set eschatology back almost 2,000 years.

Theologians have created a smorgasbord of fancy, and the Antichrist is the central figure. The wildest imaginations of man have paired this Antichrist with the beast. As we have seen, some have even called it the abomination of desolation. And, as we've stated, the Scriptures say nothing of the sort. What they do say is that the harlot which we have been studying is seen riding on a beast. We know that Jerusalem is the harlot, and we know that the beast she is riding on is Rome, personified in the evil Nero, whose name adds up to – 666 – as we will soon see.

Book 5, Chapter 28: The Distinction to be made Between the Righteous and the Wicked. The Future Apostasy in the Time of Antichrist, and the End of the World.

2: And for this reason the apostle says: Because they received not the love of God, that they might be saved, therefore God shall also send them the operation of error, that they may believe a lie, that they all may be judged who have not believed the truth, but consented to unrighteousness, 2 Thessalonians 2:10-12. **For when he (Antichrist) has come, and of his own accord concentrates in his own person the apostasy, and accomplishes whatever he shall do according to his own will and choice, sitting also in the Temple of God, so that his dupes may adore him as the Christ.**

Irenaeus, never at a loss for words nor ever lacking imagination, gives us another example of his exquisite writing skills when he says that Antichrist "concentrates in his own person the apostasy." He earlier had said that Antichrist "concentrates in himself all satanic apostasy." He also repeats his erroneous statement that the Antichrist will "sit in the Temple" (the fourth time he said that). That isn't to mean that he is resting; it is to mean that he is supposedly *ruling* from the Temple. Chiliasts say that Christ, when He comes back for His thousand-year reign, will rule from the Temple. So, as we see, on this the futurists are not even in agreement; and that twist, in one form or another, has been repeated for nearly two-thousand years. It is one of the tenets of futurism, and it is one which has really stuck in the craw of this author since 1985, which has led to the writing of this book.

Now we come to the apex of Irenaeus' writings "on all things eschatology and Antichrist," Book 5, Chapter 30, from whence his *notorious statement* is taken (it is the last two sentences of paragraph three). It should be pointed out beforehand, that that notorious statement had not been uttered as of yet by Irenaeus, and it appears that it is not uttered again by him. We will cover each paragraph individually in an attempt to capture the context, as well as point out more of the flawed thinking which results from adhering to the late-date.

Book 5, Chapter 30: Although Certain as to the Number of the Name of Antichrist, yet we should come to no Rash Conclusions as to the Name Itself, because this Number is Capable of being Fitted to Many Names. Reasons for This Point being Reserved by the Holy Spirit. Antichrist's Reign and Death.

> 1: Such, then, being the state of the case, and **this number** being found in all the **most approved and ancient copies [of the Apocalypse]**, and those men who **saw John face to face** bearing their testimony [to it]; while reason also leads us to conclude that **the number of the name of the beast,** [if reckoned] according to the Greek mode of calculation by the [value of] the letters contained in it, **will amount to six hundred and sixty and six;** that is, the number of tens shall be equal to that of the hundreds, and the number of hundreds equal to that of the units (for that number which [expresses] the digit six being adhered to throughout, **indicates the recapitulations of that apostasy**, taken in its full extent, which occurred at the beginning, during the intermediate periods, and which shall take place at the end)…Now, in the first place, it is loss to wander from the truth, and to imagine that as being the case which is not; then again, as there shall be no light punishment [inflicted] upon him who either adds or subtracts anything from the Scripture, Revelation 22:19 under that such a person must necessarily fall. **Moreover, another danger, by no means trifling,**

shall overtake those who falsely presume that they know the name of Antichrist. For if these men assume one [number], when this [Antichrist] shall come having another, they will be easily led away by him, as supposing him not to be the expected one, who must be guarded against.

Irenaeus has such a wonderful way with words. He writes superlatively about some of the most tantalizing subject matters that Revelation has to offer. He is what is known as *deep water*. In paragraph one, above, the point he is making is that the number of the beast is 666 rather than 616, which had been found in some manuscripts and had created controversy.[20] His reasoning skills are evident and well-rounded as he goes into quite an elaborate soliloquy as to how and why that error could have possibly occurred. The fact is that he was talking about the number of the beast, *not as to when John saw the Revelation*.

In any event, according to his account regarding the number, all those multiples of the number six indicate *the recapitulations of that apostasy*. The recapitulations of that apostasy? What? There could be plural apostasies to recapitulate? What in God's creation is that anyway? Well, believe it or not, there actually is something called *Irenaeus' Doctrine of Recapitulation* which is a subject for another day and which we will not go into here.

Irenaeus *is* deep water, almost mind-numbingly deep. There is also a language problem. For the English-speaking world, trying to understand what he is talking about as he was writing in

---

[20] "It is a hallelujah moment when discrepancies like this pop up. Man has only the best standard of originality and authenticity he can muster. Comparison of manuscripts for errors show that, far and away, the New Testament, with its tiny number of (human) errors for a number of manuscripts so large, in comparison to the number two place-holder writing, *is evidence of God*." (emphasis author)–Josh McDowell, *Evidence That Demands a Verdict;* Here's Life Publishers, Inc.; San Bernardino, Ca. 92402; 1988; pp. 41-46.

second-century Greek, which was then translated into Latin and finally into KJV-style English, is not an easy task. As deep as he is and as intricately involved as he writes, and considering the nature of the material of the Revelation, not to mention some of the strange interpretations he is known to have about the Antichrist and other eschatological things, do not lose sight of the fact that he was using all his powers of persuasion to impress upon his readers that the correct number was to be 666, not 616. That is the subject of his writing; we must not lose sight of that.

Understanding what the Revelation is saying about the number is difficult enough, but then understanding what Irenaeus is saying about what he thinks the Revelation is saying about it is even more difficult. Finally, especially for the 21st century American reader, we must grapple with the cumbersome KJV-type prose. Most give up, relying instead on what the "experts" say. That is a large part of the problem, for Irenaeus himself was confused from the beginning about the Revelation; and remember, he is the source of all of those experts. As a result, the futurist view has become entrenched from the beginning. Irenaeus set the stage, so to speak, for all of the fantastic hyperbole of the end times.

The number of the beast is a form of gematria, which is a method of assigning a numerical value to letters of a name, resulting in a number for a name, but nothing more or less—or supernatural, and it is done in Hebrew and in Greek. As we also noted, Nero was long gone by the time of Irenaeus, as was John, who reportedly lived out his life in Ephesus after he was supposedly freed by the harsh emperor Domitian from exile at Patmos.

But the persecution had never stopped; it was still happening in real time, and that is why the persecution under Domitian is cited by many as "confirmation," or validity, of his era being the era of the Antichrist. He was very cruel as an emperor, but he was no Nero; he actually freed John and gave others amnesty. What is confirmed is that during his reign was the ongoing distress, persecution, and tribulation which began with the murder of Stephen, culminating under Nero and the following desolation and destruction of 70, then continuing until the time of the emperor Constantine, who finally ended it in the year 313.

Domitian may have had some of the evil and cruelty of Nero, but, as we stated, *he was no Nero*. And more importantly, Domitian's era had none of the unprecedented events of the earlier first century. So, considering the circumstances at the time when John received the Revelation which, for our study is pre-70AD and most likely late in the reign of the monster Nero or the following tumultuous one-and-one-half year period before Emperor Vespasian, in which three more emperors ruled (see Timeline), and Vespasian himself, who was the destroyer of Judea and father of the abominator, Titus, who completed the destruction and desolation,[21] it would have been suicidal for John to put Nero's name in the public square! Therefore, the coded number, 666.

Irenaeus *did* issue a "supernatural" warning to those who might *presume* to know the name of the Antichrist, advising his readers *not* to attempt to determine who it may be. He would soon ignore his own warning. But nowhere in all of this does he even mention Nero, or the destruction of the city, or the Temple. It is as though they never occurred, or as though they were insignificant events. Remember, Irenaeus is the earliest of the more frequently referenced church fathers and his views are regarded as foundational. It appears as though a century was not enough elapsed-time for an objective 20/20 hindsight view—unless Irenaeus feared for his own life! After all, he was a Christian and he was living the persecution.

---

[21] On 9 June 68, amid growing opposition of the Senate and the army, Nero committed suicide and with him the Julio-Claudian dynasty came to an end. Chaos ensued, leading to a year of brutal civil war known as the Year of the Four Emperors, during which the four most influential generals in the Roman Empire—Galba, Otho, Vitellius and Vespasian—successively vied for imperial power–Wikipedia

Here, we must again remind ourselves that our study is about the harlot, and that she is seen riding on a beast with seven heads and ten horns (17:3,7). There is also a beast from the sea which has seven heads and ten horns (13:1), and there is the red dragon of 12:3, and it too has seven heads and ten horns. Until now we have been concerned with the harlot and beast of chapters 16 through 19. Is there a relationship between these two beasts and the dragon?

We will sort it out, but Irenaeus is talking about yet a different beast – a beast with a number. That is the beast of the earth (13:18), and it has only two horns, but it *spoke* as a dragon (13:11). So, the dragon is related to all. The beast with the number is the number of a man, the number is 666 (13:18), and that number equals that of Nero.[22]

As we've been pointing out, the dragon and the beast from the sea each have seven heads and ten horns. The seven heads of the dragon and the ten horns of the beast are seven and ten diadems, respectively. But the seven heads and ten horns of the beast upon which the harlot sits are each seven and ten kings. Diadems are crowns worn by kings. What is actually being said here?

It should also be pointed out that the woman of 12:1-4 before whom the red dragon stood, ready to devour the child of which she was about to deliver, was our woman – the harlot – the woman seen riding on the beast (17:3,7). The woman with child is Israel – Judah, from whom the Messiah–the child – the Lion of the tribe of Judah, comes, and whom Satan was once again attempting to destroy. The woman riding on the beast is also Israel – Judea–the harlot–whom the woman with child had become.

So again, we see three beasts, two have seven heads and ten horns, as does the red dragon. But the beast from the earth only has two horns and it speaks as a dragon–and that is the beast with the number which is the beast that Irenaeus is talking about. *He was*

---

[22] Chilton, *Days of Vengeance*, pp. 344-352; Gentry, *Before Jerusalem Fell*, pp. 198-201; Russell, *Parousia*, pp. 462-465; Terry, *Biblical Hermeneutics*, pp. 476-477.

concerned only with the number of the beast and he believed that that beast was the Antichrist.

There are several visuals that can be seen here, but they all tell the same story which God has been telling throughout in the Scriptures. That story is: that God chose the Israelites to be His people, that He brought them to Jerusalem, His city, and had His Temple built. He made a covenant with them and gave them the law but they turned from Him to other gods so He sent the prophets. When they killed the prophets, He sent His Son. When they killed Him too, He came in judgment against them, destroying the city and Temple, ending the old covenant, and ushering in the new.

Throughout, Satan–who has opposed God from the beginning and has tried to prevent or destroy the coming of Messiah, first through the actions of Jezebel and Athaliah, then Herod–tried to kill Him himself. When he finally succeeded in having Him crucified, His glorious resurrection gave birth to the church, the saints of which he became the accuser of, and which he tried to eliminate through the efforts of the harlot and the beast.

The harlot–apostate Israel; the beast with the number – Nero; and the beast from the sea, which is the beast the harlot rides upon– the Roman Empire, all give power and authority to the devil–the red dragon, who is Satan.

Continuing with *Against Heresies*: **Book 5, Chapter 30**

> Paragraph 2: These men, therefore, ought to learn [what really is the state of the case], and go back to **the true number of the name,** that they be not reckoned among false prophets. But, knowing **the sure number declared by Scripture, that is, six hundred sixty and six,** let them await, in the first place, **the division of the kingdom into ten;** then, in the

next place, **when these kings are reigning,** and beginning to set their affairs in order, **and advance their kingdom,** [let them learn] to acknowledge that **he who shall come claiming the kingdom for himself,** and shall terrify those men of whom we have been speaking, **having a name containing the aforesaid number, is truly the abomination of desolation...**

Here we see Irenaeus continuing and saying that they need not worry about trying to determine the name. "These men," he says, "therefore, ought to learn what really is the state of the case, and go back to the true number of the name." He is reasoning with them – saying that they should not worry about the actual name of the beast, and that what he is talking about is the *correct number* as declared in the Scriptures–666–not 616. That is the context in which he has been writing, and that is the backdrop for what he said next, which has something to do with the division of the kingdom into ten and so on, and that they need to acknowledge that "he who shall come claiming the kingdom for himself, is truly the abomination of desolation." That is a mouthful, it is truly an incredible statement, it is fanciful, and it is wrong.

Irenaeus, as we noted, creates such beautifully flowing prose. This ability of writers, men and women who truly love God and who write so insightfully and heartfeltly (?) about topics in the Bible is amazing, and comforting. But that insightfulness and beautifully flowing prose, in this case and in others when it comes to eschatology, is often just filler to cover a lack of understanding or fact. Irenaeus, who had just previously equated the beast (666) with the Antichrist, now equates it with the abomination of desolation. He is obviously confused and at a lack of ability to decipher Revelation, which would not be a problem were it not for the results of such a lack of understanding over the last 2,000 years.

Now, it may be stated that in Irenaeus' mind the abomination of desolation is the Antichrist, who is the beast, whose number is 666 – not 616. That is his mindset in the matter to which he is speaking. He was correct in pointing out the discrepancy about the number, and he identifies the correct number, but the rest of his statement is incorrect.

We correctly identified from the Scriptures that the abomination of desolation was the destruction and overrunning by strangers of Jerusalem and the Temple and its profaning. Jesus told the people to look for it, that they would recognize it, and they did, and got out of harm's way. The old, which had been growing old, was ready to disappear (Hebrews 8:13)–the new had come. It was the conclusion of the Old Covenant.

3: **It is therefore more certain, and less hazardous, to await the fulfilment of the prophecy, than to be making surmises, and casting about for any names that may present themselves, inasmuch as many names can be found possessing the number mentioned; and the same question will, after all, remain unsolved**. For if there are many names found possessing this number, it will be asked which among them shall the coming man bear. It is not through a want of names containing the number of that name that I say this, but on account of the fear of God, and zeal for the truth: for the name *Evanthas* (ΕΥΑΝΘΑΣ) contains the required number, but I make no allegation regarding it. Then also *Lateinos* (ΛΑΤΕΙΝΟΣ) has the number six hundred and sixty-six; and it is a very probable [solution], this being the name of the last kingdom [of the four seen by Daniel]. For the Latins are they who at present bear rule: I will not, however, make any boast over this [coincidence]. ***Teitan*** too, (**TEITAN**, the first syllable being written with the two Greek vowels ε and ι, among all the names which are found among us, is rather worthy of credit... Inasmuch, then, as this name Titan has so much to recommend it, there is a strong degree of probability, that from among the many [names suggested], we infer, that perchance he who is to come shall be called **Titan. We will not, however, incur the risk of pronouncing positively as to the name of Antichrist; for if it were necessary that his name should be distinctly revealed in this present time, it would have been announced by him who beheld the apocalyptic vision. For that was seen no very long time since, but almost in our day, towards the end of Domitian's reign.**

Now we have come to paragraph three, the home of his notorious statement. It is at the end, but the paragraph begins with Irenaeus continuing in his discourse, giving good advice in saying that they should not surmise as to the name as many names could have that number and the question would still remain unresolved. Good advice indeed, except that he mentions two names himself before latching onto a third–Titan (how similar to Titus!), and then, ignoring his own sage advice he proceeds to go into a rather lengthy and elaborate discussion as to its merits. It is *then,* and in *that* context, that he says this:

> *"We will not, however, incur the risk of pronouncing positively as to the name of Antichrist;* **for if it were necessary that his name should be distinctly revealed in this present time, it would have been**

> *announced by him who beheld the apocalyptic vision. For that (he?) was seen no very long time since, but almost in our day, towards the end of Domitian's reign."*

Rest assured, some grammarian will disagree, but *Him who beheld the apocalyptic vision* is a phrase whereby "him" is the subject and "the apocalyptic vision" is the object. *Him*, who saw it, was John; it–the object, in this case, the apocalyptic vision, does not and cannot announce anything, for it is only the event–the vision. Only the subject, in this case John, the actual living and breathing human being, the "him" who is actually *able* to speak, would have and could have announced *anything*. And it was *he*, "him" – **John** – *who was seen no long time since, in the reign of Domitia*n!

So, it was John who was available to those whom Irenaeus is talking about. They could have talked to him personally and inquired to their heart's content. As baffled as Irenaeus was about things concerning the Revelation, he was not baffled about this. *There is no conceivable way he was talking about **when** the apocalypse was seen.*

That is the simplest, most logical, and God-honoring scenario–but man has refused to accept it. What he has done instead is chosen to follow the way into idol worship by worshipping self, playing the harlot himself, putting himself in the place of God, or, as Irenaeus said, seating himself in the Temple of God, showing himself to be God.

God's way is more plausible. Man's way is too convoluted because of all the different things of what they wrongly perceive to be that which Revelation is saying. Those things don't fit together, so man has compounded his error by forcing them to fit. Just by saying that the *apocalypse* was seen in the time of Domitian instead of putting the emphasis on John has created an entire false narrative – the ziggurat. We have been enticed, and it is we who have been duped.

So, there you have it–that notorious statement–the statement which everybody cites, and the building block of the futurist view. It, and it alone, has placed the receiving of the apocalypse *after* 70AD – in the reign of Domitian.

> 4: **But he indicates the number of the name now, that when this man comes we may avoid him, being aware who he is: the name, however, is suppressed, because it is not worthy of being proclaimed by the Holy Spirit.** For if it had been declared by Him, he (Antichrist) might perhaps continue for a long period. But now as he was, and is not, and shall ascend out of the abyss, and goes into perdition, Revelation 17:8 as one who has no existence; **so neither has his name been declared, for the name of that which does not exist is not proclaimed. But when this Antichrist shall have devastated all things in this world, he will reign for three years and six months, and sit in the Temple at Jerusalem; and then the Lord will come from heaven in the clouds, in the glory of the Father, sending this man and those who follow him into the lake of fire; but bringing in for the righteous the times of the kingdom, that is, the rest, the hallowed seventh day**; and restoring to Abraham the promised inheritance, in which kingdom the Lord declared, that many coming from the east and from the west should sit down with Abraham, Isaac, and Jacob. Matthew 8:11.

Finally, in paragraph four, we come to the end of Irenaeus' material of which we have been examining, but we are far from done with him. He begins, "But he indicates the number of the name now..." He? Who is Irenaeus referring to as *he*? Why, it is John. Irenaeus rightly identifies the speaker as John in saying *he,* and, as his paragraph four follows paragraph three, he is still speaking about the same "he" as the "he" who beheld the apocalyptic vision – John!

So, going back to his notorious statement of paragraph three, where he says, "we (which included himself) won't take the risk of pronouncing the name of the number at this time... for if it were necessary to do so... it would have been announced by *him* who saw the apocalyptic vision..." The "him" is, again, John.

Continuing, at the beginning of paragraph four: "But *he* (John) indicates the *number* now." And at that point Irenaeus goes into one of his elaborate, wordy soliloquies. The point of all of this, and it must be repeated time and again, is that Irenaeus was referring to John – not when the Revelation was seen.

Continuing, he states: "When the Antichrist comes, he will sit in the Temple at Jerusalem and he will reign for three years and six months." This is the fifth time that Irenaeus has made the statement of the Antichrist sitting in, or at, the Temple. He repeatedly makes that statement; it is central to his thesis; it is a cornerstone of the futurist view; and therefore, it must repeatedly be repudiated.

It really is an incredible statement because there is no Temple for Antichrist to sit in or at. So, what Temple was Irenaeus talking about? He lived well after the Temple had been destroyed in 70AD so there was no Temple when he wrote and there still is no Temple. He doesn't even talk about the Temple that was destroyed, or Nero, or the persecution, for that matter.

Having been born in either Smyrna, now Izmir, Turkey as some say, or in France, as do others, Irenaeus was of Greek descent and a Roman citizen. He became bishop of Lyon, France, he was not a Jew, and he did not come from the area of the Holy Land. He obviously did not understand the significance of the Temple and its destruction – or he was scared to death!

His statement of Antichrist seated at the Temple and reigning for three-and-one-half years in Jerusalem is at the core of almost all of futurism and leads to the "they're ready to go" remark concerning a possible building of another Temple. Even the thought of building another Temple because we're so unwaveringly certain that that has to be done in order for it to be the house from where either Jesus will rule when He comes back, as the chiliasts say, or, as Irenaeus said, from where the Antichrist will sit when he reigns– is preposterous.

If another Temple were to be built, would the sacrifices be re-instituted? That is also preposterous even though it is an obvious first question because, that being the reason for the Temple in the first place, all Christians know that Jesus made the final sacrifice so there is no need for a Temple. We also know that Christ, being God, does not live in an abode built with human hands.

Another question is this: If John, being told to measure the Temple (Revelation 11:1) was shown the apocalypse in the reign of Domitian which was *after* 70AD, how could he measure it? There would have been no Temple to measure! But, according to Irenaeus, Antichrist will supposedly sit at the Temple. So, how could that be? Let us look at this scenario again:

We have shown that Antichrist the beast–a person–is a product of Irenaeus; he is not of Scripture–for Irenaeus did not write under inspiration. How could Antichrist then sit at a Temple which does not exist? The only possible answer is that another Temple must be built–and we, *we,* must build it. That is the scenario being bandied about. We have put ourselves at the center of this elaborate scheme. That is idolatry, but that is the futurist view.

Let's try again–what Temple was Irenaeus talking about? Could it be the one that those who say they are "ready to go" are talking about? If so, think about this for a moment: if an attempt to build another Temple were even announced, it would most assuredly start a major war–most likely world war three–because that would mean demolition of the Islamic Dome of the Rock, which has been built on the site of the Temple mount! The entire idea is ludicrous.

Man refuses to humble himself before the Almighty God. If he did, most of his problems would be solved. The answers to life lie in the Scriptures but we are in a quest to be as God–therefore we don't, or we won't, recognize them. That does not have to be. Man is capable of loving both God and self, in that order, at the same time; but also, at the same time, man is fully capable of destroying himself – and God will save a remnant.

Irenaeus the historian was writing about Antichrist or, *the* Antichrist. Let us look at his notorious statement yet again, "We will not, however, incur the risk of pronouncing positively as to the name of Antichrist; for if it were necessary that his name should be distinctly revealed in this present time, *"it would have been announced by him who beheld the apocalyptic vision. For that was seen no very long time since, but almost in our day, towards the end of Domitian's reign."*

The English translation from the Greek verb that Irenaeus used that has created this entire mess was: *that*, or *it*, *was* seen…in the reign of Domitian. That may be grammatically correct but it is not contextually so. Unlike English, where we have the choice of using separate masculine, feminine, or neuter pronouns, Greek does not. We know that Irenaeus used the correct Greek verb, because that quotation has survived in the original Greek.[23] So, why was it incorrectly translated? (which is why context is needed).

A choice was made, and it was made by the translators. It could not have been at Irenaeus' direction or discretion, for he was long gone. It may or may not have been done with devious intent, but

---

[23] Gentry, *Before Jerusalem Fell*–pp. 46-47.

malevolent intent is not implied here. Only God knows Irenaeus' beliefs and opinions about whether he would have preferred John or the apocalypse to have been seen in the time of Domitian, but it is highly unlikely that the translators knew of Irenaeus' intent.

In this case, the way Greek grammar works, the single word is, as explained earlier, a third-person, singular verb meaning *he, she,* or *it – was seen.* Irenaeus didn't choose *it* or *that.* He simply wrote the Greek word. But for some reason, the worst possible choice was made in the translation–the neuter form rather than the masculine.

Furthermore, the correct neuter translation would have been the pronoun *it*, but we see that the word is *that*. So somehow, even the "correct" incorrect word was not used. The simplest and most logical solution would have been the best solution. Just look at the mess this has created and the myriad possible scenarios presented in the alternative. Now, let us make the substitution using "he" for "it," and present the argument as thus:

> *"We will not, however, incur the risk of pronouncing positively as to the name of Antichrist; for if it were necessary that his name should be distinctly revealed in this present time, it would have been announced by **him** who beheld the apocalyptic vision. For **he was seen** no very long time since, but almost in our day, towards the end of Domitian's reign."*

It now says that *John* was seen in the time of Domitian. This makes perfect sense and causes no controversy. Keep in mind, Irenaeus himself dare not state outwardly the name of Antichrist, for the Romans were persecuting Christians in the worst possible way.

Here, in the correct case, as just presented, *Irenaeus would have been giving no indication of when the Revelation was seen.* There would have been no reason to give any such indication. All those who were concerned knew that John saw it, and there he was, in the flesh, in Ephesus–in the time of Domitian.

Irenaeus' words were silent on the *content of the vision, and when it was seen.* They said much about *who* saw it, in this case John–*the one who beheld the apocalyptic vision.* Under those circumstances, the date of the Revelation is irrelevant. It was the farthest thing from Irenaeus' mind. It would have been totally uncalled for, and frankly, the idea borders on the absurd. Irenaeus was talking about the number of the beast!

And yet, here we are. What has been created out of that little twist is man's, and ultimately Satan's, attempt at usurping God. If Irenaeus was saying that *John* was seen instead of the apocalypse, questions would have been easily answered, and two thousand years of effort would have been focused in a different direction–a better direction–God's direction. The answers are that the story remains God's story, as we have been showing. The Scriptures back it up.

It can be safely stated that Irenaeus is the foremost source because he is the only historian that we know of who actually knew someone (Polycarp and possibly Papias) who knew a disciple of the Lord (John) possibly one hundred years prior–well before Irenaeus was even born. Irenaeus is quoted profusely by Eusebius, another historian who was born some forty years after Irenaeus died, and he, very importantly, lived past Emperor Constantine's reign (337), who decreed to finally stop the persecution of the Christians–after almost three-hundred years.

The thread-of-relationship from John through Polycarp to Irenaeus is of utmost importance in that there are not others of that significance. Those who say that "the early church fathers all come down on the side of the late-date of the Revelation" invariably cite Irenaeus and Eusebius. It is time to reject Irenaeus' futurism.

So, as we've been saying, it was *John* who was seen in the time of Domitian. Most scholars acknowledge that he was in Ephesus after he was pardoned by Domitian from exile on Patmos. Here is more misinformation that has been circulating throughout the years:

Most Americans, if you ask them to describe Patmos Island, would liken it to Alcatraz Island, location of the former notorious American prison. They would create the simile: Patmos Isle is as Alcatraz Island. They would be wrong. In fact, Alcatraz Island, depending on your source, is between twenty-two and forty-seven **acres** in size, big enough for a prison building, and not much more; and which can only be gotten to by boat or airlift, as it is little more than an out-cropping of rock in the middle of San Francisco Bay, which is why it was nick-named "the Rock." Also, six-hundred forty acres equals one square mile.

Patmos, on the other hand, is slightly over **thirteen square-miles** in size, which makes it *approximately two-hundred forty times larger than Alcatraz Island*. That's a whopping disparity. There were indigenous people there; there were actually temples to the gods there, which means the people who were there were doing the same things that God's people were doing and which got them judged. It was also on a known sea-route from Ephesus to Athens or Corinth. People who were banished to Patmos were not necessarily kept in a prison cell or a cave; they basically had the run-of-the island, but they had to fend for themselves. The entire futurist portrayal is fraudulent.

The world has been fooled into believing that Irenaeus was talking about the Revelation having been seen in the time of Domitian, rather than John having been the one seen. It is probable that no one ever expected to see John again after he was banished, but there he was, live and in color; they could talk to him and ask him questions. That is a much more plausible scenario. God's story, His story, is always the best story.

The actual *seeing* of the Revelation could have taken place in an instant. John *was in the spirit* and writing as the angel instructed. That John was on Patmos when he saw the vision is a fact. That it was a time of tribulation is a fact (Revelation 1:9). That he was seen in Ephesus at the time of Domitian is also (supposedly) a fact. But those facts do not make it a fact that John saw the Revelation when he was seen during the reign of Domitian!

Man has never, and will never, be able to replicate the events of history to produce a more significant impact on all of mankind in such a way as what God was able to accomplish from the birth of Jesus to the desolation. Those events are: the virgin birth, crucifixion, resurrection, the birth of the church, the persecution, desolation, and the scattering.

The virgin birth and the resurrection are impossibilities for man. The others are of man, and they are atrocities, except for the birth of the church, which was born of atrocity. Those seventy years changed the world – they changed history. The futurist view dismisses all of that out-of-hand and instead makes it all about future events – events of no consequence. Read their books and see their movies on this subject. They are fiction.

If the case was that the *Revelation* was seen in the time of Domitian, it was still only seen by one person – John! What would that have accomplished? It came and it went, seen by John, and the emphasis would remain to be about John, as it is now. If, on the other hand, the emphasis was on the Revelation, it accomplishes nothing, other than to take the emphasis off God and put it on man, which is from Satan.

It, the apocalypse, as we stated, could not have told anybody anything because it was an *it* – a thing – only *seen by* John, and *he* was the one seen in the reign of Domitian. And only John, being a person – and *the* person, the *only* person to see the Revelation, as we also stated, could have told anybody anything he chose, anything that they wanted to know because he was the one who saw it, and he was the one who was there, in Ephesus, in the time of Domitian. This absurd minutiae is necessary because somehow, we have allowed ourselves to be duped for thousands of years, and man has been blinded by the construction of his own enormous ziggurat.

What are the implications of all of this? Think about this: there have been thousands of books written on the Revelation. A very large percentage of those books are written on the premise of the late-date based on the words of Irenaeus, and to a lesser extent, Eusebius. Without that premise, there would be no tangible choice but God's way, as described in the Scriptures, and that can only mean good things for us, because He will always be faithful to His Word – *and we have His word.*

Irenaeus wrote a fair bit about Antichrist and the idea that he sits at the Temple. He appears to have been rather consumed with him, as though he were an actual person who epitomizes all that is evil and bad, and against God, as though he were a demon or the devil himself–the recapitulation of the apostasy, whatever that is. Now, look again at what John said in his first two letters about "antichrist." His characterization is incompatible with that of Irenaeus.

So again, Irenaeus believed that Antichrist would rule from the Temple *as* Christ. There was no Temple. There is no Temple. The thought of a person such as Irenaeus, and how he depicts *the* Antichrist, ruling from a Temple in Jerusalem and being able to dupe everyone into worshipping him as Christ, is pretty far out there. The bottom line is that for all that Irenaeus wrote about Antichrist and things of the end, it is the two sentences that he wrote at the end of paragraph three above – the notorious statement–which have been reiterated by others, and which have perpetuated the error.

Eusebius – Ecclesiastical Histories

So, who was Eusebius?[24] He was born some forty years after the passing of Irenaeus, and he died in the year 339, some twenty-six years after Emperor Constantine ended the persecution, so he has a unique perspective. He became bishop of Caesarea, Israel and may have been Palestinian. He published his famous *Ecclesiastical Histories*,[25] the history of the first-century church, from about 312-324. He's the second-most cited early church historian, as far as our study is concerned, after Irenaeus. He, himself, quotes Irenaeus, and talks about Irenaeus quite frequently, referencing Irenaeus' "notorious statement" several times. Eusebius will shed much light on Irenaeus' writings on eschatology, and will provide some of his own, which will be helpful in understanding the gist of this book. We will look at particular chapters of his referenced *Heresies*, and we will try and make better sense of Irenaeus' statements as a result.

Book 3–Chapter 18. **The Apostle John and the Apocalypse**:

---

[24] Eusebius of Caesarea, also known as Eusebius Pamphili, was a historian of Christianity, exegete, and Christian polemicist. He became the bishop of Caesarea Maritima about 314 AD. Together with Pamphilus, he was a scholar of the Biblical canon and is regarded as an extremely learned Christian of his time.–Wikipedia

[25] http://www.newadvent.org/fathers/2501.htm

> It is said that **in this persecution** the apostle and evangelist John, who was still alive, was condemned **to dwell** on the island of Patmos in consequence of his testimony to the divine word. **Irenaeus, in the fifth book of his work Against Heresies, where he discusses the number of the name of Antichrist which is given in the so-called Apocalypse of John, speaks as follows concerning him: "If it were necessary for his name to be proclaimed openly at the present time, it would have been declared by him who saw the revelation. For it was seen not long ago, but almost in our own generation, at the end of the reign of Domitian."** To such a degree, indeed, did the teaching of our faith flourish at that time that **even those writers who were far from our religion did not hesitate to mention in their histories the persecution and the martyrdoms which took place during it.** And they, indeed, accurately indicated the time. For they recorded that in the fifteenth year of Domitian Flavia Domitilla, daughter of a sister of Flavius Clement, who at that time was one of the consuls of Rome, was **exiled with many others to the island of Pontia in consequence of testimony borne to Christ.**

Here, we see several items of interest: a. he mentions "this persecution" just as John had mentioned "the tribulation" (Revelation 1:9). Eusebius even provides two examples, which we will look at; b. he questions the authenticity of the Revelation, calling it the "so-called" apocalypse; and c. he promptly makes reference to Irenaeus and his notorious statement, furthering the notoriety of it.

The two historians are linked by that statement in that nearly anyone researching Revelation invariably cites Irenaeus and Eusebius as though they are providing the same information when they, in reality, are not. There is no original information on our topic here from Eusebius, so we can see the strength of Irenaeus' words as *he* is the bridge to the Apostolic Age and it is *his* notorious statement that is repeated. It all turns on his testimony.[26]

But it is a curious remark by someone such as Eusebius in that he appears to doubt the veracity of the apocalypse. There apparently was a difference of opinion between the two on the subject of the Revelation, as we will continue to see. The galling fact of this is that Eusebius is mentioned in the same breath with Irenaeus by nearly everyone as 'the emphatic witness of the early church fathers all being in agreement regarding the late-date of Revelation' when that does not appear to have been the case at all. God's word has continued to be perverted ever since to where nearly everyone who has a futurist inkling of the "end times" thinks along the lines of Irenaeus.

Eusebius opened the chapter by bringing attention to the ongoing persecution and goes on to say that *even those who were not of their religion didn't hesitate to mention the martyrdoms for Christ which had been taking place*.

Directly quoting Irenaeus and the notorious statement, Eusebius appears to say, and to agree, that the Antichrist which Irenaeus alluded to could actually be the then-current Roman emperor Domitian. The link is that John *returned from his exile on Patmos during the reign of Domitian*, who had also exiled the daughter of a sister of Clement to the isle of Pontia.

To the untrained eye it may appear odd that Irenaeus' notorious statement is used in that context, but in reality, it is not odd at all. In fact, it strengthens our case that *Irenaeus was not talking about*

---

[26] Terry; *Hermeneutics*; p.237

when the Revelation was seen, for in his second sentence Eusebius is emphasizing the point which Irenaeus was making – that he was discussing the number of the name of the beast! It could not be more straightforward than that.

This was Eusebius, the expert first-century-church historian, verifying what we just previously discussed, that *John was released from his exile* and seen, supposedly, in Ephesus in the time of Domitian. Notice, the subject matter, to repeat, *is not about the date* of the Revelation. But that is the statement (the notorious one) that Eusebius used, and that is the statement which others rely on as they make their case regarding the authority of the early witness attesting to the late-date. The authority of those early witnesses is not reliable when it comes to Revelation. In any case, the great persecution was ongoing and it was extreme.

Book 3–Chapter 39. The Writings of Papias:[27]

> Paragraph 1: There are extant five books of Papias, which bear the title Expositions of Oracles of the Lord. **Irenaeus** makes mention of these as the only works written by him, in the following words: **"These things are attested by Papias, an ancient man who was a hearer of John and a companion of Polycarp, in his fourth book.** For five books have been written by him." **These are the words of Irenaeus.** But **Papias himself** in the preface to his discourses **by no means declares that he was himself a hearer and eye-witness of the holy apostles, but he shows by the words which he uses that he received the**

---

[27] Papias was a Greek Apostolic Father, Bishop of Hierapolis, and author who lived c. 60–163 AD. It was Papias who wrote the Exposition of the Sayings of the Lord in five books–Wikipedia

doctrines of the faith from those who were their friends. He says: "But I shall not hesitate also to put down for you along with my interpretations whatsoever things I have at any time learned carefully from the elders and carefully remembered, guaranteeing their truth. For I did not, like the multitude, take pleasure in those that speak much, but **in those that teach the truth**; not in those that relate **strange commandments**, but in those that deliver the commandments given by the Lord to faith, and springing from the truth itself. **If, then, any one came, who had been a follower of the elders, I questioned him in regard to the words of the elders**, – what Andrew or what Peter said, or what was said by Philip, or by Thomas, or by James, or by John, or by Matthew, or by any other of the disciples of the Lord, and what things **Aristion and the presbyter John**, the disciples of the Lord, say. **For I did not think that what was to be gotten from the books would profit me as much as what came from the living and abiding voice."**

Here, the first key point Eusebius addresses in the writings of Papias is whether or not he (Papias) was actually a hearer of John. He "bookends" his point immediately by quoting Irenaeus and ends it by saying, "These are the words of Irenaeus." It all turns on Irenaeus.

What instantly becomes clear is that Eusebius contradicts Irenaeus, who said that Papias was a hearer of the apostle, and then he offers up his own insight in saying, "But Papias himself in the preface to his discourses by no means declares that he was himself a hearer and eyewitness of the holy apostles, but he shows by the words which he uses that he received the doctrines of the faith from those who were their friends." That is no ringing endorsement of Irenaeus on this score.

What we are seeing here is Eusebius putting a little space between himself and Irenaeus by pointing out right from the start that he was not in agreement with him. Let us note also, once again, that they were not writing under inspiration, and although they are two of the most highly regarded historians, they were not in agreement on things concerning eschatology and the apocalypse!

So, Papias considered himself *not* to have been a "seer or hearer" of the apostles, but of their friends. He talks about how he would question those who knew the apostles, naming them all in the process. At this point, it must be stated that there are also differences of opinion about whether "John the Presbyter" was the same person who wrote the Gospel, the three letters bearing that name, and the Revelation. Papias himself, as we will presently see, did not consider that this John, the man that *he* believes had seen the apocalypse, was the same man who wrote the Gospel and the epistles.

Despite the apparent differences of opinion by these early fathers, it must have been a wonderful experience to have known the friends of the apostles and to have learned from them as the zeal and passion for the Lord enabled Christianity to conquer the world with the message of redemption and salvation. We saw previously the connection between Irenaeus and the apostle John through Polycarp, and now we see Eusebius indicating that Irenaeus also had a connection to Papias and that he, too, knew John, as well as Polycarp.

> P2–It is worthwhile observing here that **the name John is twice enumerated** by him. **The first one** he mentions in connection with Peter and James and Matthew and the rest of the apostles, clearly meaning the evangelist; but **the other John** he mentions after

an interval, and places him among others outside of the number of the apostles, putting Aristion before him, and he distinctly calls him a presbyter. This shows that the statement of those is true, **who say that there were two persons in Asia that bore the same name, and that there were two tombs in Ephesus, each of which, even to the present day, is called John's**. It is important to notice this. **For it is probable that it was the second, if one is not willing to admit that it was the first that saw the Revelation,** which is ascribed by name to John. And **Papias**, of whom we are now speaking, **confesses that he received the words of the apostles from those that followed them, but says that he was himself a hearer of Aristion and the presbyter John**. At least he mentions them frequently by name and gives their traditions in his writings.

Here in paragraph two Eusebius quotes Papias, who goes into quite an elaborate explanation about the two men named John and why he believes John the Presbyter was the one who received the Revelation, and that it was *this* John whom he heard, not the apostle. In the end, as far as our study is concerned, it doesn't matter if there were more than one person named John back then involved in spreading the Gospel. Two-thousand years later, after everything that has been written and said about the Revelation and the end times, we still don't understand much. How can we, in all honesty, objectively rely solely on the mistaken words of Papias and Irenaeus on matters of the end times, such as building another Temple in which the Antichrist will sit, as per Irenaeus, or from which Jesus will rule during His thousand-year reign, as per Papias?

P3–These things, we hope, have not been uselessly adduced by us. But it is fitting to subjoin to **the words of Papias which have been quoted**, other passages from his works in which he relates some **other wonderful events which he claims to have received from tradition**. That Philip the apostle dwelt at Hierapolis with his daughters has been already stated. But it must be noted here that **Papias, their contemporary**, says that he **heard a wonderful tale from the daughters of Philip**. For he relates that in his time's one rose from the dead. **And** he tells **another** wonderful story **of Justus**, surnamed Barsabbas: that he **drank a deadly poison, and yet, by the grace of the Lord, suffered no harm**. The Book of Acts records that the holy apostles after the ascension of the Saviour, put forward this Justus, together with Matthias, and prayed that one might be chosen in place of the traitor Judas, to fill up their number. The account is as follows: "And they put forward two, Joseph, called Barsabbas, who was surnamed Justus, and Matthias; and they prayed and said."

P4–**The same writer** (author: Eusebius is still writing about Papias) **gives also other accounts which he says came to him through unwritten tradition,** *certain strange parables and teachings* **of the Saviour,** *and some other more mythical things.* **To these belong his statement that there will be** *a period of some thousand years after the resurrection of the dead, and that the kingdom of Christ will be set up in material form on this very earth.* **I suppose** *he got these ideas through a*

> *misunderstanding of the apostolic accounts,* **not perceiving that the things said by them were spoken** *mystically in figures.* **For** *he appears to have been of very limited understanding,* **as one can see from his discourses. But** *it was due to him that so many of the Church Fathers after him adopted a like opinion,* **urging in their own support the antiquity of the man;** *as for instance Irenaeus and anyone else that may have proclaimed similar views.*

We include paragraph three for the reader but move to paragraph four for our discussion, which is the crown jewel of Eusebius' writings about Papias. He begins by calling those views which Papias portrays as: "certain strange parables and teachings of the Lord, and some other *mythical* things ...," and that, "...to these (the strange teachings) belong his (Papias') statement that *there will be a period of some thousand years after the resurrection of the dead, and that the kingdom of Christ will be set up in material form on this very earth.*"

The doctrine of Christ setting up a kingdom here on earth for a thousand years is known as chiliasm... thousand year-ism, aka millennialism, and has always been considered heretical by Protestantism as well as Roman Catholicism, but that is the very essence of futurist thought. Millennialism has its own problems in the realm of futurism, as some cite pre-millennialism, a-millennialism, and post-millennialism, whereby the millennium, which is the thousand-year reign of Christ, occurs, supposedly, before, during, or after the rapture, which, supposedly, occurs at the second coming of Christ and which can occur, supposedly, before (pre), during (mid), or after (post) the Great Tribulation – phew!

The idea of "setting up a kingdom" comes straight from Daniel 2:44, when he was interpreting King Nebuchadnezzar's dream.

That prophecy, as we showed (Part II), was fulfilled at the resurrection. The old system has since been taken out, the new has come, and God's Kingdom has been set up, although futurists will deny that and argue and complain that that couldn't possibly be the case, pointing out how sinful the world is. They are missing the point. There is a reason that a large portion of the world, which was once considered Christian, is no longer considered so, and they need to look in the mirror as to why.

It should be noted that the only other times Daniel uses the expression 'set up' is 11:31 and 12:11, where he talks about 'setting up' the abomination of desolation. We showed and established the fact that Irenaeus emphatically stated that the abomination of desolation was a person, the Antichrist, the beast–and we showed why that was wrong. We also showed that the people Jesus was addressing in Matthew 24 would recognize the abomination of desolation (24:15-20). Irenaeus was way off, as was Papias.

Another thing, Daniel also saw God and the thrones in heaven 'set up' in 7:9-10. The significant point here is that this 'setting up' occurred during the time of the fourth beast which again, as we showed, takes us to the same place in history as his other visions and dreams and interpretations. And that place is the time of the resurrection, Roman Empire, the little horn being Nero, the trampling down of the remainder being the great persecution, and the 'setting-up' of the kingdom being the age of the church – the new covenant.

Eusebius opines of Papias: *"I suppose he got these ideas through a misunderstanding of the apostolic accounts, not perceiving that the things said by them were spoken mystically in figures. For [he] appears to have been of very limited understanding, as one can see from his discourses."*

This is a rather astonishing statement, for Eusebius appears to be taking a swipe at Papias and his intellect, saying that he was of "limited understanding." He goes so far as to "suppose" that

Papias *misunderstood the apostolic accounts* and characterizes his discourse (writings) in an insulting manner. Remember, by Papias' own account, those apostolic accounts came not from the apostles themselves, but from their friends, so it was second-hand information at best.

In this life there is nothing one-hundred percent, but God's hand is in everything, and man must see it and continually make decisions regarding God. If you say *yes* to God, life goes so much easier. Futurism is a house built on sand (Matthew 7:24-27).

Eusebius continues, *"But it was due to him that so many of the Church Fathers after him adopted a like-opinion, urging in their own support the antiquity of the man; as for instance Irenaeus and anyone else that may have proclaimed similar views."*

That is a mouthful and it is damning to the futuristic view. First, Eusebius places the blame for chiliastic futurism at the feet of Papias for, "…it was due to him that so many of the church fathers after him had adopted a like-opinion…." That like-opinion was futurism, either in the form of chiliasm (thousand-year-ism (Papias)), or otherwise (Irenaeus).

Remember, also, it was Eusebius himself who dubbed the apocalypse the "so-called" apocalypse, so apparently he did not think it was inspired. There was disagreement all around, but Eusebius was right on this: *so many of the Church Fathers after him* (Papias) *adopted a like-opinion*. That is how futurism began, and through Irenaeus it is how it continued. Futurism was wrong from the beginning, and therefore it would be a mistake not to re-consider the futurism which was given birth by Papias and Irenaeus. Man has since constructed a massive ziggurat.

Second, Eusebius mocked Papias' use of the term *mythical things* when he (Eusebius) referred to the apostolic accounts as having been spoken *mystically in figures*. This was not simply a play on words. "Mystically in figures," as stated by Eusebius, is correct (Revelation 11:8), as it implies something of a spiritual nature. But "mythically" is something else (see Glossary); in fact, it implies nothing real. A myth is something that is false; therefore, something mythical or mythically is something relating to a myth. If Papias truly meant to use the word "mythical" he was indeed pretty far out there. The 'doctrine' of building another Temple is based on a myth, which is a pretext. Remember, text without context is pretext, as if Revelation isn't hard enough to decipher on its own.

Third, Eusebius supposes that Papias *misunderstood the apostolic accounts because of his very limited understanding*. He does not show much respect for Papias' intellect at all. By the same token, modern scholars cited earlier in the article by Sim, the majority of whom are probably futurists and who disagree with Papias, probably do so because he is considered to be a chiliast, which, as we said, is thought of as heresy.

So, there is a rather large body of thought, including Eusebius, who disagree with Papias on this topic for various reasons. And even as chiliasts believes Christ will set up a physical kingdom on earth and will rule for a thousand years as opposed to Irenaeus' belief that Antichrist will sit at some future Temple and rule, showing himself as Christ–both propositions are mythical.

Summarizing: Papias was a chiliast and therefore, a futurist. He attributed the Revelation to the presbyter John, not the apostle John. Irenaeus, although not a chiliast, was a futurist nonetheless; and because he was such a prolific writer, he alone is the voice of antiquity, with an assist from Papias. Eusebius had doubts about what he called the so-called Revelation. He was also a prolific writer, and came afterward – perpetuating, inadvertently (?) the entire futurist narrative, even as he was in disagreement with the other two.

On more than just a few occasions Eusebius quotes Irenaeus, and those are the writings that most historians go to and cite as justification for the futurist view. Only fragments remain of Papias' writings, and a few are pertinent to our discussion in that he, and

Polycarp, were two of the earliest credible sources with connections to the disciples. Josephus' writings don't address the subject directly, as he became a war correspondent with the Roman army after he was captured by them; some say he actually became a traitor. Therefore, it is the writings of Irenaeus and Eusebius upon whom everyone relies, yet they actually do not agree with each other on the apocalypse or eschatology!

Taken together, Irenaeus, Papias, and Eusebius are the fathers of the futurist view, yet Eusebius should not be. The fact that Irenaeus is held in such high regard in his other writings, and the fact that he is quoted so frequently by Eusebius, who is himself a very respected historian and writer, most believe that the two are in agreement on eschatology when they are not.

Book 5 – Chapter 8 – The Statements of Irenaeus in Regard to the Divine Scriptures

> Paragraph 1–Since, in the beginning of this work, we promised to give, when needful, the words of the ancient presbyters and writers of the church, in which they have declared those traditions which came down to them concerning the canonical books, **and since Irenaeus was one of them, we will now give his words** and, first, what he says of the sacred Gospels: "**Matthew** published his Gospel among the Hebrews in their own language, while **Peter** and **Paul** were preaching and founding the church in Rome. After their departure **Mark**, the disciple and interpreter of Peter, also transmitted to us in writing those things which Peter had preached; and **Luke**, the attendant of Paul, recorded in a book the Gospel which Paul had declared. Afterwards **John,**

> the disciple of the Lord, who also reclined on his bosom, **published his Gospel, while staying at Ephesus in Asia**." He states these things in the **third book** of his above-mentioned work. **In the fifth book he speaks as follows concerning the Apocalypse of John, and the number of the name of Antichrist:** "As these things are so, and this number is found in all the approved and ancient copies, and those who saw John face to face confirm it, and reason teaches us that the number of the name of the beast, according to the mode of calculation among the Greeks, appears in its letters.... " And farther on, he says concerning the same: (here's that notorious statement – author) **"We are not bold enough to speak confidently of the name of Antichrist. For if it were necessary that his name should be declared clearly at the present time, it would have been announced by him who saw the revelation. For it was seen, not long ago, but almost in our generation, toward the end of the reign of Domitian."**

Here, in paragraph one, Eusebius spends his opening argument once again quoting and building up the stature of Irenaeus. It is incredible to this author how quickly he does this. There appears to not be much originality from Eusebius on this subject.

It is, as always, a wonderful description by Irenaeus as he tells what Matthew, Peter, Paul, Mark, Luke, and John did regarding the spreading of the Gospel. Irenaeus also says that John, "the disciple who reclined on Christ's bosom," that is, the apostle John, wrote his Gospel when he was staying at Ephesus. He is stressing the point that John published his Gospel when he was there in Ephesus, *but he does not say when that was.*

In his Gospel, John, at 5:2, talks about a pool by the sheep gate in the present tense. That is where the sheep were brought into the Temple for sacrifice. That may not seem significant, but, considering that this is inspired writing and is therefore correct, it is highly unlikely that John would write in the present tense if the Temple had been destroyed.

As we've so noted, he published his Gospel when he was there at Ephesus, and he was supposedly there during the reign of Domitian, but that does not mean that they were both the same time, nor does it mean that he wrote either or both of those books at either time. He could have, but we don't know for certain. In fact, there really is no definitive indication that when John was seen in the time of Domitian that the location was Ephesus when that occurred.

There is also the question of why John–having quoted Jesus saying He would destroy the Temple and rebuild it in three days (John 2:18-22) and making other references to the Temple – never said one word about it actually having been destroyed, or that it just wasn't even there anymore. Remember, the Romans destroyed it in 70. If John wrote his Gospel when he was in Ephesus in the time of Domitian, after 90AD, would he just ignore the fact? The thought is ludicrous and the entire argument is ludicrous. Nobody knows for certain, but an entire doctrine has been concocted on the premise of post-70.

Eusebius himself does not say, in his own personal opinion, that John was there during the reign of Domitian – he quotes Irenaeus, and he doesn't indicate Ephesus either. Many, possibly even himself included, say that John wrote his Gospel when he was there at Ephesus, and they surmise that it was after being freed by Domitian. But that is speculation–just as they surmise that he wrote the apocalypse in Ephesus in the time of Domitian – which is also speculation. We will show that it is very possible that John was freed during the reign of Nerva, who *succeeded* Domitian – which makes the argument even more ridiculous.

It is interesting how Eusebius begins his next few sentences: a) "He (Irenaeus) states these things in the *third* book of his above-mentioned work" (talking about what we just covered); b) "In the *fifth* book, he (Irenaeus) speaks as follows concerning the Apocalypse of John, and the number of the name of Antichrist:.."

Eusebius doesn't spend much time talking about Irenaeus' third book, going right to his fifth and the discussion about the Antichrist, and his notorious statement. But it is also incredible that, in citing the "ancient presbyters and writers of the church," Eusebius not only begins with Irenaeus, he begins with exactly the material we have been covering – namely, what he had to say about the number of the beast!

Eusebius, quoting Irenaeus, "As these things are so, and this number is found in all the approved and ancient copies, and those who saw John face to face confirm it, and reason teaches us that the number of the name of the beast, according to the mode of calculation among the Greeks, appears in its letters …." This is precisely what we've spent so much time talking about, and Eusebius makes the same argument that we have: that Irenaeus was discussing not only the number of the beast, but the *correct* number (666 vs. 616). That, as we have been exhaustively attempting to show, is the context of what Irenaeus was writing about. And that, obviously, is also the point Eusebius is making. But that, unfortunately, is not what has been put forward.

Continuing, Eusebius says: "And farther on he (Irenaeus) says, concerning the same: *'We are not bold enough to speak confidently of the name of Antichrist. For if it were necessary that his name should be declared clearly at the present time, it would have been announced by him who saw the revelation. For it was seen, not long ago, but almost in our generation, toward the end of the reign of Domitian.'"*

So, there it is again, the notorious statement, and not only, as we've said, is he quoting it in the same context as we have (the number of the beast) it is being used for the second time by Eusebius. That makes a total of three times, and those will be the first three that any serious student of the subject of eschatology will encounter because the date of the Revelation will most certainly come up immediately; as will the Antichrist, the abomination of desolation, the Great Tribulation, and the Rapture.

> P2–He (**Irenaeus**) states these things concerning the Apocalypse in the work referred to. He (**Irenaeus**) also mentions the First Epistle of John, taking many proofs from it, and likewise the First Epistle of Peter. And he (**Irenaeus**) not only knows, but also receives, The Shepherd, writing as follows: "Well did the Scripture speak, saying, 'First of all believe that God is one, who has created and completed all things,'" etc. And he (**Irenaeus**) uses almost the precise words of the Wisdom of Solomon, saying: "The vision of God produces immortality, but immortality renders us near to God." He (**Irenaeus**) mentions also the memoirs of a certain apostolic presbyter, whose name he passes by in silence, and gives his expositions of the sacred Scriptures. And he (**Irenaeus**) refers to Justin the Martyr, and to Ignatius, using testimonies also from their writings. Moreover, he (**Irenaeus**) promises to refute Marcion from his own writings, in a special work. Concerning the translation of the inspired Scriptures by the Seventy (author: Septuagint), hear the very words which he (**Irenaeus**) writes: "God in truth became man, and the Lord himself saved us, giving the sign of the virgin but not as some say, who now venture to translate the Scripture, 'Behold, a young woman

shall conceive and bring forth a son,' as Theodotion of Ephesus and Aquila of Pontus, both of them Jewish proselytes, interpreted; following whom, the Ebionites say that he was begotten by Joseph."

Beginning paragraph two, Eusebius says, "He (Irenaeus) states these things concerning the Apocalypse in the work referred to." It appears here that Eusebius cobbled together various writings and displayed them as they were originally written. His own opinions on this subject are scant, if non-existent. He says, "He (Irenaeus) also mentions the First Epistle of John…" and goes on from there. He refers to Irenaeus no less than a half dozen more times.

The problem (as we noted earlier) in sorting out a very difficult subject such as Revelation is that Irenaeus is quoting and describing what John or Polycarp or even Papias is saying, and then Eusebius is quoting Irenaeus quoting them all. Trying to decipher all the pronouns (all the he's) jumbles things so that a difficult subject becomes more difficult and nearly impossible to untangle.

P3–Shortly after he adds: "For before the Romans had established their empire, while the Macedonians were still holding Asia, Ptolemy, the son of Lagus, being desirous of adorning the library which he had founded in Alexandria with the meritorious writings of all men, **requested the people of Jerusalem to have their Scriptures translated into the Greek language. But, as they were then subject to the Macedonians, they sent to Ptolemy seventy elders, who were the most skilled among them in the Scriptures and in both languages. Thus, God accomplished his purpose. But wishing to try them individually,** as he feared lest, by taking counsel together, they might conceal the truth of the Scriptures by their interpretation, **he separated them from one another, and commanded all of them to write the same translation**. He did this for all the books. But when they came together in the presence of Ptolemy, and compared their several translations, **God was glorified, and the Scriptures were recognized as truly divine**. For all of them had rendered the same things in the same words and with the same names from beginning to end, so that the heathen perceived that the Scriptures had been translated by the inspiration of God. And **this was nothing wonderful for God to do, who, in the captivity of the people-trader Nebuchadnezzar, when the Scriptures had been destroyed, and the Jews had returned to their own country after seventy years,** afterwards, in the time of Artaxerxes, king of the Persians, inspired **Ezra the priest**, of the tribe of Levi, to relate all the words of the former prophets, and to restore to the people the legislation of Moses." **Such are the words of Irenaeus.**

What we see here is the wonderful talent of Irenaeus again on display, who is so concise and so clear as he relates how the Septuagint came into being: how seventy elders were chosen, how they did their work, and how God was glorified–and thus, we have the LXX. More importantly, it is a testament to God and a lesson to man as to the inspiration and authenticity of the Scriptures. But in seeing the talent of Irenaeus, it translates to problems for our study in that he has used that writing talent and, in this case his supposed understanding of the apocalypse and matters of eschatology, to unfortunately weave a web of misunderstanding.

Book 7 – Chapter 25 – The Apocalypse of John

Paragraph 1–Afterward **he** speaks in this manner of the Apocalypse of John. "Some before us have set aside and rejected the book altogether, **criticizing it chapter by chapter, and pronouncing it without sense or argument, and maintaining that the title is fraudulent**. For **they say that it is not the work of John, nor is it a revelation, because it is covered thickly and densely by a vail of obscurity**. And **they affirm that none of the apostles, rend none of the saints, nor anyone in the Church is its author**, but that Cerinthus, who founded the sect which was called after him the Cerinthian, desiring reputable authority for his fiction, prefixed the name. For the doctrine which he taught was this**: that the kingdom of Christ will be an earthly one**. And as he was himself devoted to the pleasures of the body and altogether sensual in his nature, he dreamed that that kingdom would consist in those things which he desired, namely, in the delights of the belly and of sexual passion; that is to say, in eating and drinking and marrying, and in festivals and sacrifices and the slaying of victims, under the guise of which he thought he could indulge his appetites with a better grace. **"But I could not venture to reject the book, as many brethren hold it in high esteem. But I suppose that it is beyond my comprehension, and that there is a certain concealed and more wonderful meaning in every part. For if I do not understand I suspect that a deeper sense lies beneath the words. I do not measure and judge them by**

my own reason, but leaving the more to faith I regard them as too high for me to grasp. And I do not reject what I cannot comprehend, but rather wonder because I do not understand it."

The "he" whom Eusebius is talking about here is Dionysius the Areopagite,[28] a man the "experts" can't seem to determine the time in which he lived. Paul mentions him (Acts 17:34), and Eusebius quotes him talking about Paul and his revelation (as we will see); and some even say he was under the tutelage of Paul for a few years. But the "modern" scholars say that although the writings attributed to him are 'highly esteemed' as a first-century writer, they think the writings were forged and they arbitrarily give him a sixth-century date. Absurd.

He was a critic of chiliasm, mentioning Cerinthus and his "fiction," which is *that the kingdom of Christ will be an earthly one*; which means he was a chiliast. just as Papias–the struggle against futurism was ongoing. Dionysius said that, "some who came before him had rejected the book (the apocalypse) altogether." As we see, it is becoming clear that, as divergent views of futurism took hold, the early church fathers were indeed totally confused about the apocalypse.

Continuing on in his first paragraph, Eusebius, quoting Dionysius, who immediately following what he had said about those who had rejected it altogether, described, in painstaking detail, just how they did so. They: a) criticized it chapter by chapter, b) pronounced it without sense or argument, c) maintained that the title was fraudulent, d) said that it was not the work of John,

---

[28] Saint Dionysius the Areopagite was a judge at the Areopagus Court in Athens who lived in the first century. As related in the Acts of the Apostles, he was converted to Christianity by the preaching of Paul the Apostle during the Areopagus sermon. According to Dionysius, Bishop of Corinth, as quoted by Eusebius–Wikipedia

e) said that it was not a revelation (not inspired–author) because it was covered thickly and densely by a veil of obscurity, f) affirmed that none of the apostles, saints, nor anyone in the church was its author, and g) said that it was the work of Cerinthus, the heretic. That is quite a mouthful, but that was the state of affairs concerning the understanding of the content of the Revelation.

After all of that, Dionysius goes on to say that he doesn't reject the book (the Revelation), "as many before him held it in high esteem," but he supposes that it is beyond his comprehension and that *because he does not understand it he suspects a deeper sense beneath the words.* He therefore places those that do understand it on a higher level of faith than himself, but he does believe that the writer received "knowledge and prophecy."

So, Dionysius admits that the Revelation is beyond his comprehension while not doubting that the writer received knowledge and prophecy, whereas Eusebius doubts its inspiration, and Irenaeus and Papias – well, they're both trapped in the no-man's land of futurism..., caught between the heretics, on the one hand, and God's truth, on the other.

P2–After this, he examines the entire Book of Revelation, and having proved that it is impossible to understand it according to the literal sense, proceeds as follows: [at this point his description of writing style is omitted for its length–author]. **But the Apocalypse is different from these writings and foreign to them; not touching, nor in the least bordering upon them; almost, so to speak, without even a syllable in common with them.** Nay, more, the Epistle, for I pass by the Gospel, does not mention nor does it contain any intimation of the Apocalypse, nor does the Apocalypse of the Epistle. **But Paul, in his epistles, gives some indication of his revelations**, though he has not written them out by themselves. "Moreover, it can also be shown that the diction of the Gospel and Epistle differs from that of the Apocalypse. **For they were written not only without error as regards the Greek language, but also with elegance in their expression, in their reasonings, and in their entire structure.** They are far indeed from betraying any barbarism or solecism, or any vulgarism whatever. For the writer had, as it seems, both the requisites of discourse, that is, the gift of knowledge and the gift of expression, as the Lord had bestowed them both upon him. **I do not deny that the other writer saw a revelation and received knowledge and prophecy. I perceive, however, that his dialect and language are not accurate Greek, but that he uses barbarous idioms, and, in some places, solecisms. It is unnecessary to point these out here, for I would not have any one think that I have said these things in a spirit of ridicule, for I have said what I have only with the purpose of showing clearly the difference between the writings."**

Dionysius, having compared the writing style of the apocalypse to that of the Gospel and epistles of John, does not believe that John, the writer of the Revelation, is the same person as that of the epistles or Gospel of John–neither did Papias. This continues the debate over the interesting differences of opinion of Papias, Irenaeus, Eusebius, and now Dionysius. Remember, Eusebius even called it the "so-called" apocalypse, therefore doubting its inspiration, and he also recognized two people named John, drawing attention to the two tombs in Ephesus bearing those names. Likewise, Dionysius is also endorsing the two-John theory. Confusing? God's way is so much simpler. All you have to do is believe and accept the statements of Scripture.

After a lengthy discussion about the writing-style of the Gospel and letters from John the apostle, Dionysius juxtaposes them with the style of the writing of the Revelation and says they are foreign to each other. He then shows serious doubt as to the style of the apocalypse, almost to the point of ridicule. The point of all of this is that it is further proof that the early church fathers didn't get it right when it came to the Revelation or eschatology. They didn't understand it, as there was a lot of heresy going around, hence the title of Irenaeus' several-volume works, *Against Heresies*.

An interesting tidbit about Dionysius the Areopagite is that he got his moniker, *the Areopagite*, from the name of a giant rock near the Acropolis in Athens called the Areopagus, which the Romans renamed Mars Hill, after their God of War, which was also the name of the Greek Supreme Court, *and from where Paul made his plea* (Acts 17:16-34).

Judaea in the Age of Nero

Written by Yulssus Lynn Holmes
March 16, 2015

Alexander the Great seized the land of Judaea (territory around Jerusalem) from the Persians in 332 B. C. and began the Greek-inspired cultural transformation known as Hellenization.** Judaea would thereafter be ruled by various dynasties – the Greek Ptolemies and Seleucids, the Jewish **Maccabee/Hasmoneans, and** even Antony and Cleopatra–before the Roman Empire absorbed it as part of the province of Palestine. **The last stages of this process took place under Augustus Caesar, the Roman Senate appointing Herod as king.**

Throughout those generations, Hellenistic multi-culturalism continued to grow in Judaea. This change can be seen in commonplace objects; traditional pottery from Israel stands in contrast to mass-produced amphorae jars with Greek factory stamps. **Everyday life in Judaea became little different from the rest of the Mediterranean, from house construction, eating utensils, exercise and personal hygiene, funeral rites, and even the Koiné (common) Greek used in the writing of the Gospels.**

The first Roman imperial dynasty, the descendants of **Augustus or his wife Livia, ruled the Mediterranean for a full century, 31 B.C. to A.D. 68. It was a time of internal peace (Pax Romanum), prosperity, and broad cultural homogeneity – but also of an increasingly authoritarian government. The last of

the family, Claudius Nero Caesar, became a despot, though he was very popular and considered to be a good emperor during his first five years. He was a lover of performing arts, classical culture, and all things Greek. **But he hated republican virtues, his generals, and especially Christians in Rome, whom he tried to exterminate in A.D. 64 after the Great Fire there.** While Nero's persecution of the Christians did not extend beyond Rome (he was looking for a scapegoat to deflect blame that he had caused the fire), he caused the deaths of his step-brother, his mother, his wife, and thousands of innocents. **He was a monster.**

In the last years of Nero's reign, his misgovernment dangerously undermined Roman authority: he refused to support adequately the Roman army, and he appointed unqualified friends and flatterers as provincial authorities. **In Palestine, the incompetence and injustice of imperial procurators (administrators) over Judaea led to the Great Jewish Revolt. In A.D. 68, the army finally turned against him; his overthrow and suicide soon followed.** Nero had built a huge, opulent palace complex in the center of Rome. Overlooking it was a huge statue of himself as a god, rivaling one of the ancient Wonders of the World, the Colossus of Rhodes. After his death, the statue was destroyed. Near its pedestal was erected the largest public amphitheater in the empire, from its location nicknamed the "Coliseum." In a sense, Nero's egoistic dream lives on.

The Great Jewish Revolt, which had started against Nero's rule, climaxed in A.D. 70 when a large Roman army under Titus, son of the new emperor Vespasian, finally captured Jerusalem. As punishment, the Temple of Jahweh was destroyed. Unrest would lead to the city becoming a Roman colony, from which Jews were barred after the Bar Kochba revolt in A.D. 132-135. **Later, religious practices in Judaea changed dramatically after emperor Constantine re-unified the empire, legalized Christianity, and in 330 built a new capital at the old Greek city of Byzantium.**

The ancient Greco-Roman-Near Eastern polytheism slowly faded away. **The Christian capital was called Constantinople, but historians refer to the new civilization as Byzantine.** In Judaea, this society would end with **the surrender of Jerusalem to Muslim Arabs** in 637. **Since then, Judaea has been populated by Jews, Christians and Muslims**, and each group further divided quarreling over scriptural interpretation and religious sites.

The above article "Judea in the Age of Nero" is useful to our study in that it broadly summarizes some of what we discussed in Parts II and III regarding historical context, and it also helps to describe life in the 'silent period'–that period of approximately four-hundred years–from the end of the ministry of the last prophet Malachi, and thus, the Old Testament–until John the Baptist.

The article gives us a glimpse into the silent-period from a different standpoint to help the reader of this book gain some sense of feeling, or insight, of that oh-so important period of time, to help in our understanding of eschatology. Most importantly, the words of Jesus, His teachings and sayings, and those of Paul and the other inspired writers, are steeped in that centuries-old transition period from Persian rule, through the Greek Hellenization, into Roman rule.

The silent-period creates a conundrum for most Christians because it is a four-hundred-year hole in the timeline between the Old and New Testaments, and this was the all-important time of the Hellenization of Judea. The apocryphal writings, especially the Maccabees, for our study, tell us a lot about what life was like back in that time. And as the following end-note shows, while this author would not go as far as Mr. McKnight in endorsing his entire required reading list, the reader should get the point.[iv]

While the Old Testament was written in Hebrew and Aramaic, Greek was the common language during the silent-period and Gospel times. Those were the three primary languages spoken during that time and in that area of the world. But the language of the Romans is Latin, and the Roman Empire had been firmly in power during the time of Christ, so we can see that there was a confluence of civilizations which had been occurring. That is why we have the Septuagint, which is the Greek translation of the Hebrew and Aramaic Old Testament; and the Vulgate, which is the Latin translation of the Old and New Testaments plus some apocryphal writings.

For any reader who regularly reads and studies his or her Bible, whether over a few years, ten, twenty years, or even a lifetime, and even if he becomes proficient in both the Old and New Testaments, and is schooled and become 'learned' – not being connected in any way by heritage to the Babylonian to Persian, then to Greek, and finally to Roman transitions, and all the while the Jews strictly adhering to their Jewish customs – understanding the things Jesus prophesied during His ministry about eschatology without much knowledge of that four-hundred-year period puts a reader at a great disadvantage.

We all suffer from that handicap. The point is, when we read our New Testament, the Gospels come first, and we invariably read where Jesus says 'the sun will be darkened and the moon turned to blood and the stars will fall from the sky' and all sorts of other apocalyptic things such as never occurred since the beginning of time–and then the end will come. The end of what? The end of the world? Only if we read the KJV and listen to the futurists. That happened to this author–early-on. But that is not the message of the Scriptures–which message is redemption and salvation. It is not about the end of the world!

Think about this: we approach the New Testament as though it just simply follows the Old–as chapter two follows chapter one, even as we intellectually acknowledge that there is a four-hundred-year gap between the two. It's like going to a three act play and missing all of act two. The point of this is that it's a significant amount of time. Four-hundred years is longer than from the beginning of the reign of King David until well past the desolation of Samaria–almost to that of Judah. It would also be as the time when, beginning from the period when God was cleansing the royal bloodline from the devilish shenanigans of Jezebel and her daughter Athaliah (Part I), *to* the silent-period.

Four-hundred years is a long time. America isn't even four-hundred years old yet. In fact, it would take 157 more years for America to reach four-hundred years old. That is longer than the period of time between the overthrows of Samaria by Assyria, until that of Judea and Jerusalem by the Babylonians, which is 'only' 136 years.

Recall from Part I how we referenced everything under the backdrop of Jeremiah 50:17-20 and Romans 13:1-7, whereby God ultimately controls the events of the nations. God expected that what had happened to Samaria and the kingdom of Israel would be taken as a warning by the people of Judah and Jerusalem.

So, how would the people of Judah comprehend that what had happened to Israel had anything to do with them, let alone to be taken as a warning, if it had happened so many years prior? These are large periods of time and they are considerably so for man, but not so for God.

In that context, how are we to live our lives today? Drawing an analogy to modern-day America–what could we, living in the year 2019, looking back 136 years to the year 1883, see and draw an analogy as to what could be a warning to us? What was happening back then in America? We were already nearly twenty years past the end of the Civil War. How could the events of then affect us today, or shortly?

It is a hard concept to fathom for man because it is in the abstract, but to God, those periods of time would certainly be quite insignificant in length. In the context just elaborated, 2 Peter 3:3-9 is a neater fit than the context the futurists like to use it in.[29] They take the concept of "a day is as a thousand years, and a thousand years is as a day," and apply it to anything regarding time in which they cannot explain, and in such a way (another variable "x"), that under their scenario, time actually means nothing–and if that be the case, God's word becomes incomprehensible, which is their description; such is the futurist view. But the fact is, God expected Judah to learn from her sister's mistakes - and when they don't, He always takes a remnant to Himself (Jeremiah 3:8,10,15-18).

As far as our study of the harlot, eschatology, and the persecution is concerned, the writings of Eusebius show that there are important works which are and have been available to man, and which should have helped us to rightly interpret the Revelation and the events of the great persecution. There are more than several pages which the reader will soon consume where Eusebius, that noted and beloved early church father and historian, will outline for us just how real and intense that persecution was. And yet, as we will show, he has been largely ignored in that respect.

For too long, nearly two-thousand years, in fact, we have been lulled to sleep by the siren song of Satan which has kept us from the truth. That siren song is this: a. the apocalypse was seen *after* Jerusalem fell, in the time on Domitian; b. *aión* means *world*, meaning Jesus was talking about the end of the world instead of the end of the age; c. *generation* means an indeterminate amount of time instead of the generation that Jesus was talking to; and d. we should all read the KJV only, the translation that carries the *aión* error forward instead of more accurate and faithful Bible translations.

Also part of the siren song are all of the writers, historians, and theologians who quote Eusebius, who in turn quotes Irenaeus

---

[29] Terry, *Biblical Hermeneutics* Pg. 496

– who, as we've shown, is the source of futurism. Those writers, historians, and theologians have either failed to read what Eusebius wrote about the persecution, or failed to understand what he wrote about it, or worse still, just flat-out ignored or rejected it. They have, in fact, only perpetuated futurism and exacerbated the problem of understanding the Revelation and the persecution.

They have failed to take the inspired Scriptures at face value where, as we have referenced and will continue to reference: a. the time of distress as prophesied by Daniel was indeed the Great Tribulation as prophesied by Jesus, and b. the Great Commission has indeed been fulfilled and is constantly being fulfilled (Colossians 1:6,23). For if the Gospel has gone out to all the world, then the Great Commission has been fulfilled. The literal interpretation of having to preach the Gospel "to every creature" (Mark 16:15–KJV), another erroneous translation of that version of the Bible, is not only ludicrous – it's literally impossible.

These writers, historians, and theologians have also failed to acknowledge that the Great Tribulation is the great persecution of Acts 8:1. What that implies, as we have noted, is that the futurist view would create the need to have a fulfillment of all three of those events, which is absurd. But, as we have seen and will continue to see, the persecution was very intense and very long-lived, and satisfies all that needs to be satisfied to fulfill the prophesies of Daniel and Jesus. And as the rest of the book of Acts spells out, step by step, we will soon see how that persecution affected the Apostle Paul and the implications of that.

Because we know that the apostle Peter was executed by Nero, we know that the destruction of 70AD hadn't occurred yet when he made that statement about a thousand years being as a day.... That could very well have been the "coming of the Lord" he was talking about–in other words, it was His coming in judgment. That is a scenario which makes perfect sense. It was near; it would immediately, soon, or shortly, come to pass; it was close at hand; it was at the door. Peter was addressing mockers and scoffers. The futurists are mockers and scoffers; they mock the suggestion that 'all those things' were fulfilled; they scoff at the very idea.

The latter stages of the transition from Greek to Roman rule took place under Augustus Caesar, who was in power during the time of John the Baptist and when Christ began His ministry. According to the above article, the last of the descendants of Augustus (or his wife) to rule the Roman Empire was Nero, the despot, who is also described as a monster. His suicide was followed by four more emperors, in what must have been a tumultuous span of less than two years, as we've noted. That fourth emperor was Vespasian, whom we know became famous as a general for his military campaign against Judea. We also know that he was succeeded as general by his son, Titus, who was the one who destroyed Jerusalem and the Temple for the final time.

So, the time period from Nero to Vespasian, then to Titus and the destruction, was a maelstrom–the cataclysmic climax–of the great persecution. But Nero didn't happen in a vacuum. We know that the persecution began with the killing of Stephen (Acts 8:1). If that occurred within a few years of the crucifixion, say somewhere between 30-35AD (exact dates can be rather nebulous), then there were approximately twenty years between then and 54AD, when Nero took the reins. We know from the above article that, although that was a time of "internal peace, prosperity, and broad cultural homogeneity" for the Empire–it was anything but that for Christians – or Jews.

We will now attempt to demonstrate how the Great Tribulation occurred.

Part V–Persecution

The Story of Stephen– We Meet Paul

(Acts 6:1–8:4)

At this point, we have studied how the people played the harlot throughout their history–in the Old Testament (Part I), through the Gospel time (Part II), and in the Revelation (Part III). We also pointed out that a study of Revelation could not be done without coming to grips with the writings of Irenaeus, who wrote extensively on the apocalypse, mostly about the beast and Antichrist, and Eusebius, who also had much to say about the Revelation, and about what Irenaeus said about it. Eusebius also had quite a bit to say about the persecution, which the Christians suffered at the hands of the Jews and the Romans.

We begin this section during the period shortly after the crucifixion and resurrection of Jesus, and so we are at an important point in time. Jesus' ministry had come to an end, and all those who were found written in the Lamb's Book of Life from the foundation of the world were saved (rescued). Jesus had given the Great Commission (Matthew 28:16-20), the Holy Spirit had been given at Pentecost (Acts 2:1-4), and the fledgling church was about to get a big boost.

According to the writer of Acts, who is the same writer as that of the Gospel of Luke, writing in hindsight and under inspiration, he attests to the Great Commission by stating that the apostles were to be Christ's witnesses: first in Jerusalem, then in Judea and Samaria, and to the remotest parts of the earth (Acts 1:8). At this point they were still primarily in Jerusalem.

After Jesus had been resurrected, He appeared to Mary Magdalene, who immediately went to the disciples to tell them that she had seen Him (John 20:16-18). They were in the house with the doors shut because they feared the Jews! (John 20:19) who had never stopped pursuing and provoking them.

This is a most important point, for now that Jesus had been crucified, and supposedly dead, after all the harassment that they had endured – they now feared for their own lives! The religious leaders, who had been intimidated by the healings and other miracles done by Jesus and the disciples, now that Jesus was 'dead,' would have felt less constrained to plot and scheme against them.

> **Acts 6:1-15** ¹Now at this time while the disciples were increasing in number, a complaint arose on the part of the Hellenistic Jews against the native Hebrews, because their widows were being overlooked in the daily serving of food. ² So the twelve summoned the congregation of the disciples and said, "It is not desirable for us to neglect the word of God in order to serve tables. ³ Therefore, brethren, select from among you seven men of good reputation, full of the Spirit and of wisdom, whom we may put in charge of this task. ⁴ But we will devote ourselves to prayer and to the ministry of the word." ⁵ The statement found approval with the whole congregation; and **they chose Stephen, a man full of**

faith and of the Holy Spirit, and Philip, Prochorus, Nicanor, Timon, Parmenas and Nicolas, a proselyte from Antioch. [6] And these they brought before the apostles; and after praying, they laid their hands on them. [7] **The word of God kept on spreading, and the number of the disciples continued to increase greatly in Jerusalem**, and a great many of the priests were becoming obedient to the faith. [8] And **Stephen, full of grace and power, was performing great wonders and signs among the people.** [9] But **some men** from what was called the Synagogue of the Freedmen, including both Cyrenians and Alexandrians, and some from Cilicia and Asia, **rose up and argued with Stephen.** [10] But **they were unable to cope with the wisdom and the Spirit with which he was speaking.** [11] Then **they secretly induced men to say, "We have heard him speak blasphemous words against Moses and against God."** [12] And **they stirred up the people, the elders and the scribes, and they came up to him and dragged him away and brought him before the Council.** [13] **They put forward false witnesses** who said, "This man incessantly speaks against this holy place and the Law; [14] **for we have heard him say that this Nazarene, Jesus, will destroy this place and alter the customs** which Moses handed down to us." [15] **And fixing their gaze on him, all who were sitting in the Council saw his face like the face of an angel.**

Stephen was a disciple of the Lord and His teachings, and he was one of seven chosen by the other disciples for the task given them by the apostles: to see to the complaint that the widows of the Hellenistic Jews were being overlooked in the daily serving of food (Acts 6: 1-7). He was a man of faith (6:5), and he was performing signs and great wonders (6:8), but when some men rose up against him to argue with him, they found they couldn't cope with the wisdom and the Spirit by which he spoke (6:10), so they secretly induced others to make up lies against him–to bear false witness against him (6:11). That is reminiscent of the experience which Jesus endured at the hands of the religious leaders (Part II).

They stirred up the people, the elders, and the scribes, and they came up to him and dragged him away and brought him before the Council (6:12). Think about that for a moment. How long a period of time would it have taken for the events of 6:11-13 to take place: from the inducing of men to say lies about him, to the stirring up of the people, and to the time they actually dragged him away and brought him before the Council–hours? days? weeks? months? It is too easy to read through that as though it was minutes. This was no small matter, for it was not only a continuation of the harassment which had been happening while Jesus was still amongst them. They had killed Him and were now arresting His followers. This could not have been a pleasant time for the new Christian church.

There is a pattern at what the false accusers actually said and did, though. They said they heard Stephen say that Jesus said, that He would destroy the Temple and alter the customs which Moses had handed down to them (Acts 6:14). Jesus did say that He would destroy the Temple and rebuild it in three days (John 2:18-22). As to the altering of customs, that is addressed in Hebrews chapter 8, where the writer is making the case as to why those customs would even have to be altered, or how that would even come about. In the end, that writer said the old was fading away and was ready to disappear (Hebrews 8:13)–the new had come.

The inspired writer of Hebrews, who was not only writing in retrospect but also in the then present tense saw fit to write what he did. There should be no reason to believe that those words, or

The Story Of Stephen–We Meet Paul

words to that effect, hadn't been spoken by others, or even by Jesus Himself. The Bible doesn't contain every word that Jesus spoke (John 21:24-25; Acts 1:1-3), but every word that He did speak – every word that proceeded from His mouth–was the bread of God (Matthew 4:1-4, John 6:35).

So, the irony is that while the false witnesses were, in fact, correct about what Stephen said – the fact is that *they* didn't hear him say it–they were put up to saying that they did, just as in the case of Jesus. The implications of what Stephen said were such that the religious leaders couldn't conceive of the Temple being destroyed (John 2:20). After all, it was God's holy Temple – it would be nothing short of blasphemy.

It was also an escalation of the violence against the Christians when he was physically dragged away, for that was an assault on him personally. The Council was nothing more than a kangaroo court; but Stephen, the man of God that he was, full of grace and power and faith, and full of the Holy Spirit–shined like an angel (Acts 6:15)!

> **Acts 7:1-60** ¹**The high priest said, "Are these things so?"** ²**And he said, "Hear me**, brethren and fathers! The God of glory appeared to our father **Abraham when he was in Mesopotamia, before he lived in Haran**, ³ and said to him, 'LEAVE YOUR COUNTRY AND YOUR RELATIVES AND COME INTO THE LAND THAT I WILL SHOW YOU.' ⁴Then he left the land of the Chaldeans and settled in Haran. From there, after his father died, **God had him move to this country in which you are now living**. ⁵But He gave him no inheritance in it, not even a foot of ground, and yet, even when he had no child, He promised that HE WOULD GIVE IT TO HIM AS A POSSESSION, AND TO HIS

DESCENDANTS AFTER HIM. ⁶ But God spoke to this effect, that **his DESCENDANTS WOULD BE ALIENS IN A FOREIGN LAND, AND THAT THEY WOULD BE ENSLAVED AND MISTREATED FOR FOUR HUNDRED YEARS.** ⁷ '**AND WHATEVER NATION TO WHICH THEY WILL BE IN BONDAGE I MYSELF WILL JUDGE,**' said God, '**AND AFTER THAT THEY WILL COME OUT AND SERVE ME IN THIS PLACE.**' ⁸ And He gave him the covenant of circumcision; and so Abraham became the father of Isaac, and circumcised him on the eighth day; and Isaac became the father of Jacob, and Jacob of **the twelve patriarchs**. ⁹ "The patriarchs became jealous of Joseph and sold him into Egypt. Yet God was with him, ¹⁰ and rescued him from all his afflictions, and granted him favor and wisdom in the sight of Pharaoh, king of Egypt, and he made him governor over Egypt and all his household. ¹¹ "Now a famine came over all **Egypt** and **Canaan**, and great affliction with it, and our fathers could find no food. ¹² But when **Jacob** heard that there was grain in Egypt, he sent our fathers there **the first time**. ¹³ **On the second visit, Joseph made himself known to his brothers**, and Joseph's family was disclosed to Pharaoh. ¹⁴ Then Joseph sent word and invited Jacob his father and all his relatives to come to him, seventy-five persons in all. ¹⁵ **And Jacob went down to Egypt and there he and our fathers died.** ¹⁶ From there they were removed to Shechem and laid in the tomb which Abraham had purchased for a sum of money from the sons of Hamor in Shechem. ¹⁷ "But as the time of the promise was approaching which God had assured to Abraham, the people increased and multiplied in Egypt, ¹⁸ until **THERE AROSE ANOTHER**

The Story Of Stephen–we Meet Paul

king over Egypt who knew nothing about Joseph. **¹⁹ It was he who took shrewd advantage of our race and mistreated our fathers so that they would expose their infants and they would not survive**. ²⁰ It was at this time that Moses was born, and he was lovely in the sight of God, and he was nurtured three months in his father's home. ²¹ And after he had been set outside, Pharaoh's daughter took him away and nurtured him as her own son. ²² **Moses was educated in all the learning of the Egyptians, and he was a man of power in words and deeds**. ²³ But when he was approaching **the age of forty**, it entered his mind to visit his brethren, the sons of Israel. ²⁴ And when he saw one of them being treated unjustly, he defended him and took vengeance for the oppressed by striking down the Egyptian. ²⁵ **And he supposed that his brethren understood that God was granting them deliverance through him, but they did not understand**. ²⁶ On the following day he appeared to them as they were fighting together, and he tried to reconcile them in peace, saying, 'Men, you are brethren, why do you injure one another?' ²⁷ But the one who was injuring his neighbor pushed him away, saying, 'Who made you a ruler and judge over us? ²⁸ You do not mean to kill me as you killed the Egyptian yesterday, do you?' ²⁹ At this remark, Moses fled and became an alien in the land of Midian, **where he became the father of two sons**. ³⁰ "**After forty years had passed,** an angel appeared to him in the wilderness of Mount Sinai, in the flame of a burning thorn bush. ³¹ When Moses saw it, he marveled at the sight; and as he approached to look more closely, there came the voice of the Lord: ³² 'I AM THE GOD OF YOUR FATHERS, THE GOD OF ABRAHAM AND ISAAC AND JACOB.' Moses shook with fear and would not venture to look. ³³ BUT THE LORD SAID TO HIM, 'TAKE OFF THE SANDALS FROM YOUR FEET, FOR THE PLACE ON WHICH YOU ARE STANDING IS HOLY GROUND. ³⁴ I HAVE CERTAINLY SEEN THE OPPRESSION OF MY PEOPLE IN EGYPT AND HAVE HEARD THEIR GROANS, AND I HAVE COME DOWN TO RESCUE THEM; COME NOW, AND I WILL SEND YOU TO EGYPT.' ³⁵ "This Moses whom they disowned, saying, 'WHO MADE YOU A RULER AND A JUDGE?' is the one whom God sent to be both a ruler and a deliverer with the help of the angel who appeared to him in the thorn bush. ³⁶ This man led them out, performing wonders and signs in the land of Egypt and in the Red Sea and in the wilderness for forty years. ³⁷ This is the Moses who said to the sons of Israel, 'GOD WILL RAISE UP FOR YOU A PROPHET LIKE ME FROM YOUR BRETHREN.' ³⁸ This is the one who was in the congregation in the wilderness together with the angel who was speaking to him on Mount Sinai, and who was with our fathers; **and he received living oracles to pass on to you. ³⁹ Our fathers were unwilling to be obedient to him but repudiated him and in their hearts turned back to Egypt,** ⁴⁰ SAYING TO AARON, 'MAKE FOR US GODS WHO WILL GO BEFORE US; FOR THIS MOSES WHO LED US OUT OF THE LAND OF EGYPT — WE DO NOT KNOW WHAT HAPPENED TO HIM.' ⁴¹ At that time they made a calf and brought a sacrifice to the idol, **and were rejoicing in the works of their hands. ⁴² But God turned away and delivered them up to serve the host of**

heaven; as it is written in the book of the prophets, 'IT WAS NOT TO ME THAT YOU OFFERED VICTIMS AND SACRIFICES FORTY YEARS IN THE WILDERNESS, WAS IT, O HOUSE OF ISRAEL? ⁴³ YOU ALSO TOOK ALONG THE TABERNACLE OF MOLOCH AND THE STAR OF THE GOD ROMPHA, THE IMAGES WHICH YOU MADE TO WORSHIP. I ALSO WILL REMOVE YOU BEYOND BABYLON.' ⁴⁴ "Our fathers had the tabernacle of testimony in the wilderness, just as He who spoke to Moses directed him to make it according to the pattern which he had seen. ⁴⁵ And having received it in their turn, our fathers brought it in with Joshua upon dispossessing the nations whom God drove out before our fathers, **until the time of David. ⁴⁶ David found favor in God's sight and asked that he might find a dwelling place for the God of Jacob. ⁴⁷ But it was Solomon who built a house for Him. ⁴⁸ However, the Most High does not dwell in houses made by human hands;** as the prophet says: 'HEAVEN IS MY THRONE, AND EARTH IS THE FOOTSTOOL OF MY FEET; WHAT KIND OF HOUSE WILL YOU BUILD FOR ME?' SAYS THE LORD, 'OR WHAT PLACE IS THERE FOR MY REPOSE? WAS IT NOT MY HAND WHICH MADE ALL THESE THINGS?' ⁵¹ **"You men who are stiff-necked and uncircumcised in heart and ears are always resisting the Holy Spirit; you are doing just as your fathers did. ⁵² Which one of the prophets did your fathers not persecute? They killed those who had previously announced the coming of the Righteous One, whose betrayers and murderers you have now become; ⁵³ you who received the law as ordained by angels, and yet**

did not keep it." ⁵⁴ Now when they heard this, they were cut to the quick, and they began gnashing their teeth at him. ⁵⁵ But being full of the Holy Spirit, he gazed intently into heaven and saw the glory of God, and Jesus standing at the right hand of God; ⁵⁶ and he said, "Behold, I see the heavens opened up and the Son of Man standing at the right hand of God." ⁵⁷ **But they cried out with a loud voice, and covered their ears and rushed at him with one impulse. ⁵⁸ When they had driven him out of the city, they began stoning him; and the witnesses laid aside their robes at the feet of a young man named Saul.** ⁵⁹ They went on stoning Stephen as he called on the Lord and said, "Lord Jesus, receive my spirit!" ⁶⁰ Then falling on his knees, he cried out with a loud voice, "Lord, do not hold this sin against them!" Having said this, he fell asleep.

When the high priest asked Stephen whether those things were so, that opened the floodgates as Stephen began a recounting of the entire history of God's people: from the time of Abraham when God set him apart, to the time of Solomon who built the first Temple (Acts 7:1-47). A point to make here is that this 'recounting of history' is something that is done repeatedly in Scripture. It is God's way of keeping His story in front of man–for man to see what is important.

But man has still managed to miss it, as His people continued to play the harlot, just as man has missed it regarding eschatology. Remember, this is inspired writing and therefore correct, so when history is being recounted, those things which are important to God are the things which are being recounted–therefore they are important to us. Additionally, those things from verses 7:38-47 are the things we covered in the entirety of Part 1, all of which were covered here in just ten verses.

The Story Of Stephen–We Meet Paul

Of interest is the fact that Moses was eighty years old when he led the people through the wilderness, and then for an additional forty years, so he was more than one-hundred twenty years old when he died (Acts 7:23,30,36). The reason they were even in the wilderness is that they had been enslaved for four-hundred years in Egypt and Moses was now leading them out to the Promised Land. God, after He freed the people, judged Egypt (Jeremiah 46:2), the nation that enslaved them (7:6-7), just like we saw that He did later with Babylon, which we saw when we studied Daniel's fourth kingdom (p 72).

God doesn't change. Going back one step further, the reason they were enslaved in the first place is that they had sold their brother Joseph into bondage in Egypt (7:9). It appears that no one-particular group of people is innocent of selling or placing his fellow man into bondage–it is in all of us as sinners, and we are all too eager to carry it out.

Even though 7:47 tells of Solomon being the builder of His house, the very next verse contrasts that with, "however…" and then goes on to say that God, the builder of the entire universe, was not to be confined to anything built with human hands. As important as the Temple was, it had to go, and it did.

So, after reciting everything of significance from the very beginning–from the time when Abraham left Mesopotamia (going back to Genesis 12), to the time when God revealed to His people that He, God, does not live in human-made structures (He lives in our heart in the person of the Holy Spirit), we come to the point where Stephen, just like Jesus when He turned to His accusers and indicted them–accused the Council members (the religious leaders) of not only being the sons of the murderers of the prophets before them, but that they themselves were the betrayers and murderers of the Righteous One – Jesus (Acts 7:52; see also Matthew 23:34)!

On the whole, you will know that what you are saying is the last thing your hearers want to hear when they gnash their teeth, cover their ears, cry out, and then rush you–because that's exactly what the religious leaders did to Stephen. They drove him out of the city, then stoned him to death (Acts 7:54-60).

What a horrific set of circumstances and events that was. That is what the character of the attitude toward Christians was at that time, and that is what was taking place to those first Christians, who didn't even know they were considered Christians until they were called such, later, in Antioch (Acts 11:26).

> **Acts 8:1-3** ¹Saul was in hearty agreement with putting him to death. **And on that day a great persecution began against the church in Jerusalem, and they were all scattered throughout the regions of Judea and Samaria**, except the apostles. ² Some devout men buried Steph*en, and made loud lamentation over him.* ³ **But Saul began ravaging the church, entering house after house, and dragging off men and women, he would put them in prison.**

So, who were the witnesses of Acts 7:58, and whose robes did they throw at the feet of Saul, and why would those "witnesses" even be mentioned here in this context? Why, they were the false witnesses of verse 6:13, the witnesses who lied and falsely accused Stephen, which resulted in the horrendous act that cost him his life. They were either taking part in the stoning, or protecting the property of those who were–and look at whose feet they laid the coats.

Saul was in hearty agreement (Acts 8:1). Of course, he was–he was one of them. He was one of the religious leaders, although not a member of the Council, but a leader nonetheless – and he was in with the murderers. Who else would be entrusted to guard the robes? It would have to be someone who was considered trustworthy by those collecting them, and to whom they belonged. Christ had turned the world upside down, and so many of the Jews were now becoming Christians. But the unbelieving religious leaders were stiff-necked and uncircumcised of heart and ears, always resisting the Holy Spirit (7:51); and they were continuing to kill the prophets–continuing to play the harlot.

And on that day a great persecution began against the church in Jerusalem, and they were scattered throughout the regions of Judea and Samaria, except the apostles (8:1). That single verse contains considerable information about eschatology and the persecution. Two things come to mind: a) the great persecution (Great Tribulation?) began that day – in Jerusalem, and b) the Christians were scattered throughout Judea and Samaria–the second part of the Great Commission (Acts 1:8).

Many dismiss and try to explain away that God-inspired statement–the one about the great persecution which started that day–because it flies in the face of what the futurists say. Why would that not be the Great Tribulation spoken of by Jesus in Matthew 24:15? Or, why would it not be the time of distress spoken of by Daniel 12:1? Those are three named events, three entities–and the three are one and the same.

"But wait!" you say. "It's about the end times, the end of the world;" or, "The armies of God must meet in battle against the armies of Antichrist at Armageddon – the Great Tribulation!" and, "The armies of God win! A new Temple will be built, and Jesus will rule the world from it! The sacrifices will re-start. The new Jerusalem will come down from heaven and we'll all live happily ever after!" And on and on it goes.

Countless books have been written on variations of that theme–conjecture–all conjecture. It is sad to see so many well-intentioned and learned scholars so wrong on this subject. The whole story was about what Christ did at the cross. Salvation was now for everybody who believed on Him. It was about His people, as it always had been. It is not about great cataclysmic events that will always happen, such as wars and rumors of wars, earthquakes, famines, volcanic eruptions and such. And man may yet manage to destroy himself in spite of himself. But, the great persecution – the great tribulation – the time of distress – was about the persecution of the new-born church, which all came to a head and exploded in 70AD.

From Stephen to Nero

(From the Book of Acts)

We ended the last section with the great persecution beginning on the day that Stephen was killed, the robes of the killers laid at the feet of Saul, and with the believers being scattered throughout Judea and Samaria. Two verses later, in Acts 8:3, we see the horrible depiction of the man named Saul. Looking again at that verse we see: *But Saul began ravaging the church, entering house after house, and dragging off men and women, he would put them in prison.* How horrible is that? And how wonderful it is to live in America, or any freedom-loving country, where we don't have to worry about mobs or the government breaking down our door and taking us away for political or religious reasons, yet.

But Saul did just that, entering house after house dragging people away and throwing them in prison. The next time we see him is Acts 9:1 where he was *breathing threats and murder against the disciples of the Lord*. Whoa! That is pretty intense–breathing threats and murder! That is the picture of someone bent on doing harm. Saul was not the man you wanted after you.

People often talk about how when Paul got saved when he was on the road to Damascus, and that he got blinded by the light when Jesus appeared to him, and how he had scales on his eyes. But he was on the road to Damascus because *he was on his way there to ask for papers from the high priest* (one of the religious leaders), *permitting him to haul away any Christians from the synagogues in Damascus, bound, to Jerusalem* (9:2). Saul was a horrible man.

And what an abrupt turn-around he would make after meeting Jesus on the road to Damascus (Acts 9:3-6). His Roman name was Paul, and he went by that name after his conversion, becoming the apostle who would author more of the New Testament than all the others combined. But Paul, still Saul at this time, was a man on a mission. The verve that he showed in his epistles he also showed in the intensity by which he persecuted the church.

We will trace the persecution through Paul in his travels as he, being an apostle and responsible for much of the evangelizing throughout the Empire through his missionary journeys, was himself persecuted, and he is representative of what occurred to Christians in general. His zeal, first for Judaism and then for the Lord will shine through.

God chose exactly the right man for His work. Paul was a Roman citizen, a Jew, and well educated, as he became a Pharisee– and no one wrote more of the New Testament that he. He was not strident, not radical, but feisty. He had a zeal, an enthusiasm – for the Lord. The dichotomy of Paul being the person at whose feet the coats of those who stoned Stephen were laid (thus beginning the great persecution), and his imprisonment and ultimate martyrdom at the hands of the beast Nero for the cause for Christ–is stark. Only Christ can change a person in that way.

The Jews were the ones who began the persecution. We saw that Saul (Paul, before his conversion), was in hearty agreement with putting Stephen to death (Acts 8:1); that he began ravaging the church (8:3); and that he was also breathing threats and murder against them, pursuing them all the way to Damascus (9:1-2)–*but he met the Lord along the way and was converted, and he began preaching and proving that Jesus was the Christ*! Then "when many days had elapsed" the Jews were plotting to kill him (9:22-23).

How many days were "many" is not known, but that was an escalation into open and outright hostility against Paul and people like him – the Christians. Remember, at that time it was mostly Jews who were being converted, and as a result, as they were persecuting the Christians, they were actually persecuting their own. So, the persecution was from the Jews, including the Hellenistic Jews (the husbands of the women that Stephen was charged with overseeing before being brought before the council), who also joined in and were plotting to kill him (9:29).

An interesting verse is 11:19, where it says that *those who were scattered because of the persecution that occurred in connection with Stephen made their way to Phoenicia* (just north of Israel), *Cyprus* (an island off the coast of Turkey, Phoenicia, and Israel), *and Antioch* (in Turkey). Yes, the persecution, which we documented as having begun with the killing of Stephen is mentioned *as* the persecution *again*. Why this detail is consistently overlooked by those who look for a future Great Tribulation and fail to accept the plain facts stated by the inspired writers is beyond comprehension. *The persecution began at the feet of Saul with the killing of Stephen!*

Also, we see that those who had been scattered from Jerusalem to Judea and Samaria made their way to other parts of the Roman Empire – they were beyond the Holy Land. That fact is clearly spelled out and emphatically stated. The Christians were scattered to Phoenicia, Cyprus, and Antioch (Asia) – they were now in the uttermost parts of the earth, just as Jesus said would occur–the Great Commission was accomplished.

Saul and Barnabas teamed up in Tarsus (in Turkey) and stayed at Antioch, where they were first called Christians (11:22-26). They traveled by sea and land as they preached Jesus, and were being pursued and persecuted by the Jews in the process. This was the beginning of his first missionary journey.

The Jews began contradicting Saul and the others, and blaspheming God because of jealousy over crowd size, of all things (13:45). They incited devout women of prominence and the leading men of the city *and instigated a persecution* against Saul and Barnabas, driving them out of their district (13:50). The persecution has now been mentioned for a third time here in the book of Acts by the inspired writer. Saying, "No, that's not it," and looking to the future for another Great Tribulation is a fool's game.

It seems unimaginable, having grown up in America, that such was the state of peoples' open hostility to Christians at that time. The church was growing fast: first, the twelve; then, Jesus send out the seventy (Luke 10:1); then, Peter and one-hundred-twenty in the upper room (Acts 1:15); three-thousand more were added (2:41); then, five-thousand (4:4); and it continued to increase (9:31); the word of the Lord continued to grow and to be multiplied (12:24); increasing in number daily (16:5); by thousands (21:20). Despite man's worst efforts, and Satan's, God's plan would not be stopped!

At Iconium, Saul, now called Paul (13:9), and his entourage entered the synagogue, which was their normal practice, but the unbelieving Jews "stirred up the minds of the Gentiles and embittered them against the brethren" (14:1-2). Now, under 'normal circumstances,' that would have been enough to scare most people off, but 14:3 says that, "Therefore they spent a long time there, speaking boldly, with reliance upon the Lord…"

Not only did they stay a long time there, they stayed *because* the Jews were stirring up the peoples' minds against them. They did not turn tail and run. Jesus taught to turn the other cheek, and that the meek shall inherit the earth; but we are not to be silent, nor afraid. Verse 14:3 begins with "Therefore," which is an adverb that means 'for that reason,' or 'because of that.' So, they stayed there *for that reason* or *because of* the fact that the peoples' minds had been stirred up.

They were not meek–they were bold. Eventually, as the city became divided, the Jews, Gentiles, and the rulers (the Romans) made an attempt "to mistreat and stone them," so they fled (14:4-6). Once the government joined in with the Jews against the Christians, the heat of the persecution was turned up.

At Lystra, some of the Jews actually came from Antioch and Iconium (from where Paul had just fled), won over the crowds, and "stoned Paul, dragging him out of the city and leaving him for dead" (14:19). These events don't happen instantaneously; it takes some 'doing' to stir up a crowd or to win them over. It was a concerted effort to weed out certain types of people – in this case, the Christians, who were not thought too highly of.

Paul, now on his second journey, came to Thyatira in Macedonia, a Roman colony (16:12), which was is Europe (Oh! how the gospel was spreading). There, they met a slave girl who had a spirit of divination. Paul cast the spirit out of her but her masters, who had been profiting from her condition, "seized him and Silas, dragging them before the authorities." Because the authorities were the Romans, and because Paul and Silas were ordered to be beaten with rods and thrown into prison where they were kept in the inner prison, their feet fastened with stocks (16:16-24), we now see the Roman Empire conclusively joined with the Jews in the persecution of the Christians.

So, what we have seen so far is that as fast as the church was growing, the unbelieving Jews, along with the Gentiles, and now the Romans, were all persecuting the apostles and their disciples. But now, in prison, they were freed by "the earthquake" (16:26) and, seeing how they had acted peacefully during the time of chaos, the authorities ordered them to be released.

But Paul showed his feisty spirit–his moxie–the stuff of which is the reason God chose him for the work that had to be done. He was a man who had the characteristics that God needed for His work, that He Himself instilled, and that Paul utilized. Remember, he was a Jew–a Hebrew of Hebrews–and a Pharisee at that, so he was learned in the Law and the Prophets. As to zeal? *A persecutor of the church*. As to righteousness? Found blameless, *blameless!* (Philippians 3:4-6); he was also a Roman citizen, (Acts 21:39). He was not going to go quietly out the back door (Acts 16:35-40)!

At Thessalonica, the city whose church he would later write two letters to, Paul, for weeks, went to the synagogue and *reasoned* from the Scriptures with the Jews that Jesus is the Christ. When many of the people, including Greeks, were persuaded and joined Paul and Silas, the unpersuaded, along with some (I love how the KJV says it) "lewd fellows of the baser sort" formed a mob, set the city in an uproar, and attacked the house where they were staying. But when they found that they weren't there, they dragged the owner and some brothers and sisters before the city authorities and extorted a "pledge" from them before releasing them (Acts 17:1-9).

It is easy to just read over these things because God's word is so packed with 'stuff,' and nobody can grasp it all, so it's only reasonable to say that we are missing the severity of the persecution. Not to mention the fact that most people are looking to a future tribulation anyway. Imagine an angry mob looking for someone and, thinking that person or persons were in your house, "attacked" your house and then dragged you and others before the authorities because those they were seeking weren't in your house!

They went to Berea, whose people have become famous. They were more noble-minded than the others, "for they received the word with great eagerness, examining the Scriptures daily to see whether these things were so" (17:11). That is sound advice to anyone who listens to others regarding God's word, or, to anyone who studies God's word.

But when the Jews of Thessalonica heard that the word of God was proclaimed there, they came there as well and started "agitating and stirring up" the crowds. How were they to feel safe when they were being pursued by people from city to city who wished to do them harm? (see Matthew 23:34)

Paul went to Athens, where he addressed the men of the city at Mars Hill. He was "preaching Jesus and the resurrection" but the subject of "the resurrection of the dead" made some of the people begin to sneer (17:32). We know, as Christians, that without the resurrection of the dead, then even Jesus isn't resurrected – and if Jesus isn't resurrected, our faith is in vain (1 Corinthians 15:12-19).

He made his way to Corinth where he was "solemnly testifying to the Jews that Jesus was the Christ," but when they resisted and started blaspheming, he "shook out his garments" and said, "From now on, I will go to the Gentiles" (18:5-6). Christianity was now open to all–it is inclusive. Then God said to him in a vision, and here's an example for us, *"Do not be afraid... but go on speaking and do not be silent*, for I am with you and no man will attack you to harm you, for I have many people in this city" (18:7-10).

What a powerful message! And what courage Paul must have derived from that. All Christians should too. That's what we're known for. We're to be "wise as serpents, and gentle as doves" (Matthew 10:16). Jesus said that just after He had said He was sending them out as "sheep in the midst of wolves." But we are not supposed to go 'as sheep, to the slaughter.' Jesus did that, and He did it to make atonement for us—we cannot do that because we are not God. Always be ready to make a defense to anyone who asks you to give an account for the hope that is in you (1 Peter 3:15 paraphrased).

The Jews, "with one accord" rose up against Paul and brought him before the Judgment Seat. But the (Roman) "proconsul" said he didn't want to be a judge in these matters and drove them away, *so they took hold of someone else instead and beat him in front of the Judgment Seat* (18:12-17) Incredible! – That's as bad as the vicious attack on the person's house (previously)!

They were so rabid and had whipped themselves into such a frenzy that they had to beat *somebody*. And also, in this case, as the Romans chose not to get involved, the people on the street must have felt empowered as they were taking their hatred out on the Christians, and the Romans were not doing much, if anything, to stop it and were, in fact, joining in. There was serious persecution going on against the Christians.

At this point, Paul was beginning his third journey, and Nero, the man whose number adds up to 666–the beast–was soon to become the Roman Emperor. In Ephesus, as he usually did, Paul went into the synagogue, "reasoning" with them and persuading them about the Kingdom of God. But some became "hardened and disobedient," speaking evil about the Way before the people (19:8-10). He spent more than two years there, and although the Jews pursued and confronted them, there was no violence recorded against them, as per the Scriptures.

In Greece, the Jews formed a plot against him (20:2-3) but he was able to find a way to leave. Back in Miletus he sent for the elders of the church at Ephesus, and as he was stating his business to them and talking about his "tears and trials" at the hands of the Jews, "and their plots against him" (20:17-19), one can see that Christians clearly had 'targets on their backs.' It didn't matter where Paul went. Ephesus and Miletus were in Asia, Greece was in Europe, and they were separated by the Aegean Sea –but the Jews relentlessly continued to go after them.

Despite being warned by the disciples of Tyre not to return to Jerusalem, then by the prophet Agabus, and even by those who were traveling with him, Paul, in vintage Pauline fashion said, "What are you doing, weeping and breaking my heart? For I am ready not only to be bound, but even to die for the name of the Lord." At that point, being unable to persuade him otherwise, they fell silent and deferred to him and the Lord (21:1-14). It is sometimes the right decision to defer rather than to argue–it is not always best to appeal to the basest instincts of man, or at least not to do so for long. God did not pick a weak man for His work; he picked a strong man, a man of courage, a man who would stand for something.

Paul returned to Jerusalem (21:17), for he wanted to be there for Pentecost (20:16), and he entered the Temple (21:26). but it didn't take long when the Jews from Asia (remember them?), upon seeing him in the Temple, "began to stir up the crowd and laid hands on him" (21:27)–they were not praying over him for healing! They rushed him and grabbed him, and "dragged him out of the Temple where they were seeking to kill him." Upon winding up in the hands of the Romans, the mob stopped beating him (so nice of them), and he was bound in chains. Then the crowd became violent again, shouting, "Away with him!" (21:30-36), just like they did with Jesus and Stephen, but Paul was 'safely' in the hands of the Romans. Fine welcome back to Jerusalem, Paul.

Now Paul, being a Roman citizen, beseeched the Roman commander to allow him to speak to the people. Permission was granted and he addressed them in Hebrew (21:37-40). He began by appealing to them, not as a Roman, but as a Jew, and what a bad person he had been earlier (just as they were). He told them that he had been raised in Jerusalem and educated under the best–Gamaliel (22:3).[30] He reminded them that he was one of them, that he was the one watching over the coats of those who stoned Stephen to death. He told them just how horrible he was, that he was 'primo' as a persecutor of Christians, that he would terrorize them to the death, throw them into prison, and would go even as far as Damascus to bring them back to Jerusalem for punishment (22:4-5; 9:1-2).

And then he told them how the Lord appeared to him, how he was saved, and what he was thenceforth instructed to do, which was

---

[30] **Gamaliel** I, also called Rabban **Gamaliel** (rabban, meaning "teacher"), (flourished 1st century AD), a tanna, one of a select group of Palestinian masters of the Jewish Oral Law, and a teacher twice mentioned in the New Testament–Britannica.com.

to go to Damascus and wait to be told what to do (22:6-10). There had been an instantaneous change in Paul. Only Jesus can do that; this author can attest to it. He told them what he was instructed to do by God through the mouth of one Ananias: first, *he, Paul, was appointed by God to know His will, to see the Righteous One, and to hear an utterance from His mouth;* and then *he would be a witness to all men to what he had seen and heard* (22:14-15).

Oh, my Lord; how wonderful! He had been led to Damascus after he was "blinded by the light" of Jesus, then God restored his sight when he met with Ananias. He told them that when he returned to Jerusalem and that when he was in the Temple praying, that he fell into a trance and saw Jesus, and the Lord spoke to him, telling him to leave Jerusalem, and that He would send him far away to the Gentiles (22:17-21).

The people had been listening to him up to that point, but now they would have no more of it. They raised their voices shouting, "Away with him from the earth, for he should not be allowed to live!" (22:22-23). Look at that statement: *he should not be allowed to live.* In other words, 'we want him dead.' Remember Jesus' accusers? *Crucify Him!* And Stephen, when the Council members gnashed their teeth, covered their ears, cried out, and rushed him!

How horrible, one should ask, is it for one group of people to single out, or label, another for the purpose of persecuting them; even to the point of death? And for what reason? In this case because of different religious beliefs. But what about next time? For racism? For no crime at all? For allegations?

A curious comment occurs in 22:24, where it talks about "examining" him by scourging, and it shows just how cruel the Romans were. But when Paul challenged the commander about the legality of scourging an "un-condemned Roman citizen" (as they were stretching him out to do so), the commander revealed the corrupt way in which he obtained his own citizenship (Paul was natural born (22:28)), then released him the next day (22:30).

But Paul's troubles were far from over. The commander, investigating further as to why he was being accused by the Jews, ordered the Council to assemble and brought him back to sit before them. An interesting point here is that the commander was Roman and the Council was the Sanhedrin, the ruling body of the Jews under the Roman yoke. Paul no sooner opened his mouth when the high priest Ananias (a different Ananias than the good one earlier), ordered him struck on the mouth. At that, Paul didn't meekly succumb but answered back that God would strike *him*, calling him a whitewashed wall in the process (Jesus called them whitewashed tombs (Matthew 23:27)).

Paul exposed the high priest's hypocrisy in trying him "according to the law" while ordering him struck "in violation of the law" (Acts 23:1-3). Paul also succeeded in turning the council against itself because of the split in their own religion into two sects, the Pharisees and Sadducees (we used to have a little joke about the Pharisees being fair, you see, because they believed in the resurrection, while the Sadducees were sad, you see, because they didn't). The Council meeting broke up, but Paul was still in custody (23:6-10).

The Lord came to him the next night and said he must be His witness at Rome, just as he had been in Jerusalem (23:11). By now, it was the year 57 or 58, Paul had completed his third missionary journey, and Nero the beast, 666, who gained the title of Caesar in 54, was firmly in power. But the Jews in Jerusalem, more than forty of them, formed a conspiracy and "bound themselves under an oath that they would neither eat nor drink until they had killed Paul" (23:12). They were fanatical in their pursuit of persecuting him.

But Paul was in the custody of the Romans, so the conspiring Jews, with the help of the chief priests, devised a plan to dupe the commander into bringing him before the Council again, so they could ambush him along the way. Hopefully, and with the grace of God, man will remain more civilized than that. Paul found out about the plot through a nephew and had him inform the commander, who arranged to have Paul escorted, along with a letter, to Felix, Governor of Judea, in Caesarea (23:16-30).[31]

So, Paul was brought to Caesarea before Felix, who was to give him a hearing after his accusers, the Jews from Jerusalem, arrived (23:35). The high priest, the same one who had ordered Paul struck on the mouth back in Jerusalem, came with some elders and a lawyer (24:1). The charges they brought were that he was "a real pest" who stirs up dissension among "all the Jews throughout the world" and that he tried to desecrate the Temple (24:5- 6). Paul made his defense, stating that he believes everything in the Law and the Prophets, and that there would be a resurrection of the righteous and the wicked, *but that the Jews from Asia* (remember them?) *should have been the ones making the accusations,* not those from Jerusalem.

He should have been able to confront his actual accusers, for those who came had no misdeeds that they could levy (24:10-21). But Felix was a corrupt official too, who was looking for money from Paul because he had allowed him some freedom of visitation. So, spitefully, he held him for two more years; and when he was replaced by Festus, he left Paul imprisoned, "wishing to do the Jews a favor" (24:24-27). Corrupt officials have no regard for human life.

Incredibly, when Festus, who had succeeded Felix, went to Jerusalem, the Jews again brought charges against Paul, and asked that he be brought there where they were setting an ambush to kill him along the way (this was the second time they concocted that sort of plot) for he was being kept in Caesarea (25:1-4). So, Paul was once again brought before the court, this time before Festus in

---

[31] Caesarea was built by Herod the Great about 25–13 BCE as the port city, Caesarea Maritima. It served as an administrative center of Judaea Province of the Roman Empire, and later the capital of the Byzantine Palaestina Prima province during the classic period–Wikipedia

Caesarea; and the Jews from Jerusalem once again brought their false charges against him; and Festus, just like Felix, in "wishing to do the Jews a favor," asked Paul if he was willing to go to Jerusalem to stand trial on those charges (again?).

But Paul, not being one to be idly pushed around, said that he *was* standing before Caesar's tribunal and, recognizing that this was nothing more than a kangaroo-court, said, "I appeal to Caesar." And Festus replied, "To Caesar you shall go" (25:6-12). Caesar was, at that time, Nero; the year was about 61, and he was already ruling for about seven years, with about seven more years before he would become so debauched that he committed suicide in 68.

So, up to this time, Paul had had to defend himself before the Council (Sanhedrin), Felix, and Festus. Now, along comes King Agrippa and Bernice, passing through Judea, "paying their respects" to Festus (25:13), and of course, while spending "many days" there, Festus "laid Paul's case before the king" (25:14), and the king, *ahem*, after much consideration, wanted to "hear from the man himself" (25:15-22). And, so he did, the next day, "amid great pomp."

Comically, these two (Festus and Agrippa) conducted a circus as they entered the auditorium "accompanied by commanders and *the prominent men of the city*," and Festus proceeded to blather-on to the king about how the Jews declared that "Paul ought not to live" but that he (Festus) could find nothing worthy of death. Furthermore, he (Paul) had appealed to Caesar, but that he (Festus) has nothing to write to Caesar *and it seems absurd sending him with no charges,* so you, king Agrippa, *please find something* (Acts 25:23-27). Absurd, indeed.

So Paul had to defend himself yet again when he should not have had to do so at all, and all because the king "just happened through." In his defense, Paul began by again identifying with his accusers as being a Jew; and that *all* Jews knew his manner of life growing up in Jerusalem, in the strictest sect of his religion (26:4-5). Then he described his former mindset as "having had to do many things hostile to the name of Jesus," and that *that was what he had done*, such as trying to force them to blaspheme, *being furiously enraged at them, and pursuing them even to foreign cities* (26:9-11; Matthew 23:34).

Then he told the king how he met Jesus, and the calling He put on his life (Acts 26:12-18). In verses 26:19-20, Paul, now standing before the king, said something interesting–that he had been declaring the heavenly vision: first to those of Damascus and *Jerusalem*, then throughout *Judea*, and even to the *Gentiles* (the fulfillment of the Great Commission).

Again! the Scriptures declare that the Great Commission has been fulfilled, but it is continually ignored. It is as two magnetic north or south poles repelling each other, one with the truth of stated Scriptural facts, facing a like-pole of 'the futurist view.' Truth and folly repel each other. To go through the arduous task of researching this subject for oneself is difficult, but that is no excuse. The church fathers were wrong on this account, and that wrong has 'served' us for two-thousand years, but that doesn't make it right.

An interesting exchange then took place between he and the king (26:24-29). As Paul got to the high point of his defense, the resurrection of Christ, the governor, Festus, blurted out that Paul was out of his mind–that "his great learning was driving him mad." The king, after Paul alluded to the fact that he knew that the king knew about the things that he (Paul) was saying, sarcastically (?) said that "Paul was going to persuade him to become a Christian."

As the king and all the officials stood and the people were dismissed, they turned and talked to one another and then the king told Festus that *he might have set Paul free* had he not appealed to Caesar (26:30-32). Those are the types of situations that people can find themselves in at any time, but in this case, there is really nothing that Paul could do about it. He had no idea he might have been set free, so he did what he felt he needed to do, which was to appeal to Caesar. And, in this case, once the Romans had him in custody, he was theirs anyway. Things happen which are out of a person's control all the time. Most are insignificant but some are not. Those that go to one's core and force decisions are when a choice for God can make all the difference in the world.

So, Paul could have been free, but he didn't know that, and so he wasn't free. He still had free will, but he didn't do something regretful. He could have shaken his fist at God and blamed Him, like many people have done and still do. He could have used these things as a pretext to deny God and to choose not to believe in God, but he chose to go into the mouth of the lion, the belly of the beast, Nero, 666.

He chose to obey God. We talked about obedience earlier, at the very end of Part I, mentioning the fact that man actually bristles at the thought of having to obey (see Part I Summary). Jesus had told Paul that he would be a witness of Him in Rome just as he had been in Jerusalem (23:11). Undoubtedly, Paul would rather not have been in custody in doing so. It also would have been all-too-easy for Paul to give up and get it over with, but then God would have chosen someone else. God's will, will be done. Paul chose to do it His way, to go through the Roman Empire. The Gospel went out to the entire world because they *were* the world. The Gospel went out His way, because it is His story. History.

Meanwhile, Paul was bound for Rome, literally (27:1), in what was a harrowing journey, and which took considerably more than three months (28:11).[32] Some call this his fourth missionary journey but Paul the prisoner was bound (literally) for Rome.

After finally arriving in Rome, and still under guard by a Roman soldier (28:16), he called together the leading men of the Jews (28:17). What transpired is jaw-dropping. Keeping in mind that he was 'on hold' waiting to meet the dreaded Nero, and not for a

---

[32] The time period used in this book for the entire trip to Rome from Caesarea was from 60-63AD.

state-dinner at that—his first appeal was again to the Jews. At every step along the way he has pleaded with them, but they would not listen. Would they play the harlot to the bitter end?

He began his appeal to them by stating that he had done nothing wrong to their people, the Jews, which were also his people. Yet, he was delivered into the hands of the Romans *by* the Jews—which was why he was making his plea *to* them (28:17). Then, he told them the Romans wanted to release him but the Jews objected, *forcing* him to appeal to Caesar. So, here he was, one last time, pleading with them, *for the sake of Israel*. Regardless of what was going to happen to him when he went before Nero, he wanted to make it right by his own people, God's people. That is why he was speaking to them (28:18-20).

Their answer was stunning, "We have neither received letters from Judea concerning you, nor have any of the brethren come here and reported or spoken anything bad about you" (28:21). Wait! Nothing? Nada – zilch – zero? "I know notteeng?" Total abandonment! So, looking objectively at this: Paul was no "angel;" nor was he just another local leader. And, even though he was more than just local—so-what? Whoa! Paul was not just *anybody*; he was shaking up the entire Jewish religion and the entire world. But they acted as though they didn't know anything about him, as though he was no big-deal. How calloused they were, and that man can be.

What a horrible charade this had been from the beginning. The religious leaders *were* playing the harlot to the bitter end. Satan has succeeded from the beginning in perverting the date of the apocalypse and therefore the meaning of prophecy and eschatology, but God's will, will not be thwarted. Jesus said, "Get thee behind me, Satan!" (Luke 4:8 KJV). We should not think too highly of ourselves for it is not about us; and remember—God always keeps a remnant.

The day that was *set* for Paul was in all probability his date to see Nero. And "they" who came to him, and all that that entailed

(Acts 28:23-25) were the Jews – again! Paul kept trying to convince his people of the Christ; but in the end, he realized that this people was a stiff-necked and obstinate people, and so he quoted Isaiah 6:9-10 to them (Acts 28:26-27; see also 2 Chronicles 7:14).

Paul was allowed to preach the Kingdom of God unhindered, and he stayed there for two more years doing so (Acts 28:30-31). The Book of Acts, at this point ends–but our biblically-based historical narrative is not over. It is a wonderful but interesting end to the book because Paul had more to say in 2 Timothy 4:16-17. There, he said, "At my first defense no one supported me, but all deserted me... and I was rescued out of the lion's mouth." It is generally accepted that Paul's letters to Timothy and to Titus were written after Acts was written, so the just referenced verses are considered to mean that he stood before Nero at least twice, escaping with his life on the first and being able to write about it, but finally paying the ultimate price and going home to the Lord on the second. [33]

What has been shown is a concerted effort, first by the Jews, then joined by the Romans and probably by anybody else who saw fit, to systematically snuff out Christianity from the very beginning. One can see the spark and the ensuing fanning of the flames in the Gospels from the religious leaders–the Jews–the very descendants of the fathers described in the Old Testament who we have shown to be the harlot–Babylon the Great–the Mother of Harlots of Revelation.

We have seen the persecution continue and intensify from its simmer early in the Gospels, rise to the killing of Jesus, then the killing of Stephen–the beginning of the persecution–and then the all-out attempt to exterminate the Christians from that point on. We have seen, in the writings of Eusebius, who–used initially by

---

[33] According to *The People's Chronology,* Paul was beheaded with a sword near Rome, possibly on this day – June 29, 67. This date is open to dispute. Paul's death has been variously placed between 62 and 67. We shall probably never know for sure–Christianity.com

this author as an example of how meager the 'understanding of the apocalypse' was to the earliest and best of our church fathers—*did not hesitate to inform his readers of the ferocity and longevity of the persecution.*

The fact is, the great persecution didn't end until the Edict of Milan, which was a proclamation and political agreement concluded in Milan between the Roman emperors Constantine I and Licinius (from the western and eastern kingdoms, respectively) in February, 313AD. That proclamation permanently established religious toleration for Christianity within the Roman Empire. Here is another fact—the great persecution may have lasted well past 70AD, but for the purposes of this book, the year 70 was the end of the seventy-year period which is not only unprecedented in its scope and character—it is unduplicable! Messiah came; Jesus changed the world; His resurrection is what allows for man to be saved; the old has gone; the new has come.

On a lighter note, we know that the Bible has its own numerology. In our case, we can say that the persecution started with the killing of Stephen, arguably, around 33AD, and that it ended with the Edict of Milan in 313AD, which means it lasted 280 years. That number equals four times seventy; four seventies; four sevens, times ten. Those numbers are significant to God, which discussion is beyond the scope of this book. However, mention has been made previously about God's blessings for obedience and curses for disobedience, which are listed in Leviticus 26 and Deuteronomy 28.

If we look at Leviticus 26:18,21,24, and 28, we see that God said—four times—that if the people did… (then He tells us what that is), He would punish them, increase the plague on them, or strike them—seven times. Again, He said—four times—that He would punish them seven times. That is four sets of seven, or, four sevens. That isn't the only place that we see those numbers. In our own study of Revelation, we see it again: there are the letters to the seven churches; there are the seven seals; seven trumpets; and seven bowls–four sevens. God's hand is everywhere.

The punishments of the law were unleashed on God's people in Daniel's time, and again in 70AD. Each one brought desolation, and each one had an abomination that causes desolation, by Babylon and Rome, respectively. The difference between the two is that, although the Temple had to be rebuilt after the first desolation, it did not have to be so after the second. The old had become obsolete and was growing old, and it was ready to disappear.

Summarizing, the Harlot of Revelation is Jerusalem; the beast she is riding on is Rome; the number of the beast, 666, represents Nero. Antichrist is not a person; Antichrist is not the abomination of desolation, nor is it the beast; the imaginary Antichrist cannot sit at the Temple for there is no Temple. The Great Commission has been fulfilled.

FROM NERO TO CONSTANTINE

(FROM THE WRITINGS OF EUSEBIUS)

In Part IV, in the very beginning of the first of his writings that we listed from Eusebius, at Book 3 Chapter 18 of his works *Ecclesiastical Histories*, he made mention of the persecution. It had been ongoing since Stephen was killed (Acts 8:1). The apostle John, at Patmos when he received the vision of the apocalypse, also mentioned the tribulation (Revelation 1:9). But since Eusebius didn't begin to publish his works until 312 and afterwards (see Timeline), and the fact that the persecution was nearing its end at 313, he had a unique perspective and a lot to say about it. He was actually said to be a court advisor to Emperor Constantine.[34]

The Book of Acts covers matters up until the time of Nero, who eventually executed the Apostles Peter and Paul. Prior to that time, persecution came mostly from the Jews, but the Romans were contributing, as we noted. The Romans probably only tolerated the Christians, as they did the Jews, giving authority to the religious leaders to tend to their own internal affairs–up to a point.

But when the Great Fire broke out in Rome in the summer of 64, burning a large part of the city, and the people started to put the blame on Nero, the Christians, hated by all because "they turned from their idolatrous ways and worshipped only one God," were the perfect scapegoats. Tensions were also increasing between the

---

[34] Gentry; *Before Jerusalem Fell*; p. 101

Jews and Romans until all-out war finally broke out in 66. So, now everybody was killing everybody, and the Christians were getting it from both sides.

As the persecution raged on, Eusebius records the historical import of what occurred in his writings.

BOOK 2 – CHAPTER 25 – The Persecution under Nero (54-68) in which Paul and Peter were honored at Rome with Martyrdom in Behalf of Religion

> **When the government of Nero was now firmly established, he began to plunge into unholy pursuits, and armed himself even against the religion of the God of the universe. To describe the greatness of his depravity does not lie within the plan of the present work. As there are many indeed that have recorded his history in most accurate narratives, every one may at his pleasure learn from them the coarseness of the man's extraordinary madness**, under the influence of which, after he had accomplished the destruction of so many myriads without any reason, he ran into such blood-guiltiness that he did not spare even his nearest relatives and dearest friends, but destroyed his mother and his brothers and his wife, with very many others of his own family as he would private and public enemies, with various kinds of deaths. But with all these things this particular in the catalogue of his crimes was still wanting, that **he was the first of the emperors who showed himself an enemy of the divine religion. The Roman Tertullian is likewise a witness of this. He writes as follows: "Examine

> **your records. There you will find that Nero was the first that persecuted this doctrine, particularly then when after subduing all the east, he exercised his cruelty against all at Rome.** We glory in having such a man the leader in our punishment. For whoever knows him can understand that nothing was condemned by Nero unless it was something of great excellence." **Thus, publicly announcing himself as the first among God's chief enemies, he was led on to the slaughter of the apostles. It is, therefore, recorded that Paul was beheaded in Rome itself, and that Peter, likewise, was crucified under Nero. This account of Peter and Paul is substantiated by the fact that their names are preserved in the cemeteries of that place even to the present day.**

Here, Eusebius, the writer extraordinaire, chooses not to offer detail as to just how twisted Nero was—other than to say that he destroyed myriads, including his own mother, brothers, and his wife, and many others of his own family—and indicating that many others had recorded such, He felt it "wanting" that: *he was the first of the emperors who showed himself an enemy of the divine religion*—an extraordinary statement indeed.

He wasn't the last to do so, but he was the first and the worst. Note that Eusebius mentions Tertullian,[35] who lived before him and after Nero, who wrote as follows: "Examine your records. There you will find that Nero was the first that persecuted this doctrine..."

Here is food for thought: we have previously pointed out the five occasions where Irenaeus has stated that the Antichrist would

---

[35] Tertullian (160-220) was a prolific early Christian author, from Carthage in the Roman province of Africa. Of Berber origin, he was the first Christian author to produce an extensive corpus of Latin Christian literature–Wikipedia

sit in or at the Temple. He has, in conjunction with the first four of those statements, said that Antichrist would show himself to be God, or to be Christ, referencing 2 Thessalonians 2:1-12 in the process. Now, here, we have both Eusebius and Tertullian talking about Nero as being the first to show himself to be an enemy of the divine religion, the first among God's chief enemies, and the first that persecuted this doctrine.

So, look again at paragraph 2 of Chapter 30, Book 5 of Irenaeus' *Against Heresies* (Part IV), where he writes about the division of the kingdom into ten, *that when these kings are reigning, and beginning to set their affairs in order, and advance their kingdom, and that he who shall come claiming the kingdom for himself…having a name containing the aforesaid number, is truly the abomination of desolation…,* i.e. Antichrist.

See also the fourth beast of Daniel chapter 7, where it had ten horns, which were ten kings; and it uttered great boasts, speaking out against the Most High; it was waging war with and wearing out the saints of the Highest One, trampling down the remainder; and making alterations of the law.

Now, compare that to those which Eusebius above says of what Tertullian writes concerning Nero: *…then when after subduing all the east, he* (Nero) *exercised his cruelty against all at Rome.* And then Eusebius, following Tertullian, about Nero: *Thus, publicly announcing himself as the first among God's chief enemies, he was led on to the slaughter of the apostles.*

It isn't a perfect analogy, there never is one, but Irenaeus appears to have been on to something, except for the fact that he didn't look backward to the events which had unfolded in the time leading up to and during Nero's reign in trying to decipher the riddle of the kings; instead he was erroneously looking forward to things supposedly still to come.

And Eusebius, in writing so extensively on that which Irenaeus wrote and with still more hindsight, didn't figure it out either (see our discussion about the beasts from the sea and land, and about the red dragon at paragraph 1, Book 5, Chapter 30 – Irenaeus; *Heresies* -in Part IV) ... food for thought.

BOOK 3 – CHAPTER 5 – The Last Siege of the Jews after Christ

> **After Nero had held the power thirteen years, and Galba and Otho had ruled a year and six months, Vespasian, who had become distinguished in the campaigns against the Jews, was proclaimed sovereign in Judea and received the title of Emperor from the armies there.** Setting out immediately, therefore, for Rome, **he entrusted the conduct of the war against the Jews to his son Titus**.
>
> **For the Jews after the ascension of our Saviour, in addition to their crime against him, had been devising as many plots as they could against his apostles. First Stephen was stoned to death** by them, and after him James, the son of Zebedee and the brother of John, was beheaded, and finally James, the first that had obtained the episcopal seat in Jerusalem after the ascension of our Saviour, died in the manner already described. **But the rest of the apostles, who had been incessantly plotted against with a view to their destruction, and had been driven out of the land of Judea, went unto all nations to preach the Gospel, relying upon the power of Christ**, who had said to them, "Go ye and make disciples of all the nations in My name."

But the people of the church in Jerusalem had been commanded by a revelation, vouchsafed to approved men there before the war, to leave the city and to dwell in a certain town of Perea called Pella...

Eusebius begins this chapter at the time of Vespasian, the cruel general and Emperor, who came to power after fourteen years of the wicked Nero, followed by a chaotic period of three more emperors in the ensuing year-and-a-half before Vespasian called The Year of the Four Emperors.[36] He was responsible for much of the carnage and destruction in Judea before he became emperor, but Titus his son was the one who finally finished the job and destroyed Jerusalem and the Temple.

That was the abomination of desolation; or, if it need be a person, it was Titus himself, the desolator. And isn't it curious that the name Titus is similar to Titan, the name Irenaeus became enamored with in attempting to determine the name of the number of the beast (Part IV)?

Of note, Eusebius characterizes exactly what the persecution was like and how the Christians were suffering. He said that the Jews, in addition to their crime against Jesus, which was crucifying Him, *had been devising as many plots as they could against His apostles,* and he begins with Stephen, whose death the Scriptures say began the great persecution (Acts 8:1). Then he named two apostles, James the brother of John (the Sons of Thunder), and James the lesser. It is an unfathomable thought for a group of people (the Jews) "to devise as many plots as they can" against another group of people (the Christians), to their destruction.

Eusebius continues, "But the rest of the apostles, who had been incessantly plotted against with a view to their destruction, and had been driven out of the land of Judea, went unto all nations to

---

[36] see footnote, p 131.

preach the Gospel...," thus acknowledging *himself* that the Great Commission was fulfilled–only he doesn't use those exact words.

The Jews continued to incessantly plot against the apostles in an attempt to exterminate them. They were relentless and it must have been truly horrible. But the Christians of Jerusalem who had been *commanded by a revelation* (see Matthew 24:15-21), left the city to dwell in the town of Perea called Pella, thus escaping the final conflagration of the destruction of 70.

Eusebius has delivered a power-packed and truly amazing passage! Imagine what life would be like if we were incessantly plotted against with a view to our destruction. The Christians, having been first driven out of Jerusalem, then Judea, were able to complete the command of Jesus to be His witnesses, first in Jerusalem, then Judea and Samaria, and now, to the uttermost parts of the world.

BOOK 3 – CHAPTER 20 – The Relatives of our Saviour

...Tertullian also has mentioned Domitian in the following words: "Domitian (81-96) also, who possessed a share of Nero's cruelty, attempted once to do the same thing that the latter did. But because he had, I suppose, some intelligence, he very soon ceased, and even recalled those whom he had banished." But after Domitian had reigned fifteen years, and Nerva had succeeded to the empire, the **Roman Senate**, according to the writers that record the history of those days, voted that Domitian's honors should be canceled, and that those who had been unjustly banished should return to their homes and have their property restored to them. **It was at this time that the apostle John returned from his banishment in the island and**

took up his abode at Ephesus, according to an ancient Christian tradition.

The fact is that most futurists claim that Domitian was the beast. They are patently wrong. Here, from the mouth of Tertullian, a contemporary of Irenaeus and himself a prolific writer and church historian, we have these words: *Domitian also, who possessed a* **share** *of Nero's cruelty… even recalled those he had banished*. So, even the *idea* that Domitian could possibly be the beast is absurd. He only had *a share* of Nero's cruelty, and he even softened and *showed some intelligence,* recalling those he had banished.

But, according to Eusebius, *John was not one of them*. The Roman Senate voted to cancel Domitian's "honors," (ostensibly after Domitian's rule) setting him free, and allowing him to return from his banishment. And even if Domitian was the one who exiled him, John could have been in Patmos at any time for any reason, including his banishment. He may even have been in Ephesus during the time of Domitian, but there is no definitive evidence that he saw the Revelation at that time and there is nothing to the contrary in the Scriptures or elsewhere to indicate that he did, aside from those who erroneously interpret Irenaeus that way. Just read what the Scriptures say: he was there *because of the word of God and the testimony of Jesus* (Revelation 1:9)!

Here is another issue: if, as we just stated, according to Eusebius, the Roman Senate set John free in the reign of Nerva, who succeeded Domitian – then he couldn't have possibly been seen in Ephesus during the reign of Domitian! The point being made here is that exact details are sketchy at best. The fact that the futurist view rests on the notion that John was seen during the reign of Domitian and that therefore he saw the Revelation during that time is preposterous!

BOOK 3 – CHAPTER 33 – Trajan (98-117) Forbids the Christians to be Sought After

So great a persecution was at that time opened against us in many places that Plinius Secundus, one of the most noted of governors, **being disturbed by the great number of martyrs, communicated with the emperor concerning the multitude of those that were put to death for their faith.** At the same time, he informed him in his communication that **he had not heard of their doing anything profane or contrary to the laws, except that they arose at dawn and sang hymns to Christ as a God; but that they renounced adultery and murder and like criminal offenses, and did all things in accordance with the laws.** In reply to this Trajan made the following decree: **that the race of Christians should not be sought after, but when found should be punished.** On account of this the persecution which had threatened to be a most terrible one was to a certain degree checked, but **there were still left plenty of pretexts for those who wished to do us harm. Sometimes the people, sometimes the rulers in various places, would lay plots against us, so that, although no great persecutions took place, local persecutions were nevertheless going on in particular provinces, and many of the faithful endured martyrdom in various forms.** We have taken our account from the Latin Apology of Tertullian which we mentioned above. The translation runs as follows: "And indeed we have found that search for us has been forbidden. **For when Plinius Secundus, the governor of a**

province, had condemned certain Christians and deprived them of their dignity, he was confounded by the multitude, and was uncertain what further course to pursue. He therefore communicated with Trajan the emperor, informing him that, aside from their unwillingness to sacrifice, he had found no impiety in them. And he reported this also, that the Christians arose early in the morning and sang hymns unto Christ as a God, and for the purpose of preserving their discipline forbade murder, adultery, avarice, robbery, and the like. **In reply to this Trajan wrote that the race of Christians should not be sought after, but when found should be punished.**" Such were the events which took place at that time.

It should be noted that from the time of Nerva, who succeeded the cruel Domitian, it was known as the time of the "Five Good Roman Emperors." Really! they were: Nerva (96-98), Trajan (98-117), Hadrian (117-138), Antoninus Pius (138-161), and Marcus Aurelius (161-180).

So, as Eusebius attests, Tertullian is again quoted: *When Plinius Secundus, the governor of a province, had condemned certain Christians and deprived them of their dignity, he was confounded by the multitude, and was uncertain what further course to pursue.* As Eusebius himself notes: ***So great a persecution was at that time opened against us in many places*** *that Plinius Secundus, one of the most noted of governors, being disturbed by the great number of martyrs, communicated with the emperor concerning the multitude of those that were put to death for their faith.*

It is inconceivable that anyone can deny that the great persecution was indeed the great tribulation. So, here was the governor of a province, carrying out his duties and routinely condemning Christians to death and other indignities, suddenly feeling "disturbed" and confounded by the "great number of martyrs" to where he felt compelled to communicate to Emperor Trajan – one of the 'good' emperors.

Trajan ruled shortly after Domitian, and the persecution had continued. The many martyrs did nothing wrong; instead they sang hymns to Christ as God and renounced adultery and murder and the like. Trajan, 'in the kindness of his heart,' decreed that the "race" of Christians should not be sought after, but when found should be punished. Awful!

That is still plenty horrific, "*…there were still left plenty of **pretexts** for those who wished to do us harm.*" Pretext, according to the Cambridge English Dictionary, is: *a **pretended** reason for doing something that is used to hide the real reason.* In other words, it is making false accusations, it is bearing false witness, or it could be using any pretext to 'stumble upon' Christians to do them harm.

'*Sometimes the people, sometimes the rulers in various places, would lay plots against us, so that, although no great persecutions took place, local persecutions were nevertheless going on in particular provinces, and many of the faithful endured martyrdom in various forms.*'

It didn't have to be only the government whom the Christians had to watch out for, for it was sometimes the rulers and sometimes the people. It is difficult to think about going about daily life having to worry about being accosted anywhere and at any time simply because of one's religious faith. The rooting out of Christians in order to kill them or throw them in prison for no reason at all but that they were Christians was ingrained in nearly everyone and was systematically being carried out.

In this case. it was a concerted effort which had been going on all along to stomp them out. But the Jews and Romans had already lost that battle–Christianity was spreading throughout the world; and what had started as persecution predominantly from only the Jews, then the Roman government since Nero's *becoming first among God's chef enemies*, became pretext for anybody and everybody to persecute them.

BOOK 4 – CHAPTER 9 – The Epistle of Adrian (Hadrian) 117-138, Decreeing That we Should Not be Punished Without a Trial

"To Minucius Fundanus. I have received an epistle, written to me by Serennius Granianus, a most illustrious man, whom you have succeeded. It does not seem right to me that the matter should be passed by without examination, lest the men be harassed and opportunity be given to the informers for practicing villainy. If, therefore, the inhabitants of the province can clearly sustain this **petition against the Christians so as to give answer in a court of law**, let them pursue this course alone, but let them not have resort to **men's petitions and outcries. For it is far more proper if any one wishes to make an accusation, that you should examine into it. If anyone, therefore, accuses them and shows that they are doing anything contrary to the laws, do you pass judgment according to the heinousness of the crime? But, by Hercules! if anyone bring an accusation through mere calumny, decide in regard to his criminality, and see to it that you inflict punishment.**" Such are the contents of Adrian's rescript.

Wonderful, right? Think about it for a minute–Christians should no longer be persecuted by "men's petitions and outcries," without some sort of due process from a court of law? That is our standard – our American Bill of Rights, but for them it was the Wild West. An assumption can be made that prior to this decree, you needed *no* reason the drag somebody away and beat them to a pulp or kill them. But, ahem, this was still the time of the 'Five Good Emperors.'

BOOK 6 – CHAPTER 1 – The Persecution Under Severus (193-211)

> **WHEN Severus began to persecute the churches**, glorious testimonies were given everywhere by the **athletes of religion**. This was especially the case in Alexandria, to which city, as to a most prominent theater, **athletes of God** were brought from Egypt and all Thebais according to their merit, **and won crowns from God through their great patience under many tortures and every mode of death.** Among these was Leonides, who was called the father of Origen, and who was beheaded while his son was still young. How remarkable the predilection of this son was for the Divine Word, in consequence of his father's instruction, it will not be amiss to state briefly, as his fame has been very greatly celebrated by many.

We are now a decade or more removed from the time of the 'Good Emperors' and whatever reprieve the Christians might have enjoyed was well past. It is so easy to read over this above passage and not grasp exactly what was happening. Think about the concept of "the many tortures and every mode of death" that "the athletes of God" and "the athletes of religion" suffered for a moment. It is incomprehensible just how vicious the persecution must have been. How could they live their lives when they were subject to such treatment? And yet, all this is ignored as futurists wait for the Great Tribulation.

BOOK 6 – CHAPTER 28 – The Persecution Under Maximinus (235-238)

THE Roman emperor, **Alexander**, having finished his reign in thirteen years, was succeeded by **Maximinus** Caesar. **On account of his hatred toward the household of Alexander, which contained many believers, he began a persecution, commanding that only the rulers of the churches should be put to death, as responsible for the Gospel teaching.** Thereupon **Origen** composed his work On Martyrdom, and dedicated it to Ambrose and Protoctetus, a presbyter of the parish of Caesarea, because **in the persecution there had come upon them both unusual hardships**, in which it is reported that they were eminent in confession during the reign of Maximinus, which lasted but three years. **Origen has noted this as the time of the persecution in the twenty-second book of his Commentaries on John, and in several epistles.**

There may have been a respite under Alexander, 'whose household contained many believers,' but it ended as he was succeeded by Maximinus, who decided to go after the 'rulers of the churches and preachers of Christianity.' Origen, (184-253)[37] another Christian scholar and historian, and one who, as a boy, witnessed the beheading of his father, also notes the persecution in his book, *On Martyrdom*.

Where are the modern scholars who have read Eusebius, Tertullian, Origen, and others and have read their accounts of the

---

[37] Origen of Alexandria, also known as Origen Adamantius, was an early Christian scholar, ascetic, and theologian who was born and spent the first half of his career in Alexandria–Wikipedia

persecution? Can they not deduce for themselves that the great persecution is the Great Tribulation? There are many writings available on the persecution. Unfortunately, our senses are dulled to the subject, and all that information collects dust as we ignore it.

Note the pettiness of Maximinus because of his hatred toward Alexander, and that that spitefulness and vindictiveness became a pretext for the persecution under him.

BOOK 6 – CHAPTER 39 – The Persecution Under Decius (249-251), and the Sufferings of Origen

> After a reign of seven years **Philip** was succeeded by **Decius. On account of his hatred of Philip, he commenced a persecution of the churches**, in which Fabianus suffered martyrdom at Rome, and Cornelius succeeded him in the episcopate. In Palestine, **Alexander, bishop of the church of Jerusalem, was brought again on Christ's account before the governor's judgment seat in Caesarea, and having acquitted himself nobly in a second confession was cast into prison, crowned with the hoary locks of venerable age. And after his honorable and illustrious confession at the tribunal of the governor, he fell asleep in prison**, and Mazabanes became his successor in the bishopric of Jerusalem. Babylas in Antioch, having like Alexander passed away in prison after his confession, was succeeded by Fabius in the episcopate of that church.

> **But how many and how great things came upon Origen in the persecution, and what was their**

> final result, as the demon of evil marshaled all his forces, and fought against the man with his utmost craft and power, assaulting him beyond all others against whom he contended at that time, and what and how many things he endured for the word of Christ, bonds and bodily tortures and torments under the iron collar and in the dungeon; and how for many days with his feet stretched four spaces in the stocks he bore patiently the threats of fire and whatever other things were inflicted by his enemies; and how his sufferings terminated, as his judge strove eagerly with all his might not to end his life; and what words he left after these things, full of comfort to those needing aid, a great many of his epistles show with truth and accuracy.

This is just plain horrible! For those who are still awaiting the Great Tribulation, please re-evaluate to see whether or not you have missed it. It is amazing how many times the Scriptures say something and the 'experts' say, "No, no. That's not it," then they concoct elaborate arguments as to why that's so, ignoring the simplest solution. They continue to deny, and they continue to build their ziggurat.

Note that Eusebius refers to "the demon of evil," and he again notes that 'spitefulness' was a pretext for the persecution under Decius, who hated Philip his predecessor. And he mentions the "judge" of Origen, who "strove eagerly with all his might not to end his life." In other words, he tried to keep him alive so that he could continue to torture him. People will plumb the depths of evil to do the most heinous things, sometimes because of petty grievances.

BOOK 6 – CHAPTER 41 – The Martyrs in Alexandria

THE same writer, in an epistle to Fabius, bishop of Antioch, relates as follows the sufferings of the martyrs in Alexandria under Decius: **"The persecution among us did not begin with the royal decree, but preceded it an entire year. The prophet and author of evils** to this city, whoever he was, previously moved and aroused against us the masses of the heathen, rekindling among them the superstition of their country…"

…But a sedition and civil war came upon the wretched people and turned their cruelty toward us against one another. So, we breathed for a little while as they ceased from their rage against us. But presently the change from that milder reign was announced to us, and great fear of what was threatened seized us. For the decree arrived, almost like unto that most terrible time foretold by our Lord, which if it were possible would offend even the elect.

Imagine that! A respite, as sedition and civil war set in, so 'they turned their cruelty toward the Christians against one another and ceased from their rage against them.' It is as though everyone now had cause to have someone to fight with and to kill, whether each other or the Christians–but the Christians could actually "breathe a little" as the others turned on one another. Here, also, Eusebius refers to "the prophet and author of evils." These monikers can easily be overlooked, but this is not the first time a nickname was given an emperor for his evil deeds. This is another indication of the seriousness of the persecution.

Book 7 – CHAPTER 10 – Valerian and the Persecution Under Him (253-260)

GALLUS and the other rulers, having held the government less than two years, were overthrown, and Valerian, with his son Gallienus, received the empire. The circumstances which Dionysius relates of him we may learn from his epistle to Hermammon, in which he gives the following account:

"And in like manner it is revealed to John; 'For there was given to him,' he says, 'a mouth speaking great things and blasphemy; and there was given unto him authority and forty and two months.' It is wonderful that both of these things occurred under Valerian; and it is the more remarkable in this case when we consider his previous conduct, **for he had been mild and friendly toward the men of God, for none of the emperors before him had treated them so kindly and favorably."**

If you are still reading this, you know that the beast was Rome, personified by Nero, whose name adds up to 666; but here we have Dionysius mischaracterizing Emperor Valerian as the dragon of Revelation 13:5. It is understandable from a then personal standpoint in that there is only so much misery a person can endure before he dies, so context for an individual under those circumstances is lost. The point should be made, however, that the persecution must have been horrendous under Valerian for Dionysius to make that characterization. Nevertheless, this is simply another indication of the great persecution and people, in this case Dionysius, misinterpreting Revelation.

BOOK 7 – CHAPTER 13 – The Peace Under Gallienus (260-268)

SHORTLY after this Valerian was reduced to slavery by the barbarians, and his son having become sole ruler, conducted the government more prudently. He immediately restrained the persecution against us by public proclamations, and directed the bishops to perform in freedom their customary duties, in a rescript which ran as follows:

"The Emperor Caesar, Publius, Licinius Gallienus, Pius, Felix, Augustus, to Dionysius, Pinnas, Demetrius, and the other bishops. I have ordered the bounty of my gift to be **declared through all the world**, that they may depart from the places of religious worship. And, for this purpose you may use this copy of my rescript that no one may molest you. And this which you are now enabled lawfully to do, has already for a long time been conceded by me. Therefore Aurelius Cyrenius, who is the **chief administrator of affairs**, will observe this ordinance which I have given, and not even those who were said openly to be Christians received them with such manifest hospitality and friendliness as he did at the beginning of his reign. **For his entire house was filled with pious persons and was a church of God.**"

"**But the teacher and ruler of the synagogue of the Magi from Egypt persuaded him to change his course, urging him to slay and persecute pure and holy men because they opposed and hindered the corrupt and abominable incantations.** For there are and there were men who, being present and being seen, though they only breathed and spoke, were able to scatter the counsels of the sinful demons. **And he induced him to practice initiations and abominable sorceries and to offer unacceptable sacrifices; to slay innumerable children and to sacrifice the offspring of unhappy fathers; to divide the bowels of new-born babes and to mutilate and cut to pieces the creatures of God, as if by such practices they could attain happiness."**

Note, first, that the emperor Valerian, however cruel he was, was himself *reduced to slavery* upon his overthrow. This is a condition endemic to mankind, for he constantly enslaves his fellow man, *and no one group is above enslaving another*.

Another item of interest is Emperor Gallienus' 'rescript,' which *"ordered the bounty of my gift to be declared through all the world."* This is a reminder to those whom we have made the case against who believe Jesus' disciples words were about the end of the physical world (Matthew 24:3 KJV; see Part II). Gallienus ruled the Roman Empire approximately 230 years *after* the disciples asked that question, and the empire was still considered *the world*.

This is also remarkable in that here, there was a ruler who ruled to *not* persecute, and the house of whose chief administrator of affairs *was filled with pious persons and was a church of God,* but was nevertheless turned "because they (Christians) opposed and hindered the corrupt and abominable incantations." Those corrupt and abominable incantations were practiced by the masses; and those abominable sorceries and unacceptable sacrifices were no different than those we saw that were carried out in Part I with the detestable Molech and other idols.

They were as such: they would slay their own children and sacrifice the offspring of unhappy fathers–their own offspring. They would divide the bowels of the newborn, mutilating them, cutting them to pieces. And from all of this, they would try to attain happiness!

How horrid! and how barbaric those practices are–practices of people without Christ. That is where we have come from–and that is what we can become, without Christ. Blessings for obedience and curses for disobedience are what we can count on.

Only Jesus could enlighten them, as attested to by the Christians, who would foreswear murder and adultery and sing hymns to Christ as God and live within the law, but because they opposed the corrupt and abominable incantations, they were sought out to be slaughtered!

BOOK 8 – CHAPTER 2 – The Destruction of the Churches

...It was in the nineteenth year of the reign of Diocletian (284-305), in the month Dystrus, called March by the Romans, when the feast of the Saviour's passion was near at hand, that **royal edicts were published everywhere, commanding that the churches be leveled to the ground and the Scriptures be destroyed by fire, and ordering that those who held places of honor be degraded, and that the household servants, if they persisted in the profession of Christianity, be deprived of freedom.**

Such was the first edict against us. **But not long after, other decrees were issued, commanding that all the rulers of the churches in every place be first thrown into prison, and afterwards by every artifice be compelled to sacrifices.**

It is unimaginable, and yet it happens today in other parts of the world and we shrug our shoulders and pretty much ignore it, just as they ignored it then and its significance. The leveling of churches and the burning of the Scriptures was carried out throughout the Empire. The difference today is that it happens *only* in *certain countries*–but then it was world-wide, as the Roman Empire *was* the world. It must be noted, sadly, that although we in the Western World do not see Bible burning, we do see Bible banning, and government directed, at that.

Nothing could ever compare to what was happening to the Christians at that time (we hope and pray). The optimum time to stop the spread of anything is at the onset – Christians did not exist before Jesus Christ, two-thousand years ago. But that was what was happening to Christianity–they were being subjected to eradication; and yet Christianity swept the world.

Being a Christian is a matter of the heart, and it could only happen because Jesus Christ was resurrected. Without the resurrection we have nothing; we would be practicing incantations and abominable sorceries; we would be as barbarians; we would be offering unacceptable sacrifices to God. We have seen instances where God refused sacrifices; where He turned His face from His own people – and it was always because His people would worship other gods and do those detestable things.

BOOK 8 – CHAPTER 13 – The Bishops of the Church That Evinced by Their Blood the Genuineness of the Religion Which They Preached

> **…the Emperor Constantius (305-306), who through his entire life was most kindly and favorably disposed toward his subjects, and most friendly to the Divine Word, ended his life in the common course**

of nature, and left his own son, Constantine, as emperor and Augustus in his stead.

This was the beginning of the end of the persecution.

BOOK 9 – CHAPTER 9 – The Victory of the God-Beloved Emperors

...Constantine (306-337), whom we have already mentioned as an emperor, born of an emperor, a pious son of a most pious and prudent father... **These and the like praises Constantine, by his very deeds, sang to God, the universal Ruler, and Author of his victory, as he entered Rome in triumph.** Immediately all the members of the Senate and the other most celebrated men, with the whole Roman people, together with children and women, received him as their deliverer, their Saviour, and their benefactor, with shining eyes and with their whole souls, with shouts of gladness and unbounded joy... in the most public place in Rome, he commanded that the following inscription should be engraved upon it in the Roman tongue: "By this salutary sign, the true proof of bravery, I have saved and freed your city from the yoke of the tyrant and moreover, having set at liberty both the senate and the people of Rome, I have restored them to their ancient distinction and splendor." And after this both Constantine himself and with him the Emperor Licinius, who had not yet been seized by that madness into which he later fell, praising God as the author of all their blessings, with one will and

> mind **drew up a full and most complete decree in behalf of the Christians**...

That full and most complete decree in behalf of the Christians was the Edict of Milan of 313AD. The great persecution was over! The Great Tribulation was over!

BOOK 9 – CHAPTER 11 – The Final Destruction of the Enemies of Religion

> The impious ones having been thus removed, the government was preserved firm and undisputed for **Constantine and Licinius**, to whom it fittingly belonged. They, **having first of all cleansed the world of hostility to the Divine Being, conscious of the benefits which he had conferred upon them, showed their love of virtue and of God, and their piety and gratitude to the Deity, by their ordinance in behalf of the Christians**.

Hallelujah amen! Finally! After two-hundred eighty years the great persecution was over! The time of distress such as never occurred since there was a nation until that time, as prophesied by Daniel (Daniel 12:1); the great tribulation, such as has not occurred since the beginning of the world until now, nor ever will, as prophesied by Jesus (Matthew 24:21); the great persecution which began on that day against the church at Jerusalem at the feet of Saul (Paul) (Acts 8:1)–was over! Beginning with the killing of Stephen, hitting a crescendo under Nero, and exploding at the destruction and desolation of 70–the Gospel went out to the world! Hallelujah! For the Lord our God the Almighty reigns! Amen!

APPENDICES

TIMELINE OF EVENTS FROM THE BIRTH OF CHRIST TO THE END OF THE PERSECUTION AND ROMAN EMPIRE

Data in the following charts are not exact; they are for general purposes only; data collected from various sources.

Date	0	6	27	33 (?)	34	37
Event	Jesus Born	John Born	Roman Empire Declared	Jesus Crucified	Stephen Killed Persecution Begins	Josephus Born
Emperor			Augustus <14			Tiberius (14-37)

Date	65	69	70	100	140	155
Event	Paul Executed Peter Executed by Nero	Polycarp Born Papias Born	Desolation Josephus Dies	John Dies	Irenaeus Born	Polycarp Dies
Emperor	Caligula (37-41) Claudius (41-54)	Nero (54-68) Galba (68-69) Otho (69) Vitellius (69)	Vespasian (69-79)	Titus (79-81) Domitian (81-96) Nerva (96-98)	Trajan (98-117) Hadrian (117-138)	Pius (138-161)

Date	160	163	180	184	202
Event	Tertullian Born	Papias Dies	*Against Heresies*	Origen Born	Irenaeus Dies
Emperor		Aurelius (161-180)	Commodus (180-192)		

Date	220	253	264	313	312-324
Event	Tertullian Dies	Origen Dies	Eusebius Born	Edict of Milan Persecution Ends	*Ecclesiastical Histories*
Emperor	Severus (193-211) Alexander (212-235)	Maximinus (235-238) Gordon (238-244) Philip (244-249) Decius (249-251) Gallus (251-253)	Valerian (253-260) Gallienus (260-268) Claudius II (268-270) Aurelian (270-275) Probus (276-282) Carus (282-283)	Carinus (283-285) Diocletian (284-305) Constantius (305-306) Constantine (306-337) Licinius (308-324)	

Date	339	395
Event	Eusebius Dies	Roman Empire ends; Eastern Roman Empire (Byzantine Empire) Declared
Emperor	Constantine II (337-361) Julian (361-363) Jovian (363-364) Valentinian I (364-375) Gratian (375-383) Maximus (383-388) Valentinian II (375-392) Eugenius (393-394) Theodosius (394-395)	

TABLE 1
KINGS AND PROPHETS

The Kingdom of Israel

King	Time Span	Date	Scripture	Prophet
Saul	40 years	1050 BC	1 Samuel 9	Samuel
David	40 years	1010 BC	2 Samuel 2; 1 Kings 2	
Solomon	40 years	971 BC	1 Kings 1:37 - 11:43	

Divided Kingdom

Israel			Judah			Prophet
King	**Years**	**Date**	**King**	**Years**	**Date**	**Prophet**
Jeroboam	22 Years	931 BC	Rehoboam	17 Years	931 BC	
			Abijah	3 Years	913 BC	
			Asa	41 Years	911 BC	
Nadab	2 Years	910 BC				
Baasha	24 Years	909 BC				
Elah	2 Years	886 BC				
Zimri	7 Days	885 BC				
Omri	8 Years	885 BC				
Ahab (Marries Jezebel)	22 Years	874 BC				Elijah
			Jehoshephat	25 Years	876 BC	
Ahaziah	2 Years	853 BC				
Jehoram	12 Years	852 BC				
			Joram (Marries Athaliah, daughter of Jezebel and Ahab)	8 Years	851 BC	

Jehu Slays the Kings of Israel and Judah and has Jezebel Slain

King	Years	Date	King	Years	Date	Prophet
Jehu	28 Years	841 BC	Ahaziah (son of Joram and Athaliah)			
			Athaliah	6 Years	841 BC	Elisha 841
			Joash	40 Years	835 BC	
Jehoahaz	17 Years	812 BC				
J(eh)oash	16 Years	799 BC				
			Amaziah	29 Years	796 BC	
						Jonah 790 (?)
Jeroboam II	31 Years	782 BC				
			Uzziah (Azariah)	25 Years	768 BC	
						Amos 767 - 753
						Hosea 755-725
Zechariah	6 Months	752 BC				
Shallum	1 Month	751 BC				
Menahem	10 Years	751 BC				
			Jotham	16 Years	750 BC	
						Isaiah 745-685
Pekahiah	2 Years	742 BC				
Pekah	20 Years	740 BC				
						Micah 740 - 700
			Ahaz	16 Years	735 BC	
Hoshea	9 Years	731 BC				

722BC - Samaria (Israel) Taken Captive by Assyria - End of Israel's Kingdom

Judah

King	Time	Year	Prophet	Dates
Hezekiah (good)	29 Years	729 BC		
Manassah (evil)	55 Years	687 BC		
Amon (evil)	2 Years	642 BC		
Josiah (good)	31 Years	640 BC	Nahum	640 (?)
			Habakkuk	630 (?)
			Zephaniah	630 (?)
			Jeremiah	627 - 580
			Joel	620
Jehoahaz (evil)	3 Months	609 BC		
Jehoiakim (evil)	11 Years	609 BC		
			Daniel	603 - 535
Jehoichin (evil)	3 Months	598 BC		
Zedekiah (evil	11 Years	597 BC		
			Ezekiel	593 - 570
			Obadiah	586

586BC - Jerusalem and Temple Destroyed (Desolation) - End of Kingdom of Judah (Babylonian Captivity)

Table 2

From the Captivity to the End of the Old Testament (+/- 200 Years)

Bible Book	Jewish Event	Date	Contemporary History	Prophet	Dates
				Jeremiah	627-580
Jeremiah 36-39; 46	First Captivity	605	Battle of Carchemish, Nebuchadnezzar Defeats Egypt (605) Pisistratus; Athens (605-527)	Daniel	603-535
Jeremiah 39:1-10	Second Captivity	597			
2 Kings 25:1-21	Jerusalem Captured				
Jeremiah 43-44	Temple Destroyed Third Captivity	586	Nebuchadnezzar Besieges Tyre; Pythagoras (582-507)	Ezekiel	593-570
Ezekiel 17-21	Last of Ezekiel's Prophesies	571	Evil Merodach; Babylon		
2 Kings 25-28	Jehoichin Released by Merodach	562	Nabonidus (556) Temple of Diana; Ephesus (552) Public Library at Athens (544) Cyrus Takes Babylon 539)		
Daniel 5	Belshazzar's Feast	539	First Year of Cyrus (538)		

Bible Book	Jewish Event	Date	Contemporary History	Prophet	Dates
Daniel 6	Daniel in the Lion's Den	538			
2 Chronicles 36:22-23	Decree for the Return	538			
Ezra 1:1-4					
Ezra 1:5-2:70	First Return; 50,000 under Zerubbabel				
Ezra 3-6	Foundation of Temple Laid; Long Delay	536			
Ezra 4:24	Temple Building Resumed	520	Darius in Babylon (521)	Haggai	520
Ezra 6:15	Temple Dedicated	516	70 Years from Destruction		
		510	Roman Republic Declared		
		500	Greek Classical Period (500-323)		
		490	Battle of Marathon		
			Xerxes I (Ahesuerus) (486-465)		
		483	Herodotus (485-425); Sophocles;		
		480	Invasion of Greece		
Esther 1	Feast of Ahesuerus (Xerxes I)				
Esther 2	Esther Becomes Queen	479	Socrates (470)		
Esther 3-7	Haman's Plot	474			
Ezra 7:1-26	Second Return Under Ezra	458		Malachi	458-432
			First Decemvirate (Rome) (451)		
Nehemiah 2:1	Return Under Nehemiah	445			
Nehemiah 6:15	Wall of Jerusalem	444	Pericles: Athens (444)		
			Parthenon; Athens (443-438)		
			Peloponnesian War (431-404)		
			Plato (427)		
Nehemiah 10	Reforms; Death of Nehemiah	400	Xenophon's Retreat (401)		

Glossary of Names, Places, and Events

(As They Relate to This Book)

Abel to Zechariah (A to Z) – from Matthew 23:35; the Alpha and the Omega; the first and the last (see Revelation 1:8; 21:6; 22:13).

Abomination of Desolation – the desolation was the destruction of Jerusalem and the abomination was the act of entering, profaning, desecrating, and/or destroying the Temple, committed by Nebuchadnezzar, Antiochus Epiphanes, and Titus (see Desolation).

Abraham – the one whom God chose to be the father of His people and to whom He made the Promise.

Adorn – a special word in Scripture; for our study it is how God's holy Temple is characterized as it was decked with votive gifts (Luke 21:5; Matthew 24:1), which was the case with the first Temple (2 Chronicles 3:5-7). It is used by the inspired writers to characterize the relationship between God and His people, such as: a. the way His word can adorn our lives, i.e. wisdom, knowledge, and understanding should be worn around our necks (Proverbs 3:19-22); b. how we should stand before God with eminence and dignity (Job 40:7-10); c. how God dealt with His people, or how a wife dresses-up and brightens herself for her husband (Ezekiel 16:11-13).

Against Heresies – the title of the works of Irenaeus, who was speaking out against the heresies of the day; it serves as the kernel of faulty eschatology and is an important focus of study in this book.

Ahab – a king of Israel whom Jezebel married; they became the parents of Athaliah (see Athaliah).

Aión–(age; era) – a period of time; for our study it was: the time in which Jesus, the promised Messiah to the Jews, went to the cross for the sin of mankind. From thence His disciples carried His words and teachings throughout Judea and Samaria and to the uttermost parts of the earth until the desolation of 70AD when the city and Temple were destroyed, and the Jews and Christians were driven from Judea. At that point in time the old covenantal practice of animal sacrifice for the forgiveness of sin was ended. It was the end of the old covenant age.

Allegory – a figure of speech. It is of two kinds: a) one in which it is *continued metaphor* where the *two* things are both mentioned and that what is asserted belongs to the *principal* object; and b) one of *comparison by implication* where only *one* thing is mentioned, and what is asserted belongs properly to the *secondary* object; to whom it refers, [i.e.] it is not mentioned, but implied.[38]

Alpha and Omega – the first and last letters of the Greek alphabet.

Angel of the Lord – can be either *an* angel of the Lord (an angel) or *the* angel of the Lord (preincarnate Christ).

Antichrist – a term used in the first and second letters from John in which he defines a spirit, attitude, and behavior of ill will toward Christ and things of Christ, as antichrist. The Scriptures nowhere mention *the* Antichrist.

Antiochus Epiphanes – a Greek general and ruler who destroyed the city of Jerusalem and profaned the Temple ~167BC.

Apocalypse – the original name of the Revelation.

Aristotle (384-322BC) – an ancient Greek philosopher who, along with Plato, is considered "the Father of Western Philosophy."

---

[38] *Figures of Speech Used in the Bible* – E.W. Bullinger; Baker House – 2004 (1898)

Glossary Of Names, Places, And Events

Armageddon – a literal place in Judea, translated from the Hebrew (Revelation 16:13) where futurists say the final battle between Jesus Christ and the devil, or good vs evil, will take place in the end times.

Assyria – the power of the day which overran Israel (Samaria) in 722BC.

Athaliah – the daughter of Jezebel and King Ahab of Israel, who married King Joram of Judah and later took the throne herself, becoming Queen. She proceeded to murder the royal offspring in an attempt to eradicate the lineage of the Messiah.

Atonement – a sacrifice for sin. The word appears eighty times, all in the Old Testament, and seventy-one of those are in the books of Exodus, Leviticus, and Numbers, with only seven in the Prophets, therefore it is a term related to the Law. Jesus was the final atonement for the sin of man.

Baal – a false god.

Babylon – the nation that destroyed Judah in 586BC, destroying Jerusalem and the Temple and causing the abomination of desolation for the first time

Blasphemy – something anathema to God which is said or done against Him.

Blessings and Curses – those attributes of God, given through His law, which man reaps according to his deeds (see Leviticus 26 and Deuteronomy 28).

Bondage – man's condition under slavery to sin, which is why he needs a savior.

Captivity (the) – the seventy years of bondage which the Israelites endured in Babylon after Nebuchadnezzar destroyed Jerusalem and the Temple.

Carchemish (Battle of) – a city at the north end of the Euphrates River in NE Syria/SE Turkey where a famous battle took place as Pharaoh Neco of Egypt came up to meet, and lost to, King

Nebuchadnezzar of Babylon in 605BC (Jeremiah 46; 2 Chronicles 35:20-27).

Chaldeans – Babylonians.

Chiliasm – chili, the Greek numerical prefix for one thousand. Chiliasm is thousand-year-ism, the belief that Christ will come back and reign on earth for a thousand years. It was the belief of Papias, and is futurism at its earliest.

Conjecture – speculation; supposition; fancy.

Constantine – the Roman Emperor who finally ended the persecution in 313AD.

Context – that wonderful attribute of God which He imputed to man so that we can understand what we read and hear. It is what is lost when it comes to understanding eschatology.

Controversial (**Notorious**) **Statement** – that statement, uttered one time by Irenaeus, and repeated twice by Eusebius, which is the pretext for the futurist view

Council (Sanhedrin) – the Jewish elders which met and meted out justice in Judea and Samaria (see Sanhedrin).

Covenant – that arrangement which God established with His people whereby He chose a people (the Israelites) to be His, and that they would live by His generous and loving, but also corrective, statutes.

Creation – all that God made in seven days.

Cyrus – the king of Persia under whom the Babylonian captivity ended. God stirred-up his spirit to decree that the Temple in Jerusalem should be rebuilt and that those of the Jews who cared-to might return to fulfill that purpose. With those first returning he also decreed to have sent back the sacred vessels which had been taken by Nebuchadnezzar from the first Temple (Ezra 1:1-8; 6:1-5).

Daniel – one of the four major prophets who had some very important things to say about eschatology.

Glossary Of Names, Places, And Events

Darius the Mede – the king of Babylon under the Persian king Cyrus, and under whom work on the Temple resumed after the "long pause" (Ezra 4:24).

David – the king of Israel; who succeeded the disastrous king Saul. He was "a man after God's own heart". He is listed as the father of Jesus and the son of Abraham (Matthew 1:1) – text without context is pretext.

Decemviri – a Latin term meaning *ten men*, which designates any such commission in the Roman Republic (ten decemvirs).

Decemvir – one of a body of ten Roman Magistrates, appointed in 451BC, to draw up a code of laws, which became known as the Twelve Tablets, the basis of Roman Law.

Decemvirate – the board of ten decemvirs which drew up the Twelve Tablets.

Defile – to contaminate and poison something as it relates to God, such as His word or His Temple.

Desolation – defined by Isaiah 1:7, it is total destruction, as *overthrown by strangers*. It was the actual destruction of the city of Jerusalem by Nebuchadnezzar, Antiochus Epiphanes, and Titus.

Diana (temple of) – the Temple of Artemis, also known as the Temple of Diana, which was built in Ephesus in the 6th century BC.

Disciple – a follower of Jesus.

Divided Kingdom – that which became of the original kingdom of Israel. God tore the kingdom from King Solomon and gave ten tribes to Jeroboam, who became king of the new Israel, and gave one tribe to Solomon's son Rehoboam, who became the king over the new kingdom of Judah which contained the city of Jerusalem, the city which God chose to keep a light of David to Himself (1 Kings 11:13, 31-39; and 15:4-5).

Domitian – the Roman Emperor who (possibly) released John the Revelator from his exile on Patmos Isle. Some say he actually sent John to exile. He was an extremely cruel Emperor but he ruled in an insignificant era. Domitian is mentioned by Irenaeus in what has become known as *the notorious statement* in this book.

Dynasty – a sequence of powerful leaders in the same family.

Ecclesiastical Histories – the name of the published works of Eusebius, which is the history of the 1st century church and is used as a reference in this book.

Edict of Milan (313AD) – the proclamation of Emperors Constantine and Licinius which enacted 'toleration' for Christians and finally ended the great persecution.

Egypt – an important nation in the northeast of Africa. The Israelites were enslaved there early on, and they pined to go back there as Moses led them through the wilderness, as God was directing them to the Holy Land and the city of Jerusalem. It is also one of the routes through which the Gospel spread. Manuscripts, and fragments of manuscripts found along this route were called Alexandrian in nature.

End Times – that time when Jesus supposedly comes back to earth to set up His kingdom (the thousand-year reign); it is also when the Antichrist comes and sits at the Temple, the rapture occurs, as does the great tribulation; the battle of Armageddon occurs and Jerusalem comes down from heaven.

Ephesus – the city in what is now western Turkey on the coast of the Aegean Sea where the apostle John resided after his release from banishment on Patmos Isle.

Equivocation – a double meaning. This is used many times in eschatology, making it impossible to understand. Example: partial fulfillment of prophecy.

Ephod – an idol.

Eschatology – the study of the end times.

Esther – she was instrumental during the return of the Jews from captivity; she became Queen to the king of Persia, Ahasuerus; the Bible book by that name is for her.

Glossary Of Names, Places, And Events

Eusebius – the church historian whose published works, *Ecclesiastical Histories*, one hundred forty years after Irenaeus published his, are used by others to validate Irenaeus and his futurism.

Ezekiel – one of the four major prophets.

Ezra – led the second return from captivity under King Artaxerxes of Persia.

False Witness – someone who makes false accusations against someone else or testifies against someone of a false offense.

Flog – to scourge; what the Roman soldiers loved to do to "examine" an accused.

Foundation of the World – when God created the heavens and the earth.

Free Will – God's gift to us.

Fruit of the Tree of the Knowledge of Good and Evil – the fruit which God commanded Adam and Eve not to eat. It was of the Tree is of the Knowledge of Good and Evil. Man didn't need the knowledge of good and evil until Adam and Eve ate of the fruit of the tree. They fell for the lie of Satan which is: you will be like God (Genesis 3:5). Man has been striving ever since.

Futurism – the predominant view of Biblical prophecy and Revelation, begun with Papias and Irenaeus, and erroneously adopted as accurate.

Generation – a period of time, more or less 20-50 years, from one family of offspring to the next. It is that grouping of people, i.e. those who opposed Jesus from the beginning, and those whom He lambasted in Matthew 23, those who finally had Him arrested and executed, and those who then stoned Stephen to death, beginning the great persecution.

Golden Calf – the ephod, or false god, the people made while Moses was up on Mt. Sinai receiving the commandments on God.

Great Commission – Jesus' sending out of His disciples to preach the Gospel from Jerusalem, to Judea and Samaria, and to the uttermost parts of the earth.

Great Distress – a time which Daniel prophesied would occur near the time of the Resurrection (12:1).

Great Persecution – the effort to stomp out Christianity from the outset; it began with the killing of Stephen (Acts 8:1) and ended with the Edict of Milan in 313AD.

Great Tribulation – that which Jesus prophesied in Matthew 24:21.

Greece – the third of Daniel's four prophesied kingdoms; it followed Medo-Persia and preceded Rome.

Greek Classical Period (500-323BC–refers to the period between the Persian Wars at the beginning of the fifth century B.C., and the death of Alexander the Great in 323 B.C. It was an era of war and conflict—first between the Greeks and the Persians, then between the Athenians and the Spartans—but it was also an era of unprecedented political and cultural achievement. Besides the Parthenon and Greek Tragedy, classical Greece brought us the historian Herodotus, the physician Hippokrates (who gave us the Hippocratic Oath) and the philosopher Socrates. It also brought us the political reforms that are ancient Greece's most enduring contribution to the modern world: the system known as demokratia, or "rule by the people" (democracy).

Guilt –what Jesus laid on the religious leaders for killing the prophets and playing the harlot (Matthew 23:35).

Haman – the second in command under Ahasuerus, king of Persis; a hater of the Jews.

Haman's Plot – read Esther 3.

Harlot – it is who this book is about. In the Old Testament it was the Israelites who rejected God by worshipping other gods and killing the prophets. In the New Testament it was Judea and Jerusalem and therefore the Jews who opposed Jesus and His disciples and who killed Him and the prophets, including Stephen. She is depicted in Revelation as Babylon the Great, the mother of harlots, and she was riding on a beast.

Glossary Of Names, Places, And Events

Haughty Spirit – that which goeth before a fall (Proverbs 16:18 KJV). The aura the harlot projected, as though she was as a goddess, somehow pure, as though she was as God (Revelation 18:7-9)

Hellenization – the process by which the Jews became influenced and molded into the Greek customs during the transition to Roman rule.

Hermeneutics – principles of interpretation of the Scriptures.

Herodotus (484-425) – a Greek historian who wrote *Histories*, a work on the Persian Wars (425).

High Places – those places where the people went and built their altars and temples to worship their gods.

History (His Story) – the story that God is telling through His Scriptures.

Holy of Holies – the inner sanctum of the Temple or the tabernacle, behind the veil, where the ark of the covenant is kept.

Homer – a Greek poet who lived sometime from the 12th – 8th century BC (?). He wrote the *Iliad,* possibly around 900BC. The *Iliad* is famous for having the most extant manuscripts (643), far and away more than any other of man's writing – which pale in comparison to the number of the New Testament, whose numbers exceed 24,000.[39]

Hosea – one of the minor prophets who talked about a major problem with His people, a lack of faithfulness or kindness or knowledge of God; they rejected knowledge, and they forgot the law of God (Hosea 4:1-3).

Hypocrite – a person who practices hypocrisy, which is doing or saying that which one criticizes others of doing or saying.

Idolatry – the way in which somehow, someway, man puts himself before God.

Impute – that which God credits on our behalf.

---

[39] *Evidence that Demands A Verdict*, Josh McDowell; Here's Life Publishers, Inc; 1988; Page 43

Irenaeus – he is *it*. He is why this book exists. He is the father of futurism. He believed that John of Revelation is the same John of the Gospel and the epistles.[40]

Inspired writing – the Scriptures, which are the only writings inspired by the Holy Spirit of God.

Isaac – the son of Abraham and Sarai (Sarah), and through whom is the Promise.

Isaiah – the first of the major prophets. He gave us our definition of desolation (Isaiah 1:7). He prophesied during the divided kingdom, through the desolation of Samaria, with the majority of his ministry to Judah.

Ishmael – the son of Abraham and Hagar (Sarai's maid).

Israel – the people of God and the descendants of Isaac, the son of Abraham. Israel was also the name of Jacob, the son of Isaac and Rebekah (Genesis 25:19-26).

Israelites – God's chosen people.

Jacob – son of Isaac through whom the Promise flowed.

Jehu – a mighty warrior whom God commanded Elijah to anoint as king of Israel who slew both the kings of Israel and Judah and was instrumental in the death of the reviled Jezebel, trampling her underfoot, then sitting down to eat and drink.

Jeremiah – one of the major prophets, and our book's first citation, as he is used in conjunction with the apostle Paul (at the beginning of Part I), in that Jeremiah explains how Samaria was taken by Assyria and then all of Judah and Samaria by Babylon, and tells how He would punish Babylon; while Paul states that all those nations, and what they did, were directed by God.

Jehoichin – the king of Judah when Nebuchadnezzar captured Jerusalem.

---

[40] *Jesus and the Eyewitnesses*; Richard Bauckham; William B. Eerdmans Pub. Co. 2006; Pg. 455

Glossary Of Names, Places, And Events

Jeroboam – a king of Israel who was the recipient of the ten tribes which God tore from Solomon; thus, beginning the Divided Kingdom. He was an idol worshipper who led the people astray.

Jerusalem – God's holy city.

Jezebel – the most despised person in the Bible. She is responsible for God visiting His wrath to the third and fourth generations as described in the 2nd commandment;[41] she married King Ahab of Israel; their daughter, Athaliah, married Joram, king of Judah.

John (6-100AD) – the writer of the Gospel which bears his name, the three letters which also bear his name, and the Revelation. Whether or not they are one and the same person is debated.

Josephus (37-100AD) – a Jewish priest, scholar, and historian; he was a Pharisee who later became a military leader during the Jewish War. He surrendered to Rome as Vespasian was subduing Judea. He would later join the Roman forces (a turncoat) under Vespasian's son Titus, who destroyed Jerusalem and the Temple. His *History of the Jewish War* has a detailed account of the siege of Jerusalem and its destruction.

Judah – one of the twelve sons of Jacob who settled what would become one of the twelve tribes of the Kingdom of Israel, and which later became the kingdom by that name in the divided kingdom. The Promise ran through him as Jesus was the Lion of the Tribe of Judah..

Judea – the Holy Land in the time of Christ, which was formerly known as Judah.

Juxtapose – contrast; compare; set against one another.

Kingdom of God – as per Jesus' teachings, the world in which God's people reign.

King James Version (KJV) – the first major English translation of the Bible: The New Testament (from the original Greek), and the Old Testament (from the original Hebrew and Aramaic). It became

---

[41] Exodus 20:5; 34:7; Numbers 14:18; and Deuteronomy 5:9

the predominant Bible used in America since its introduction in 1611. This helped to perpetrate the false futuristic notion held by Irenaeus and Papias as it carried the mis-translation of the Greek word ***aion***, which was translated *world* instead of *age* or *eon* in Matthew 24:2 (see Part II). This left, without a doubt, the impression that Jesus was talking about the end of the world instead of the end of the age (which was the old covenant sacrifice system).

Koine Greek – the language of the New Testament; it is considered to be a dead language, which makes its meaning "sure." Wouldn't that be God's way, to preserve His word.

Kosmos – the Greek word for *world*; the *universe*.

Lamentation – weeping; sorrow; grief; what Jesus and Daniel did over Jerusalem when, both times, it was destroyed.

Law – the Ten Commandments, and all the other various and sundry laws given by God through Moses, in Exodus and Leviticus.

Law and Prophets – God's two witnesses; everything we need to know about what God expects from us. God gave us the law through Moses; when the people strayed, the prophets came and urged them back to the law.

Longsuffering – that attribute which God displays in which He is slow to anger.

Lovingkindness – that attribute which God displays in which He shows His love for us.

Luke – a physician; a disciple of Christ; a writer of the Gospel bearing his name; a companion of the apostle Paul.

Major Prophets – Isaiah, Jeremiah, Ezekiel, and Daniel.

Marathon (Battle of) – fought in 490BC during the first Persian invasion of Greece between the citizens of Athens and a Persian force. The battle was the culmination of the first attempt by Persia, under King Darius I, to subjugate Greece–Wikipedia

Mark – a disciple of Christ; one of the original twelve; a companion and scribe of Peter; the writer of the gospel according to that name.

Glossary Of Names, Places, And Events

Mary Magdalene – a follower of Jesus, and the person to whom He first appeared after His resurrection (Mark 16:9).

Matthew – a tax collector; a disciple of Christ; one of the original twelve; a writer of the gospel according to that name.

Measure – a term used in which God is sizing up a city, such as Jerusalem (2 Kings 21:10-15; Isaiah 28:17), or a structure, such as the Temple (Revelation 11:1-2), for destruction.

Medo-Persia – the rulers of the Holy Land who followed the Babylonians and preceded the Greeks; they are the second of the four kingdoms prophesied by Daniel in his visions and dreams.

Merodach (evil) (581-560BC) – son of and successor to King Nebuchadnezzar of Babylon; he released Judah's King Jehoiachin (2 Kings 25:27).

Messiah – Jesus the Christ; the Son of the living God.

Metaphor – [a transference or carrying over or across; from meta (beyond or over) and pherein (to carry); Representation or Transference. While simile gently states that one thing is *like* or *resembles* another, metaphor boldly declares that one thing **is** the other (the Lord **is** my Shepherd). Few figures are more misunderstood than the metaphor. The two nouns themselves must both be mentioned, and must always be taken in their absolutely literal sense, *or else no one can tell what they mean*. When a pronoun which ought, *according to the laws of language,* to agree in gender to its own noun is changed, and made to agree with the noun which represents it, it is a metaphor. This is always the case in metaphors– *the figure lies in the verb, not the nouns.*][42]

Micah – a minor prophet who had something to say about the people sacrificing their children to the gods.

Minor Prophets – all the prophets other than the four major prophets.

---

[42] Bullinger; *Figures of Speech*

Molech – a despicable idol which had a place to lay an object, such as a child (which was the practice), and had a hollow area to build a fire, thus sacrificing children by fire.

Mystical – relating to the belief that there is hidden meaning in life, or that each human being can unite with God (Cambridge English Dictionary). In our case: a hidden spiritual meaning in the Scriptures as explained by Eusebius in response to writings put forth by Papias.

Mythical – Something or someone that is mythical exists only in myths and is therefore imaginary (Collins English Dictionary). In our case it refers to certain beliefs held by Papias regarding Revelation.

Nabonidus – the last king of the Babylonian Empire (556-539BC)

Naboth – Man whose vineyard Ahab coveted, Jezebel swindled, and where her corpse was eaten by dogs.

Nebuchadnezzar – the king of Babylon (605-562), who came in conquest of the Holy Land and who proceeded to destroy Jerusalem and the Temple in 586BC, committing the first abomination of desolation.

Nehemiah–the central figure of the Book of Nehemiah, which describes his work in rebuilding Jerusalem during the Second Temple period. He was governor of Persian Judea under Artaxerxes I of Persia–Wikipedia

Nero – the ruler of the Roman Empire (54-68AD) during the time of the great persecution, and who intensified it in such a way as to attempt to exterminate Christians and Christianity from the face of the earth; his reign was the height of the persecution. The ensuing destruction and desolation of 70 ended the old covenant and completed the great commission. He is the beast of Revelation; his name adds up to 666.

Notorious Statement – The statement made by Irenaeus in Book 5, Chapter 30, Paragraph 3 of his *Against Heresies* which, being

Glossary Of Names, Places, And Events

misinterpreted ever since, set the course of the futurist interpretation of eschatology.

Oholah and Oholibah – those sister cities of Samaria (the older), which God had already judged and was using as a warning to the younger, Jerusalem (Judah), which He would eventually judge (Ezekiel 23). The actual events were one hundred thirty-six years apart.

Olivet Discourse– Jesus' eschatological oratory given from the Mount of Olives (Matthew 24-25).

Origen (184-253) – an early Christian scholar, ascetic, and theologian who was born in Alexandria, Egypt and spent the first half of his career there – Wikipedia.

Overthrown by Strangers – desolation (Isaiah 1:7).

Papias (60–163 AD)–a Greek Apostolic Father, and the Bishop of Hierapolis. He wrote the *Exposition of the Sayings of the Lord* in five books–Wikipedia. He was a futurist (a chiliast) who had an influence on Irenaeus. It can safely by said that Papias is one of the pillars of futurism, along with Irenaeus, Eusebius, and the KJV.

Parable – [a placing beside for the purpose of comparison; the classical use of the word was for one of the subdivisions of *paradeigma*, i.e., *an example*; a presentation of an analogous case by way of illustration. In the New Testament it is used of a story with a hidden meaning, without pressing, in every detail, the idea of a comparison. As the name of a Figure of Speech, it is limited to what we may describe as *continued simile*, an illustration by which one set of circumstances is *likened* to another; it consists in *likeness*, not in *representation*, and therefore is not a *continued metaphor*, but a *repeated simile*. This likeness is generally in only some special point. The resemblance is to be sought for in the scope of the *context*, in the one great truth which is presented, and the one important lesson which is taught, and not in the minute details which these happen to be associated. Any lesson for ourselves must come as an *application* of it to present circumstances. The common idea is that they are intended to make things clear and plain, but they are spoken that the truth might be veiled from those who "seeing, see not," and "hearing, hear not" (Matthew 13:10-17); hence they are the most difficult portions of God's Word.][43]

Parthenon – a former temple to the goddess Athena, built on the Acropolis under the direction of Pericles (447-438BC).

Patmos – the place where John received the Revelation (1:9).

Paul – the foremost of the inspired writers. He took the Gospel to the Gentiles. A bitter enemy of the faith until his conversion. It was at his feet that the persecution officially began (Acts 8:1). It is through he and Eusebius that we trace the persecution (Part V).

Peloponnesian War – war between Athens and Sparta, won by Sparta, fought in two stages, 460-446, and 431-404BC. It occurred around the periphery of the Aegean Sea.

Peoples of the Earth – the nations of the earth other than the Israelites.

Pericles (495-429) – an idol worshipper; a Greek general who ruled during the "Golden Age;" he was a friend of Sophocles and a contemporary of Socrates.

Persecution – the collective effort to harm or kill Christians and to eradicate Christianity by the Jews and Roman Empire until the time of Constantine (Part V).

Pharisees, Sadducees, and Scribes – the religious leaders of Jesus' time; Paul was a Pharisee.

Phoenicia – a strip of land along the Mediterranean Sea north of Israel; approximately modern-day Lebanon.

Pisistratus (605-527BC) – an idol worshipper; called the "tyrant of Athens," he was instrumental in the growth of Athens.

Plato (428-347BC) – a Greek philosopher.

Playing the Harlot – really getting into something you shouldn't be really getting into.

---

[43] Bullinger; *Figures*

Glossary Of Names, Places, And Events

Polycarp (69-155) – a bishop of the early church; a disciple of the apostle John and the teacher of Irenaeus.[44]

Preterism – the belief that by the time of the desolation of 70AD, most prophecy was fulfilled.

Pretext – a reason to do something you shouldn't do.

Principle – that innate attribute which God imputes to us, and which guides us to do the right thing.

Promise (the) – that the descendants of Abraham would be as the stars of heaven (Genesis 15:5,13-14,18); that his seed would be as the stars of the heavens and the sand of the seashore, and in his seed all the nations of the earth would be blessed (22:15-18); to Isaac that his descendants would be as the stars of heaven, and by his descendants all the nations of the earth shall be blessed (26:2-4); and to Jacob that his descendants will be like the dust of the earth and in him all the families of the earth will be blessed (28:10-15).

Prophecy – an utterance of God through man.

Prophet–someone who speaks an utterance of God.

Prophesy – the act of uttering a prophecy of God.

Proverb – [from the Greek word paramia, from paroimia; from *para*, beside; and *oimos*, a way or path; hence, paramia is a wayside saying, a trite expression, or common remark, a proverb. Paramia translates from the Hebrew noun *mahshal* which belongs to the *verb* of the same name and spelling, which means to rule, control; to have or exercise control. Hence it is plain that there is a connection between a *rule* and a *proverb;* this connection may be illustrated by our phrase *a ruling principle*; and by the fact that we might term what we call the Proverbs of Solomon *Solomon's Rules*, since that is just what they are – rules for guiding life. It would seem to mean a saying most widely used and in ordinary life generally. By degrees, usage separated the words *parable* and *paramia, parable* being limited to an illustration, and *paramia* now

---

[44] see Irenaeus, Part IV.

being confined to what we call a proverb. The figure is used, therefore, of any *sententious saying,* because these are generally such as control and influence life.]⁴⁵

Pythagoras (569-475BC) – a Greek philosopher and mathematician whose principles influenced Plato and Aristotle.

Rapture – the rising of all God's people to meet Jesus in the air when He supposedly comes back to earth.

Recapitulation of the Apostasy – a term used by Irenaeus to describe the Antichrist, whom, to him, is the beast and is also the abomination of desolation. In his quest to explain Revelation, and despite his best efforts, it is clear that he did not understand it.

Recounting of History – a process by which any of the inspired writers describes those events which God orchestrated from the beginning until that current time; the point being that these are important aspects of Scripture and equally important points in history in that they are historical and repeated; therefore, they keep matters in context.

Redemption – the salvaging of what would have been lost by paying a ransom; what Jesus Christ attained at the cross, giving His life as a ransom for those who believe in Him.

Rehoboam – the son of King Solomon, who himself became king, and the first one at that of the kingdom of Judah. God gave him one tribe, Judah, for the sake of His servant David, and for the sake of Jerusalem, which He had chosen (1 Kings 11:9-13). This is the line from which Christ came.

Religious Leaders – in Old Testament times they were the "fathers," or leaders of God's people. In Christ's time, they were the Pharisees, Sadducees, and scribes whom Jesus clashed with, and whom eventually had Him executed.

Remnant – the people whom God saves from calamity to continue to further His will, i.e. the Israelites who came out of the

---

⁴⁵ Bullinger; *Figures*

Glossary Of Names, Places, And Events

Babylonian captivity, and the Christians who escaped the destruction of 70AD and scattered throughout the world.

Roman Kingdom (753-509BC)–the city of Rome was founded in 753 BC by Romulus, who became the first king of the Roman Kingdom. There was a total of seven kings over a period of 244 years before the monarchy was overthrown and replaced by the Roman Republic.

Roman Republic (509-27BC)–a period in which the power of Rome reached the whole peninsula of Italy and Roman law was founded, written by the decemviri, with the Law of the Twelve Tables written in 450 BC.

Roman Empire (27BC-476AD)–the post-Roman Republic period of the ancient Roman civilization; it was a government headed by emperors and large territorial holdings around the Mediterranean Sea in Europe, North Africa, and West Asia.

Eastern Roman Empire (Byzantine Empire) – 476-1453 – [a vast and powerful civilization with origins that can be traced to 330AD, when the Roman emperor Constantine I dedicated a "New Rome" on the site of the ancient Greek colony of Byzantium (Constantinople – author). Though the western half of the Roman Empire crumbled and fell in 476 A.D., *the eastern half survived for nearly a thousand more years*, spawning a rich tradition of art, literature and learning and serving as a military buffer between Europe and Asia. The Byzantine Empire finally fell in 1453, after an Ottoman army stormed Constantinople during the reign of Constantine XI.] – www.history.com

Rome – the fourth and final kingdom of Daniel's prophecies. The destroyer of Jerusalem and the Temple in 70AD, ending the Old Covenant era and fulfilling Jesus' command to His disciples to be His witnesses, first in Jerusalem, then Judea and Samaria, and to the uttermost parts of the earth. Rome is the beast of Revelation and of our book.

Samaria – that part of the Holy Land which was overthrown by Assyria prior to the Babylonian invasion, and which was set upon by the Assyrians in such a way as to rape and intermarry with the women, creating a race of "half-breeds" and hence, the negative view of them by the Jews of Gospel time. Samaria was a city in Judah and later in Judea; there was a general area called Samaria also; one could rightly think of Israel during the divided kingdom as Samaria.

Sanhedrin (Council) – the ruling body of the Jewish people under the Roman yoke.

Saul – the name of the first king of Israel whom the people chose, rejecting God as their king; he was a total failure. The name of the apostle Paul before he decided to go by his Roman name. The man who mercilessly persecuted the church from the very beginning as he was the man at who's feet the robes of those who stoned and killed Stephen were laid. (Acts 8:1).

Scourge – the process of whipping by which the Roman soldiers would "examine" or mete out justice either before killing, imprisoning, or releasing a prisoner.

Second Coming – as per the futurist view: the next time that Christ will come back to earth, when He will rule for a thousand years (the millennium); or when He will come back for His people who will meet Him in the air (the rapture), and from thence -? As per the view of this author: when Jesus came in judgment against Judea in 70AD, destroying Jerusalem and the Temple and ending the old covenant.

Seventy – one of those numbers, God's numbers, which just seem to appear to have special meaning. It is titillating in that seventy is the number of years of the Babylonian captivity; there are the seventy weeks of Daniel (9:24-27); that is the number of disciples which Jesus sent out in pairs (Luke 10:1); Jesus used the number in an authoritative and weighty way, talking to Peter (Matthew 18:21-22); and it was the year of the abomination of desolation, the end of the old covenant, and the fulfillment of the Great Commission (70AD). Seven is another of God's numbers, as is ten, twelve, and four.

Sight of the Lord – that attribute of God in which the kings of Israel and Judah either measured up or they didn't; they either did right or evil in the sight of the Lord.

Snare – that which is unseen, unexpected, and unplanned for, but which halts or impedes our progress, leaving us vulnerable as prey.

Socrates (469-399BC)–a classical Greek philosopher; one of the founders of Western philosophy, and credited as the first moral philosopher of the Western ethical tradition of thought.–Wikipedia

Sodom – the city which God destroyed with fire and brimstone, along with Gomorrah (Genesis 18:22-19:29). It is used in conjunction with Samaria as a warning to Jerusalem (Ezekiel 16); and it is also paired (mystically) with Egypt as a metaphor for Jerusalem (Revelation 11:8).

Solomon – the son of David who succeeded him as king of Israel and from whom the kingdom was torn, giving ten tribes to Jeroboam, who would become king of Israel, and one tribe (Judah) to Solomon's son, Rehoboam who would become king of the new kingdom of Judah.

Sophocles (497-406BC) – a famous Greek playwright.

Spiritism – Spiritism is why King Saul was an abject failure (1 Samuel 28:3-25).

Spiritist–a person who claims to speak with or for the spirits of the dead (Merriam-Webster online dictionary), and which is frowned upon in the Scriptures (Deuteronomy 18:9-13).

Stephen – a disciple of Christ, but not one of the twelve. A man of God who was falsely accused, as was Jesus, and subsequently stoned to death, in what was the beginning of the great persecution (Acts 8:1).

Tabernacle – the portable structure which served as the Temple as the people were led by Moses through the wilderness, until the Temple itself was built in Jerusalem by Solomon.

Temple – the building which was constructed in Jerusalem as the permanent structure where the people would bring their tithes and offerings to the priests, and sacrifices for their sin.

Tertullian (160-220) – a prolific early Christian author from Carthage in the Roman province of Africa. Of Berber origin, he was the first Christian author to produce an extensive corpus of Latin Christian literature–Wikipedia. He was a contemporary of Irenaeus. He eventually became a Montanist, a heresy with odd eschatological leanings.

Testify – a legal term which indicates someone giving evidence or swearing to something as to its truth, and a term which Jesus used in condemning the religious leaders of His day as being killers of the prophets (the harlot).

Testament – another legal term; tangible proof or evidence of something; a statement of belief.

Theology – the study of God (Theos).

"These Things" – those things which Jesus said would come upon "that" generation, as described in Matthew 23 and 24.

The Books – those books which God keeps (Daniel 7:10 and Revelation 20:12).

"This" Generation – the generation of people that Jesus said "all these things" would come upon as described Matthew 23 and 24.

Titus – The general who destroyed Jerusalem and the Temple in 70AD. As the commanding general, he may have been the person who planted the Roman standard in the Holy of Holies and who actually gave the command the destroy it. It was the abomination of desolation.

Tree of Knowledge of Good and Evil – the tree in the Garden of Eden, which God commanded Adam and Eve not to eat the fruit of (Genesis 2:17), but which the serpent enticed Eve to eat thereof, saying that she would be like God, knowing good and evil (3:5).

Tribulation – distress or suffering resulting from oppression or persecution (Merriam-Webster).

Two Witnesses – the Law and the Prophets.

Tyre – a city of modern-day Lebanon.

Vespasian – the Roman general who made his reputation by his military campaign against Judea and Jerusalem. He ascended to the throne as Emperor and his Son, Titus took his place as general.

Wilderness – the Sinai, where the Israelites were led by Moses for forty years when they came out of bondage in Egypt, before they went into the Promised Land.

Wing of Abominations – from Daniel 9:27, it is metaphor for what leads up to the destruction of the city and Temple of 70AD; i.e. the abominations of what the pagan Romans were doing to God's people and the land of Judea, the city of Jerusalem, and the Temple, culminating with the idolatrous army overrunning and occupying them and planting their standard in the Holy of Holies.

Witness – still another legal term; someone who testifies to something; to actually see something.

Woe – dread; gloom; misfortune.

Xenophon (431-354) – an ancient Greek philosopher, historian, soldier, mercenary, and student of Socrates–Wikipedia

Xerxes I (aka Ahesuerus) (486-465) – called Xerxes the Great, he was the fifth king of the Achaemenid dynasty of Persia. Like his predecessor Darius I, he ruled the empire at its territorial apex. He ruled until his assassination at the hands of Artabanus, the commander of the royal bodyguard – Wikipedia. He signed on to Haman's plot to exterminate the Jews (Esther 3).

Ziggurat – the imaginary structures man builds in his attempts to avoid, evade, and usurp God.

BIBLIOGRAPHY

Bauckham, Richard. *Jesus and the Eyewitnesses*. Grand Rapids: Eerdmans 2006

Bench, Tim. *False Doctrines*. Abilene, Tx.: 2015

Bullinger, E.W. *Figures of Speech used in the Bible*. Brand Rapids: Baker 2004

Chilton, David. *The Days of Vengeance: An Exposition of the Book of Revelation*. Ft. Worth: Dominion, 1987.

Cook, Steven R. *The Sin of Idolatry*. 2015.

Edwards, William D., Gabel, Wesley J., Hosmer, Floyd E., *Scourging and Crucifixion in Roman Tradition*. Mayo Clinic, Rochester: 1986.

Gentry, Kenneth. *Before Jerusalem Fell: Dating the Book of Revelation*. Ft. Worth: Dominion, 1989.

Holmes, Yulusses L. *Judaea in the Age of Nero*. March, 2015

Kik, J. Marcellus. *An Eschatology of Victory*. Philipsburg: Presbyterian and Reformed, 1971.

Knight, Kevin *New Advent* http://www.newadvent,org/fathers

Master Study Bible (NASB). Nashville, Tn.: Holman, 1981.

McKnight, Scot. *Interpreting the Synoptic Gospels*. Grand Rapids: Baker, 1988.

McDowell, Josh. *Evidence That Demands a Verdict*. San Bernardino: Here's Life, 1988

Russel, Stuart J. *The Parousia: A Study of the New Testament Doctrine of Our Lord's Second Coming*; Grand Rapids: Baker, 1887.

Sim, David C. *The Gospel of Matthew, John the elder and the Papias Tradition: A Response to R.H. Gundry*; Australian Catholic University; Melbourne, Australia 2007

Singer, Isidore, Barton, George A. *Molech*. Jewish Encyclopedia.com.

Terry, Milton. *Biblical Hermeneutic: A Treatise on the Interpretation of the Old and New Testament*. Grand Rapids: Zondervan, 1883.

ENDNOTES

i Posted on August 9, 2015 by Steven R. Cook, D. Min.

You shall have no other gods before Me. You shall not make for yourself an idol [פֶסֶל pesel – an idol or carved image], or any likeness of what is in heaven above or on the earth beneath or in the water under the earth. You shall not worship [שָׁחָה shachah – to worship, bow down] them or serve [עָבַד abad – serve, work] them; for I, the LORD your God, am a jealous God, visiting the iniquity of the fathers on the children, on the third and the fourth generations of those who hate Me. (Ex. 20:3-5)

What is idolatry?
Idolatry is the selfish sin of substitution in which we devote ourselves to worship something or someone in the place of God. It is foremost a sin of a covetous heart that leads us to desire more than what God provides, and to trust something or someone lesser than God to satisfy our wants and needs. Paul addresses the heart of idolatry when he writes that covetousness "is idolatry" (Col. 3:5). Covetousness is idolatry because the covetous heart desires things and pleasures more than God. **The believer who is satisfied with God is content with what he has (1 Tim. 6:7-11; cf. Phil. 4:11), but the covetous heart is never content and always seeks more (i.e. money, success, friends, etc.) in order to feel secure or to please the flesh.**
In a general sense idolatry is the paying of divine honor to any created thing; the ascription of divine power to natural agencies. Idolatry may be classified as follows: (1) the worship of inanimate objects, such as stones, trees, rivers, etc.; (2) of animals; (3) of the higher powers of nature, such as the sun, moon, stars; and the forces of nature, as air, fire, etc.; (4) hero-worship or of deceased ancestors; (5) idealism, or the worship of abstractions or mental qualities, such as justice.[1]

What is an idol?
Throughout Scripture, an idol is almost always a carved image, something crafted by human hand, made of wood or stone. An idol can be either a physical object that symbolizes a deity, or it can be an abstract

concept such as greed or justice. A physical idol is merely the work of a craftsman (see Isa. 44:9-19). There is no life in it (Ps. 115:1-8; Jer. 51:17; Hab. 2:18-20), nor can it deliver in times of trouble (Isa. 46:5-7). **Ultimately, an idol is the thing or person we trust more than God to provide, protect, or guide us in life.** Biblically, there is only one God, and He demands that His people worship Him (Ex. 20:3-6). The exclusive worship of God is for His glory and our benefit.

Can God's people engage in idolatry?
Yes. We can engage in idolatry. **The record of Israel's history – with the exception of a few generations – is a record of their unfaithfulness to God** as they worshipped pagan idols (Ex. 32:1-6), which, at times, included human sacrifice (Deut. 12:31; 18:10; 2 Ki. 21:6; Ezek. 16:20-21). The books of Judges, 1 & 2 Kings, Isaiah, Jeremiah, Ezekiel and Hosea (just to name a few) all reveal Israel regularly committed idolatry, **and this caused them to suffer greatly under God's discipline as He faithfully executed the cursing aspects of the Mosaic Covenant (Deut. 28:15-68).**

Idolatry is dangerous because it is connected with the activity of demons (1 Cor. 10:19-20), who seek to steal God's glory and wreck our relationship with the Lord. Many of God's people have fallen into idolatry. Aaron led Israel into idol worship (Ex. 32:1-6). Solomon, by the end of his life, bowed down to idols (1 Ki. 11:6-10), and there is nothing in the biblical record that suggests Solomon ever turned back to the Lord. The apostle Paul addressed idolatry in his letter to the church at Corinth (1 Cor. 8:1-13; 10:14-33; 2 Cor. 6:16). The apostle John twice worshiped an angel and was rebuked for it (Rev. 19:10; 22:8-9). John knew the sinful proclivity of all Christians and I believe this is why he warns us, "Little children, guard yourselves from idols" (1 John 5:21).

Why do we commit idolatry?
Even though we are born again believers with a new heart (2 Cor. 5:17; Eph. 4:22-24; 1 Pet. 1:3, 23), we still possess a sin nature (Rom. 6:6; 13:14; Gal. 5:16-17, 19; Col. 3:9), and there is always a conflict within us (Rom. 7:19-25; Gal. 5:16-17). **We commit idolatry because we seek to satisfy our sinful desires over God and His will.** In American culture we tend to worship at the altar of self-interest, greed, personal achievement, personal security and self-satisfaction.

How do we guard ourselves from falling into idolatry?
First, **realize our hearts are sinful and bent toward idolatry**. It is the natural proclivity of mankind to worship things and people in the place of God. It comes very easy to us, even as Christians. Second,

be devoted to God. Paul writes to Christians, stating, "present your bodies a living and holy sacrifice, acceptable to God, *which is* your spiritual service of worship" (Rom 12:1). This is a lifetime commitment to God in which we bring all of our life under His directive will. Third, **constantly be in God's Word**, letting it guide our thinking and behavior. As Christians, we do not worship the Bible, but neither can we worship God without it (John 4:24). The Bible is God's inerrant and enduring written revelation that tells us who He is and what He's accomplished in time and space. The Bible is written in understandable language and made acceptable by the Holy Spirit (1 Cor. 2:14-16; 2 Cor. 3:14-16; 4:3-4). Our walk with God depends on rightly understanding and applying Scripture (John 17:17; 1 Pet. 2:2; 2 Pet. 3:18). Fourth, **surround yourself with Christian friends** who will help you in your daily spiritual walk with the Lord. Our fellowship with other growing believers is paramount concerning our spiritual health and growth. The Bible is very clear when it states, "bad associations corrupt good morals" (1 Cor. 15:33). This is true in every way, and it helps us to have growing Christian friends who influence us to worship God and stay close to Him always. Fifth, **make time to worship the Lord daily**, singing to Him and praising Him for all His blessings (Ps. 95:2; 105:2; Eph. 5:18-21; Phil. 4:6; Col. 3:16-17; 1 Thess. 5:18). A heart that is satisfied with God will not seek lesser people or things to fill the void that occurs when we turn away from Him.

Steven R. Cook, D. Min.

About Steven R. Cook, D.Min.

Steven is a Christian educator. His webpages communicate evangelical Christian doctrines and topics. Steven earned a Master of Divinity degree in 2006 from Southwestern Baptist Theological Seminary and completed his Doctor of Ministry degree in 2017 from Tyndale Theological Seminary. His articles are theological, devotional, and promote a biblical worldview. Studies in the original languages of Scripture, ancient history, and systematic theology have been the foundation for Steven's teaching and writing ministry. He has written several Christian books, dozens of articles on Christian theology, and recorded more than three-hundred hours of audio and video sermons. Steven worked in jail ministry for over twelve years, taught in Bible churches, and currently leads a Bible study each week at his home in Arlington, Texas.

ii
Scourging and Crucifixion in Roman Tradition
(William D. Edwards, MD, Department of Pathology, Mayo Clinic, Rochester, MN; Wesley J. Gabel, MDiv, West Bethel United Methodist Church, Bethel,

MN.; Floyd E Hosmer, MS, AMI, Dept of Medical Graphics, Mayo Clinic, Rochester, MN; Homestead United Methodist Church, Rochester, MN; review of article and excerpts from **On The Physical Death of Jesus Christ**, JAMA, March 21, 1986 – Vol 255, No. 11). (The medical terms in this article have been edited into layman's terminology by: Carol R. Ritchie; TNCC, MSN, RN, CNOR.)

Scourging Practices

Flogging was a legal preliminary to every Roman execution, and only women and Roman senators or soldiers (except in cases of desertion) were exempt. **The usual instrument was a short whip with several single or braided leather thongs of variable lengths, in which small iron balls or sharp pieces of sheep bones were tied at intervals.** For scourging, the man was stripped of his clothing, and his hands were tied to an upright post. **The back, buttocks, and legs were flogged either by two soldiers (lictors) or by one who alternated positions.** The severity of the scourging depended on the disposition of the lictors and **was intended to weaken the victim to a state just short of collapse or death.** As the Roman soldiers repeatedly struck the victim's back with full force, the iron balls would cause deep contusions, and the leather thongs and sheep bones would cut into the skin and subcutaneous tissues. Then, as the flogging continued, the lacerations would tear into the underlying skeletal muscles and produce quivering ribbons of bleeding flesh. Pain and blood loss generally set the stage for circulatory shock. The extent of blood loss may well have determined how long the victim would survive on the cross. **After the scourging, the soldiers often taunted their victim.** https://www.cbcg.org/scourging-crucifixion.html

iii

Molech–http://jewishencyclopedia.com/articles/10937-moloch-molech

Nature of the Worship — Critical View:

The name "Molech," later corrupted into "Moloch," is an intentional mispointing of "Melek," after the analogy of "bosheth" (comp. Hoffmann in Stade's "Zeitschrift," iii. 124). As to the rites which the worshipers of Molech performed, **it has sometimes been inferred, from the phrase "pass through the fire to Molech," that children were made to pass between two lines of fire as a kind of consecration or februation; but it is clear from Isa. lvii. 5 and Jer. xix. 5 that the children were killed and burned.** The whole point of the offering consisted, therefore, in the fact that it was a human sacrifice. From Jer. vii. 31 and Ezek. xx. 25, 26, it is evident that both prophets regarded these human sacrifices as extraordinary offerings to Yhwh. **Jeremiah declares that Yhwh had not commanded them, while Ezekiel says Yhwh polluted the Israelites in their offerings by permitting them to sacrifice their first-born, so that through chastisement they might know that Yhwh**

was Yhwh. The fact, therefore, now generally accepted by critical scholars, is that in the last days of the kingdom human sacrifices were offered to Yhwh as King or Counselor of the nation and that the Prophets disapproved of it and denounced it because it was introduced from outside as an imitation of a heathen cult and because of its barbarity. In course of time the pointing of "Melek" was changed to "Molech" to still further stigmatize the rites.

Motive of Sacrifices – The motive for these sacrifices is not far to seek. It is given in Micah vi. 7: "Shall I give my first-born for my transgression, the fruit of my body for the sin of my soul?" In the midst of the disasters which were befalling the nation men felt that if the favor of Yhwh could be regained it was worth any price they could pay. **Their Semitic kindred worshiped their gods with offerings of their children, and in their desperation the Israelites did the same.** For some reason, perhaps because not all the priestly and prophetic circles approved of the movement, they made the offerings, not in the Temple, but at an altar or pyre called "Tapheth" (LXX.), erected in the valley of Hinnom (comp. W. R. Smith, "Rel. of Sem." 2d ed., p. 372). "Tapheth," also, was later pointed "Topheth," after the analogy of "bosheth." In connection with these extraordinary offerings the worshipers continued the regular Temple sacrifices to Yhwh (Ezek. xxiii. 39).

iv

From *Interpreting the Synoptic Gospels* – Scot McKnight; Grand Rapids, Mi. [Baker Book House, 1988], pp. 27-29.

The student's knowledge of the ancient world greatly affects exegesis. Just as it is important to have certain "interpretive grids" in our minds as we read the Chicago Tribune or Allan Bloom's Closing of the American Mind, so **it is crucial for the New Testament student to be able to think like first-century Jews, to hear their expressions, to share their customs, and to experience their social milieu.** Yet "background" does not imply that we need to know everything about the ancient world before we can comprehend the Gospels. In fact, the process is a circular one: as we understand more about the Gospels, we understand more about that world; and as we understand more about that world, so we understand more about the Gospels.

Background considerations are necessary if the student is to uncover elements in the text that were simply assumed by the first century writer and his audience in order to understand the intention of the author as made known in the text. By the original author and his readers, this knowledge was shared; due to historical distance, this information is arcane to us. And there is much the Gospel traveler will need to know in order to be a perceptive visitor in that world.

In this connection, discipline is necessary in background studies. The student must limit investigation to that which is pertinent for interpretation. For example, if one decides to investigate the nature and purpose of genealogies

(Matt 1:1-17), one may become overwhelmed in the attempt to access all available sources (e.g. Jewish historians and philosophers [Josephus, Philo, 1 Macc.]) to determine the importance of heritage and geographical, political, and religious connections, in addition to pertinent Old Testament passages. One's quest, particularly in the contact of sermon preparation, must be much narrower and will probably be limited to a few dictionary articles and the exegesis of a few relevant passages elsewhere in the Bible. **In that every topic is a potential doctoral dissertation, the student must learn to discard what is not directly pertinent.**

Obviously, thorough background study provides historical anchoring. The student who is familiar with a Jewish perspective on table fellowship will understand the implications of Matt. 9:9-13. **The student who knows nothing about the Maccabean revolt will fail to recognize why the Jews were so upset by Jesus' and Paul's attitudes toward the law and Temple. Interpretation which is not anchored in background studies will be historically insensitive and, therefore, simply wrong. Christians who neglect background information are in danger of denying the time-conditioned nature of revelation, both in the event and in the text.**

As mentioned above, the problem with background studies is that they can prove infeasible for pastors. Therefore, **basis sources much be mastered for quick reference to solid and responsible facts.** Again, there are basically three ways to approach background studies: (1) read the original sources (Old Testament, Apocrypha, pseudepigrapha, New Testament, Graeco-Roman sources, rabbis) and conduct and inductive study [this will take several years]; (2) peruse general surveys in standard reference works; (3) consult the best surveys, then examine the evidence. Using the latter approach, the student can become a sensitive historian.

Too few students have read Josephus, and fewer still have studied Philo, the Dead Sea Scrolls, or the rabbinical writings. Such neglect results in interpretations that are anachronistic and misleading. **It is my recommendation that every seminary student, before graduation, should read** the Old Testament Apocrypha, the Manual of Discipline (the Dead Sea Scrolls), Josephus's Jewish War, 1 Enoch, Jubilees, the Sibylline Oracles, the Odes and Psalms of Solomon, the Testaments of the twelve Patriarchs, the Babylonian Talmud (at least five Mishna tractates [including Aboth] with commentary), the Gospel of Thomas, and portions of the Graeco-Roman literature (Plato's Republic, Aristotle's Ethics, Suetonius's Augustus, Tacitus's Annals, as well as some papyri and inscriptions). At the very minimum, the student should read C.K. Barrett's the New Testament Background: Selected Documents. **Someone who possesses both ability and opportunity and who has not read this minimal amount of material is quite frankly unprepared for interpretation and insensitive to the task of New Testament exegesis.**

Scripture Index

Genesis
2:17   267
3:5   107, 251
6:11-7:24   65
12   189
15:5, 13-14, 18   261
18:22-19:29   265
19:1-29   65
22:15-18   261
25:19-26   254
26:2-4   261
28:10-15   261

Exodus
1:15-16, 22   91
13:21-22   10
14:19-20   10
16:35   7
19:16-19   10
20:1-6   7
20:3-6   39n
20:4-6   20
20:5   255n
32:1-20   7
34:1-28   7
34:7   255n

34:10-17   6
36-40   8

Leviticus
17:1-7   8
20:4-6   9
26   80, 210, 247
26:14-39   66
26:18, 21, 24, 28   210

Numbers
14:18   255n
32:6-13   7

Deuteronomy
5:6-10   7, 20, 39n
5:9   255n
18: 9-13   265
28   80, 210, 247
28:15-68   66
31:14-18   9

Judges
2:11-23   11
8:22-35   13

1 Samuel
8:4-9, 19-22   15
10:9-13   18
10:17-19   15
13:14   44
28:3-19   9
28:3-25   265

2 Samuel
5:1-10   27

1 Kings
11:9-13   262
11:13, 32, 36   44
11:13, 31-39   249
12:20   44
12:25-33   29n
15:4-5   249
16:30-31   19
18   17
18:4, 13, 19, 40   17
19:1-2. 3, 9-14, 19   17
21   18

2 Kings
8:16-18, 26   19
9:1-7, 8-10, 22   18
9:14-16, 21-22, 30, 33-37   19
9:30-33   52
11:1-3   20
12:1-3   20
14:1-4   20
17   27

21:10-15   257
21:12-13   92
25:27   257

2 Chronicles
3:5-7   245
7:12-22   16
7:14   209
12:13   85n
17:3-6   22
21:4-7   22
21:5-6   19
22:2-4   22
26:3-5   22
35:20-27   248

Ezra
1:1-8   248
4:24   249
6:1-5   248

Esther
3   253, 267

Job
40:7-10   245

Proverbs
1:7   40
3:19-22   245
9:10   99
16:18   107, 253

Scripture Index

Isaiah
1:1-31   23
1:2-4   27
1:6   27
1:7   26, 65, 249, 254, 259
1:9   26
1:9, 27   28
1:16-17   26
1:18   28, 74
1:19-20   26
1:21   26, 27
1:26-27   27
3:11   51
6:9-10   209
13   xxvi
23:13   29
23:13-17   28
28:17   92, 257
43:25   74
44:22   74

Jeremiah
2:20   29
3:6   30
3:6-10   29
3:8, 10, 15-18   176
3:10   30
25:8-12   65
29:10-14   65
46:2   189, 248
50   98
50:17-20   2, 28, 175
50:19-20   28

Ezekiel
6:1-14   30
6:2   32
6:3   32
6:4, 6, 14   32
6:8   32
6:9   32
16   265
16:1-10   34
16:1-63   32
16:11-12   52
16:11-13   34, 245
16:14-21   34
16:27   35
16:41-42   35
16:46-50   35, 107
16:60-62   35
23   259
23:1-49   35
23:3   38
23:9   38
23:22, 28   38
23:24   39
23:25   39
23:31-33   39
23:38-39   39
23:40, 42   39
23:49   39

Daniel
2:31-33   72
2:38   72
2:40-45   5

2:44   155
5:28   72
7   215
7:1   72
7:3-8   73
7:9-10   156
7:10   266
7:13-14   74
7:19-22   73
7:22   74
7:23-27   5
7:24-27   73
7:27   74
8:1   73
8:1, 20   65
8:3-4   73
8:5-9   73
8:17, 19   75
8:20   73
8:21   65, 73
8:23-25   5
9   60, 62
9:1   65
9:1-19   62, 70, 74, 110
9:2   65
9:4   66
9:11   66
9:12   66
9:14   66
9:16   69
9:20-23   65
9:23   61
9:24   68, 74, 96
9:24-27   5, 65, 67, 68, 69, 74, 95, 264
9:25   95
9:25-27   96
9:26   95
9:27   27, 65, 70, 95, 267
10:1   75
10:20   75
11:1   75
11:3   75
11:31   27, 65, 156
11:35, 40   75
12:1   69, 70, 75, 82, 100, 118, 191, 235, 252
12:1-3   5, 69
12:1-4   68
12:4   75
12:11   27, 65, 156

Hosea
4:1   40
4:1, 6, 10-19   39
4:1-3   253
4:6   40
4:12   40
4:13   40
4:14   40
4:19   40

Micah
1:1   42
1:1-16   40
1:3-4   42

Scripture Index

1:5   42
1:6-9   42
1:9, 12   42
1:16   42
6:7   275

Zechariah
3:2   85n

Matthew
1   26
1:1   249
1:1-17   15n
1:8   20
2:13, 16   91
2:16   116
4:1-4   183
4:5-6   91, 116
7:24-27   157
8:11   138
10:16   199
13:10-17   260
13:11   85
13:39-40, 49   75
16:19   86
18:21-22   264
21:33-46   xv, 85
23   47, 55, 94, 251
23-24   59, 266
23:1-12   48
23:1-39   48
23:13-21   49
23:15   51

23:22-28   50
23:27   203
23:29-36   59
23:29-39   51
23:34   70, 189, 199, 206
23:34-35   110
23:34-36   53
23:34-38   118
23:35   97, 245, 252
23:36   57, 58
23:37-38   59
23:37-39   70, 110
23:38   27
23:39   60
24   56, 156
24-25   259
24:1   55, 90n, 245
24:1-3   58
24:2   56, 256
24:3   56, 57, 75, 231
24:4-14   61
24:6, 13-14   58, 75
24:8   116
24:9   58
24:9-12   118
24:11, 24   58
24:15   27, 58, 61, 65, 68, 70, 123, 191
24:15, 34   62
24:15-18   108
24:15-21   218
24:21   70, 75, 100, 235, 252
24:29   58

24:30   58, 74
24:31   58
24:34   58
27:26   3
28:16-20   179
28:19   85
28:20   75

Mark
4:11   85
13:11   90n
13:14   27
15:15   3
16:9   257
16:15   85, 177

Luke
4:8   208
4:9   116
10:1   196, 264
18:2   124, 125
21:5   56, 90n, 245
24:44-47   104

John
2:18-22   104, 161, 182
2:20   183
4:24   273
5:2   161
5:43   124, 125
5:44   125
6:35   183
17:17   273

19:1   3
19:30   88
20:16-18   180
20:19   180
21:24-25   183

Acts
1:1-3   183
1:15   196
1:5   196
1:8   85, 180, 191
2:1-4   179
2:41   196
4:4   196
6-7   95
6:1-7   182
6:1-15   180
6:1-8:4   179
6:5   182
6:8   182
6:10   182
6:11   182
6:11-13   182
6:12   182
6:13   190
6:14   182
6:15   183
7:1-60   183
7:1-47   188
7:6-7   189
7:9   189
7:23, 30, 42
7:38-47   188

7:47   189
7:51   191
7:52   189
7:54-60   190
7:58   190
8   105
8:1   xvi, 82, 96, 100, 103, 118, 177, 178, 190, 191, 194, 212, 217, 235, 252, 260, 264, 265
8:1-3   190
8:3   193, 194
9:1   193
9:1-2   194, 201
9:2   194
9:3-6   194
9:22-23   194
9:29   195
9:31   196
11:19   195
11:22-26   195
11:26   190
12:24   196
13:9   196
13:22   44
13:45   196
13:50   196
14:1-2   196
14:3   196
14:4-6   197
14:19   197
16:5   196
16:12   197
16:16-24   197

16:26   197
16:35-40   198
17:1-9   198
17:11   198
17:16-34   170
17:32   199
17:34   167
18:5-6   199
18:7-10   199
18:12-17   199
19:8-10   200
20:2-3   200
20:16   201
20:17-19   200
21:1-14   200
21:17   201
21:20   196
21:26   201
21:27   201
21:30-36   201
21:37-40   201
21:39   198
22:3   201
22:4-5   201
22:6-10   202
22:14-15   202
22:17-21   202
22:22-23   202
22:24   202
22:28   202
22:30   202
23:1-3   203
23:6-10   203

23:11   203, 207
23:12   203
23:16-30   204
23:35   204
24:1   204
24:5-6   204
24:10-21   204
24:24-27   204
25:1-4   204
25:6-12   205
25:13   205
25:14   205
25:15-22   205
25:23-27   205
26:4-5   205
26:9-11   206
26:12-18   206
26:19-20   206
26:24-29   206
26:30-32   206
27:1   207
28:11   207
28:16   207
28:17   207, 208
28:18-20   208
28:21   208
28:23-25   209
28:26-27   209
28:30-31   209

Romans
1:24, 26   35
2:17-29   102
3:21-22   75
3:21-31   102
4:5   75
5:15-21   75
6:6   272
7:19-25   272
12:1   273
13   98
13:1-7   2, 175

1 Corinthians
2:14-16   273
8:1-13   272
10:19-20   272
10:14-33   272
14:33   84
15:12-19   99, 199
15:13-14   99
15:16   100
15:17   100
15:33   273

2 Corinthians
3:14-16   273
4:3-4   273
5:17   272
6:16   272

Galatians
5:16-17   272
5:16-17, 19   272

Scripture Index

Ephesians
1:3   86
4:22-24   272
5:18-21   273

Philippians
3:4-6   198
4:6   273
4:11   271

Colossians
1:6, 23   177
3:5   271
3:9   272
3:16-17   273

1 Thessalonians
5:18   273

2 Thessalonians
2:1-12   215
2:3   122
2:10-12   127

1 Timothy
6:7-11   271

2 Timothy
2:15   86
4:16-17   209

Hebrews
7:27   75

8   182
8:13   135, 182
9:11-12, 15, 28   75
10:12, 14

James
1:5   99
1:5-8   84

1 Peter
1:3, 23   272
2:2   273
3:15   199

2 Peter
1:3   86, 98
3:3-9   176
3:8   110
3:18   273

1 John
2:13-14   99
2:18   83
2:22   83
4:3   83
4:4   99
4:8, 16   84
5:4-5   99
5:21   272

2 John
1:7   83

Revelation
1:1   xxviii, xxiv
1:8   245
1:9   145, 148, 212, 219, 269
1:9-20   xxviii
1:11   xxviii
1:11, 19   xxviii
1:19   xxviii
2:7, 11, 17   99
2:8, 12, 18   xxviii
3:7, 14   xxviii
3:14   100
3:15-16   116
4:1-2   xxviii
5:5   15n, 99
6:1, 3, 5, 7, 9, 12   xxviii
8:1   xxviii
8:1-2   xxviii
8:7, 8, 10, 12   xxviii
9:1, 13   xxviii
11:1   140
11:1-2   92, 257
11:8   157, 263
11:15   xxviii
12   91
12:1-4   132
12:3   132
13:1   132
13:5   229
13:8   70
13:11   132
13:18   132
14:8   90, 107
14:13   xxviii
16-19   xvi, 132
16:13   247
16:17-19:6   90
16:1, 17   88
16:16   103
16:17   88
16:17-21   87
16:18   88
16:19   88, 90, 107
17:1   89, 93
17:1, 15   104
17:1-7   88, 107
17:2   90, 107
17:3, 7   89, 132
17:4   90
17:5   xxv
17:6   90, 103
17:7   89, 93
17:8   54, 97, 98, 100, 138
17:8-13   118
17:8-18   93
17:9   98, 100
17:9-12   99
17:10   99
17:13-14   99
17:14   100, 103
17:16   104
18:1-8   106
18:2   107
18:3   107
18:4   108
18:5   107

18:7   107
18:7-9   253
18:8   108, 110
18:9-24   108
18:16   110
18:17, 19   110
18:18   110
18:19   110
18:21   110
18:24   110
19:1   111
19:2   111
19:5-6   111
19:1-6   110
19:9   xxviii, 98
19:10   272
19:11   100
20:12   266
21:5   xxviii, 100
21:6   54, 100, 245
22:8-9   272
22:13   54, 245
22:16   xxviii
22:19   128

1 Maccabees
1:20-64   62

Subject Index

Note - Numbers in () are number of times word appears in the text.

Abomination (17)   24, 31-34, 37, 69, 85, 89, 90, 121, 211, 245, 267
Abomination of Desolation (48)   xxvii, xxx, 27, 58, 59, 61, 62, 65, 68-70, 95, 104, 123, 125, 126, 134, 135, 156, 163, 211, 215, 217, 245, 247, 258, 262, 266
Abraham (16)   66, 138, 183, 184, 186, 188, 189, 245, 249, 254, 261
Adorn (20)   19, 32, 34, 39, 51, 52, 55, 89, 90, 109, 110, 164, 245
Against Heresies (11)   113, 117, 119, 120, 133, 148, 170, 215, 245, 258
Ahab (15)   17-19, 21, 22, 246, 247, 255
Aion (11)   55-58, 104, 114, 176, 246, 256
Allegory   246
Alpha and Omega   246
Angel of the Lord (3)   246
Antiochus (9)   62, 68, 69, 73, 85, 245, 246, 249
Antichrist (107)   vii, xxvii, xxx, 83, 91, 92, 103, 118, 120-132, 134-136, 138-142, 146, 148, 149, 153, 156, 158, 160, 162, 163, 173, 191, 211, 214, 215, 246, 250, 262
Apocalypse (43)   xxvii, 80, 120, 128, 137, 138, 140, 142, 143, 145, 147-149, 152, 157, 159-170, 176, 179, 208, 210, 212, 246
Apostle (62)   95, 96, 99, 109, 119, 121, 122, 127, 147, 148, 150-154, 157, 158, 160, 166, 167n, 168, 170, 177, 180, 181, 190, 191, 194, 197, 212, 214-218, 250, 254, 256, 261, 264, 272
Aristion (3)   151, 153

Aristotle (3)   246, 262, 276
Armageddon (5)   xxx, 103, 191, 247, 250
Artaxerxes (3)   165, 251, 258
Assyria (28)   xxv, 2-4, 15, 25, 28, 35, 36, 38, 40, 42, 45, 54, 81, 84, 175, 247, 254, 264
Athaliah (20)   17, 19, 20, 22, 91, 116, 133, 175, 246, 247, 255
Atonement (12)   67, 68, 74, 75, 84, 85, 98, 199, 247
Baal (14)   11-14, 17, 19, 247
Babylon (78)   xxv, xxvi, 1-5, 15, 27, 36, 38, 45, 54, 60, 65, 66, 68, 72, 73, 76, 77, 81, 84, 87, 89-93, 103, 106, 107-109, 174, 175, 187, 189, 209, 211, 247-249, 252, 254, 257, 258, 263, 264
Babylon the Great (14)   xxv, xxvI, 1, 5, 87, 89-92, 103, 106, 107, 209, 252
Beast (101)   xxvi, xxvii, xxx, 49n, 72, 73, 76, 83, 89, 92-94, 97, 99, 100, 103, 111, 122, 126, 128-130, 132-135, 140, 143, 150, 156, 160, 162, 163, 179, 194, 200, 203, 207, 211, 215-217, 219, 229, 252, 258, 262, 263
Blasphemy (3)   183, 229, 247
Blessings (12)   xv, 26, 44, 80, 81, 210, 232, 234, 247, 273
Bondage (7)   7, 184, 189, 247, 267
Byzantine (Eastern Roman) Empire (7)   76, 76n, 104, 173, 204n, 263
Captivity (27)   xxv, 15, 29, 34, 38, 45, 60, 65, 66, 76, 84, 87, 93, 165, 242, 247, 248, 250, 251, 263, 264
Carchemish, Battle of   247
Chaldeans (13)   1, 28, 29, 36, 38, 62, 65, 69, 183, 248
Chiliasm (7)   85, 155, 157, 167, 248
Chiliast (10)   114, 127, 140, 157, 158, 167, 259
Conjecture (6)   xxx, 80, 98, 191, 248
Constantine (19)   76, 131, 143, 147, 172, 210, 234, 235, 248, 250, 260, 263

Subject Index

Context (53)   xiii, xxvii, xxx, 3, 26, 27, 42, 54, 55, 58, 59, 61, 64, 70, 80, 86, 91, 104, 122, 125, 126, 128, 134, 136, 141, 149, 158, 162, 173, 175, 176, 190, 229, 248, 249, 259, 262

Controversial (6)   55, 115, 248

Council (17)   181-183, 189, 190, 195, 202, 203, 205, 248, 264

Covenant (56)   xv, xix, 6, 7, 9, 12, 17, 21, 27, 32, 34, 35, 53, 56, 63, 66, 67, 77, 88, 95, 98, 99, 101, 102, 133, 135, 156, 184, 246, 248, 253, 256, 258, 263-265, 272

Creation (3)   126, 129, 248

Curses (11)   xv, 26, 63, 66, 80, 81, 210, 232, 247

Daniel (91)   xxi, 4, 5, 27, 40, 58, 60-62, 65-70, 72-77, 81, 82, 85, 100, 104, 105, 110, 120n, 123, 135, 156, 177, 189, 211, 215, 235, 248, 252, 256, 257, 263

Darius (6)   62, 64, 75, 249, 256, 267

David (25)   xxiii, 15, 21, 22, 27, 44, 78, 87n, 99, 117, 175, 187, 249, 262, 265, 269, 270

Decemvir (3)   249

Decemvirate   249

Decemviri (2)   249, 263

Defile (7)   36, 37, 39, 69, 249

Desolate (23)   3, 23, 27, 30-32, 34, 41, 42, 59, 64-67, 69, 94, 107

Desolation (46)   23, 26, 27, 32, 37, 39, 59, 62, 64-67, 77, 85, 95, 96, 99, 104, 107, 115, 119, 120, 131, 145, 175, 211, 235, 245, 246, 249, 254, 258, 259, 261

Destruction (54)   xvi, 27, 35n, 45, 57, 60, 65-67, 77, 81, 92-96, 99, 104, 105, 107, 108, 114, 120, 131, 135, 140, 177, 178, 213, 216-218, 232, 235, 245, 249, 255, 257, 258, 263, 267

Diana (Temple of) (2)   249

Disciple (50)   1, 48, 55, 56, 59, 85, 86, 90, 96, 100, 113, 117n, 143, 151, 159, 160, 180, 181, 193, 197, 200, 216, 231, 246, 249, 251, 252, 256, 257, 261, 263-265

Divided Kingdom (10)   xxv, 16, 29, 44, 78, 249, 254, 255, 264

Domitian (59)   102, 130, 131, 136-138, 140-145, 148-150, 160-162, 176, 218, 219, 221, 222, 249, 250
Dynasty (4)   131n, 171, 250, 267
Ecclesiastical Histories (5)   147, 212, 250, 251
Edict of Milan (5)   210, 235, 250, 252
Egypt (36)   7, 10, 11, 35, 36, 38, 64, 91, 184-186, 189, 224, 230, 247, 250, 259, 265
End Times (17)   xx, xxvi, xxix, xxx, 42, 55, 75, 82, 130, 149, 153, 191, 247, 250
Ephesus (27)   130, 143-145, 150, 153, 160, 161, 164, 170, 200, 219, 249, 250
Ephod (4)   13, 14, 250, 251
Equivocation   250
Eschatology (68)   xv, xvi, xx, xxi, xxiii-xxvii, xxix, xxx, xxxn, 3, 10, 26, 43, 54, 55, 57, 57, 70, 77, 80-82, 86, 89, 99, 114-116, 120, 126, 127, 134, 147, 152, 159, 163, 165, 170, 173, 174, 176, 188, 191, 208, 245, 248, 250, 258, 269
Esther (4)   45, 252, 252, 267
Eusebius (107)   113, 115, 117, 117n, 118, 120, 143, 146, 147, 147n, 148-165, 167, 167n, 168, 169, 176, 177, 179, 209, 212-215, 217-219, 221, 225, 227, 228, 248, 250, 251, 258-260
Ezekiel (6)   4, 32, 35, 251, 272, 274
Ezra (4)   45, 93, 165, 251
False Accusation (2)   222, 251
False Doctrine (4)   xxiv, 97n, 101, 269
False God (5)   8, 18, 90, 247, 251
False Narrative   xv
False Prophet (2)   58, 133
False Witness (6)   181-183, 190, 222, 251
Fathers (73)   xvi, xxvii, 9-12, 20, 25, 39n, 44, 51-54, 63, 64, 71, 78, 80, 83, 113, 116, 120, 131, 143, 147n, 149, 152, 155, 157, 157, 167, 170, 183-187, 206, 209, 210, 231, 262, 269, 271
Flog (5)   3, 251, 274

Subject Index

Foundation of the World (7)   70, 93, 100, 179, 251
Free Will (2)   44, 251
Fruit of the Tree of the Knowledge of Good and Evil (2)   43, 251
Futurism (24)   xxix, 114, 125-127, 140, 143, 155, 157, 167, 168, 177, 248, 251, 254, 259
Futurist (85)   xvi, xxv-xxvii, xxix, xxx, 1, 42, 54, 55, 73-75, 77, 81, 82, 86, 92, 96, 98, 103, 108, 110, 114, 115, 118, 119, 125-127, 130, 138-140, 144, 145, 149, 155-159, 174, 176-178, 191, 206, 219, 224, 247, 248, 256, 258, 259, 264
Generation (56)   4, 8, 20, 26, 39n, 47, 53-55, 58, 60, 62, 65, 74, 80, 92, 107, 110, 114, 116, 148, 160, 162, 171, 176, 251, 255, 266, 271, 272
Golden Calf (2)   7, 251
Great Commission (17)   xxx, 77, 85, 99, 177, 179, 180, 191, 195, 206, 211, 218, 251, 258, 265
Great Distress (3)   70, 82, 252
Great Persecution (43)   xvi, xxx, 69, 77, 82, 84, 95, 96, 99, 102, 103, 105, 108, 118, 150, 156, 176-178, 190-194, 210, 217, 220-222, 226, 229, 235, 250-252, 258, 265
Great Tribulation (32)   xvi, xxx, 70, 71, 75, 82, 103, 105, 106, 118, 155, 163, 177, 178, 191, 192, 195, 196, 221, 224, 226, 227, 235, 250, 252
Greece (16)   65, 73, 75-77, 200, 252, 256
Greek (72)   xix, xx, 56, 57, 62, 68, 76, 76n, 114, 128, 130, 136, 139, 141, 142, 150n, 160, 162, 164, 169-174, 178, 198, 246, 248, 252, 253, 255-257, 259-263, 265, 267
Guilt (17)   8, 34, 35, 40, 43, 51-54, 110, 213, 252
Haman (3)   252, 267
Harlot (182)   xvi, xxi, xxiii, xxv-xxviii, xxx, 1, 4-14, 18, 19, 22, 24, 26, 27-43, 45, 50n, 52, 55, 61, 71, 74, 78, 79, 84, 85, 87-90, 92-94, 97, 103, 107, 108, 110, 111, 126, 132, 133, 137, 176, 179, 188, 191, 208, 209, 211, 252, 253, 260, 266
Haughty (9)   34, 35, 50n, 52, 107, 253

Hellenization (14)   76, 76n, 171, 173, 180, 182, 195, 253
Herod (6)   90, 93, 116, 133, 171, 204n
Herodotus (2)   252, 253
High Places (17)   5, 20-22, 29, 29n, 30, 32-34, 40-42, 253
High Priest (6)   183, 188, 193, 203, 204
History (43)   xvii, xxx, 4, 5, 15, 43, 55, 58, 59, 69, 76, 77, 81, 82, 95, 102, 105, 117, 117n, 118, 145, 147, 156, 179, 188, 207, 213, 218, 250, 253, 255, 262, 263, 272, 273
Holy of Holies (5)   66, 69, 253, 266, 267
Holy Spirit (12)   75, 128, 138, 179, 181, 183, 187-189, 191, 252, 273
Homer   253
Hosea (4)   40, 253, 272
Hypocrite (11)   49-52, 253
Idol (47)   20, 30, 31, 33, 34, 36, 37-42, 52, 121, 186, 231, 250, 258, 271, 272
Idol Worship (6)   44, 137, 255, 260, 272
Idolater (2)   xx, 53
Idolatrous 3)   44, 212, 267
Idolatry (30)   xx, 22, 29, 43-45, 80, 87, 140, 253, 269, 271, 272
Iliad (2)   253
Impute (5)   54, 81, 248, 253, 261
Inspiration (11)   66, 97, 100, 114, 140, 152, 165, 168, 169, 180
Inspired (22)   56, 62, 75, 77, 157, 161, 163, 165, 168, 171, 173, 177, 182, 188, 191, 195, 196, 245, 254, 260, 262
Irenaeus (226)   xxvi, xxvii, 49n, 83, 92, 113-115, 117, 117n, 118-120, 122-127, 129-132, 134-137, 139-144, 146-153, 155-165, 168-170, 176-179, 214-217, 219, 245, 248, 250, 251, 254, 256, 258, 259, 261, 261n, 262, 266
Isaac (9)   138, 184, 186, 254, 261
Isaiah (13)   xxvi, 23, 25-28, 40, 254, 272
Ishmael (3)   13, 14, 254

Subject Index

Israel (121)   xxv, 2-5, 8, 11-15, 17-19, 21-23, 25, 27-32, 34, 34-42, 44, 45, 63, 78, 80, 84, 85n, 95, 97, 132, 133, 147, 171, 175, 185-187, 195, 208, 246, 247, 249, 254, 255, 260, 264, 265, 272

Israelites (33)   3, 4, 7, 9, 14, 28, 34, 43, 78, 84, 90, 91, 97, 133, 247, 248, 250, 252, 254, 260, 262, 267, 274

Jacob (15)   41, 42, 138, 184, 186, 187, 254, 255, 261

Jehu (12)   17-19, 52, 254

Jeremiah (15)   3, 4, 28, 30, 40, 62, 65, 254, 256, 272, 274

Jeroboam (8)   29, 29n, 34, 44, 78, 249, 255, 265

Jerusalem (192)   xvi, xxiii, xxv, xxx, 1, 21-23, 26-29, 32-35, 40-42, 52, 58, 67, 69, 70, 76, 77, 84, 85, 85n, 86, 87, 90-93, 95, 96, 103-105, 107, 108, 120, 122-124, 126, 132, 133, 135, 138, 139, 141n, 146, 164, 171-173, 175, 176, 178, 180, 181, 190, 191, 194, 195, 200-207, 211, 212n, 216-218, 226, 235, 245, 246-252, 254-259, 262-267, 269

Jesus (260)   xv, xxviii-xxx, 1, 3, 15, 15n, 20, 22, 26, 27, 47, 48, 50-56, 58-62, 65, 67-70, 72, 74, 75, 78, 81-90, 94, 96, 97, 99-101, 103-105, 108, 110, 111, 116, 117n, 118-120, 123-126, 135, 140, 145, 153, 156, 161, 173, 174, 176, 177, 179-183, 188, 189, 191, 193-195, 198, 199, 201-203, 206-210, 217-219, 231-233, 235, 246, 247, 249-252, 254n, 255-257, 259, 260, 262, 263-266, 269, 274, 276

Jezebel (36)   16-20, 22, 26, 44, 52, 91, 116, 133, 175, 247, 254, 255

John the Apostle   170

John the Baptist (2)   173, 176

John the Elder (3)   117n, 270

John the Presbyter (2)   152, 153

John the Revelator   249

Josephus (6)   120, 159, 255, 276

Judah (99)   xxiv, xxv, 1-5, 15, 17, 19-23, 25-27, 29, 30, 35, 38, 40-42, 44, 45, 63, 65, 78, 80, 84, 92, 99, 107, 132, 175, 176, 247, 249, 254, 255, 257, 259, 262, 265

Judea (63)   xxv, 1, 15, 76, 78, 84, 90, 93, 95-98, 102-105, 107, 110, 123, 131, 132, 173, 175, 178, 180, 190, 193, 195, 204-206, 208, 216-218, 246-249, 251, 252, 254, 255, 258, 263, 264, 267
Juxtapose (2)   170, 255
Kingdom of God (2)   209, 255
Kingdom of Heaven (2)   49, 87
Kingdom of Israel (5)   78, 175, 249, 255
KJV (16)   56-58, 75, 107, 130, 174, 176, 177, 198, 208, 231, 253, 255, 259
Kosmos (2)   56, 256
Lament (14)   41, 59-61, 108, 110, 190, 256
Law (53)   xv, xv1, 4, 18, 26, 39, 40, 44, 50, 52, 63, 64, 66, 70, 71, 78, 80, 84, 133, 181, 187, 201n, 203, 211, 215, 220, 223, 232, 247, 249, 253, 256, 257, 263, 276
Law and Prophets (6)   18, 84, 198, 204, 256, 267
Longsuffering (6)   44, 80, 256
Love (15)   xxiv, 3, 25, 40, 48, 63, 80, 84, 85, 116, 127, 134, 198, 235, 256
Lovingkindness (2)   63, 256
Luke   256
Marathon (Battle of)   256
Mark (7)   xx, xxiii, 117, 120, 159, 160, 256
Mary Magdalene (2)   180, 257
Matthew (13)   117n, 151, 152, 159, 160, 257, 270
Measure (14)   51, 53, 66, 91-93, 140, 166, 257, 265
Medo-Persia (10)   65, 72, 73, 75-77, 252, 257
Merodach (Evil)   257
Messiah (19)   5, 19, 67, 77, 91, 95, 96, 116, 132, 133, 210, 246, 247, 257
Metaphor (24)   xxv, xxvi, xxx, 5, 32, 42, 82, 87, 87n, 90, 91, 246, 257, 259, 265, 267
Micah (3)   40, 42, 257
Molech (12)   9, 231, 258, 270, 274, 275

Subject Index

Mystical (7)   xvi, 155-157, 258, 265
Mythical (11)   75, 154, 155, 157, 158, 258
Nabonidus   258
Naboth (3)   17, 19
Nebuchadnezzar (21)   xxv, 2, 5, 45, 60, 72-74, 76, 84, 85, 155, 165, 245, 247-249, 254, 257, 258
Nehemiah (3)   45, 98, 258
Nero (92)   xxiv, 96, 97, 97n, 101-105, 118, 122, 126, 130, 131, 131n, 132, 133, 139, 156, 171-173, 177, 178, 193, 194, 200, 203, 205, 207-209, 211-219, 222, 229, 235, 258
Notorious Statement (20)   114, 115, 127, 136-138, 141, 146-149, 160, 162, 250, 258
Oholah and Oholibah (6)   35, 37, 38, 259
Olivet Discourse (7)   xv, 55, 58, 72, 120, 259
Origen (11)   224, 225, 225n, 226, 227, 257
Overthrown by Strangers (7)   23, 26, 27, 59, 249, 259
Papias (70)   13-15, 17, 17n, 118, 120, 143, 150, 150n, 151-159, 164, 167-169, 248, 251, 256, 258, 259, 270
Parable (8)   xv, 81, 85, 154, 155, 159, 261
Parthenon (2)   252, 260
Patmos (14)   130, 144, 148, 149, 212, 249, 250, 260
Paul (125)   1, 82, 91, 99, 102, 103, 117n, 120, 122, 123, 126, 159, 160, 167, 167n, 169, 170, 173, 179, 193-209, 209n, 212-214, 235, 252, 256, 260, 264, 271, 272, 276
Peloponnesian War   260
Peoples of the Land (22)   5, 7, 10, 11, 15, 43, 45, 76n, 78, 90, 91, 94, 107, 196, 260
Pericles (2)   260
Persecution (143)   xvi, xxx, 69, 77, 82, 84, 91, 95, 96, 97n, 98-103, 105, 108, 118, 130, 131, 139, 143, 145, 147-150, 156, 172, 176-179, 190-198, 200, 209, 210, 212, 213, 217, 220-222, 224-230, 234-236, 248, 250-252, 258, 260, 263, 267

Peter (18)   117n, 151, 152, 159, 160, 163, 177, 178, 196, 212-214, 256, 264
Pharisee (25)   47-51, 70, 71, 78, 87, 194, 198, 203, 255, 260, 262
Phoenicia (5)   29, 195, 260
Pisistratus   260
Plato (4)   246, 260, 262, 276
Play the Harlot (20)   6-10, 22, 28, 39, 40, 78, 188, 191, 208
Played the Harlot (27)   4, 11-14, 22, 40, 79, 179
Playing the Harlot (16)   7, 9, 33, 45, 52, 74, 79, 84, 85, 92, 94, 97, 137, 208, 252, 260
Polycarp (16)   114, 119, 120, 145, 150, 152, 159, 164, 269
Premise (9)   xv, xxix, 81, 146, 161
Preterism (3)   102, 261
Preterist (3)   xvi, 108n
Pretext (20)   xiii, 54, 86, 104, 126, 158, 207, 220, 222, 223, 226, 227, 248, 249, 261
Principle (8)   xvi, xxvii, xxviiin, 54, 253, 261, 262
Promise (16)   21, 28, 79, 81, 85, 138, 159, 163, 183, 184, 245, 246, 254, 255, 261
Promised Land (4)   7, 8, 189, 267
Prophecy (45)   xv-xvii, xx, xxiii, xxvi, xxvii, 5, 32, 42, 62, 65, 67, 68, 74, 75, 79, 81-84, 97, 135, 156, 168, 169, 208, 250, 251, 261
Prophesied (25)   4, 28, 32, 40, 65, 72, 77, 82, 85, 105, 116, 118, 120, 174, 177, 235, 252, 254, 257
Prophesy (14)   4, 18, 25, 27, 30, 32, 68-70, 74, 85, 261
Prophet (122)   xv, xxi, xxv, 4, 17-19, 22, 23, 25, 26, 30, 40, 44, 51-53, 58, 59, 61-63, 65, 66, 68, 70-72, 74, 78, 80-82, 84, 85, 90, 92, 109-111, 123, 133, 165, 173, 186, 187, 191, 198, 200, 204, 228, 238, 247, 248, 251-254, 256, 257, 261, 266, 267, 274, 275
Proverb (8)   40, 44, 84, 261, 262
Pythagoras   262
Rapture (10)   20, xxviii, xxx, 58, 81, 155, 163, 250, 262, 264
Recapitulation (8)   xxvii, 83, 128, 129, 146, 262

Subject Index

Recounting of History (3)   188, 262
Redemption (5)   xxix, 152, 174, 26
Rehoboam (6)   44, 78, 249, 252, 265
Religious Leaders (31)   1, 27, 47, 52-55, 59, 78, 87, 94, 96, 97, 103, 110, 180, 182, 183, 189-191, 193, 208, 209, 212, 252, 260, 262, 266
Remnant (15)   xv, 2, 3, 5, 28, 31, 32, 116, 141, 176, 208, 262
Revelation (153)   xv-xvii, xx, xxi, xxiii, xxv-xxix, 5, 15n, 79, 80, 82, 83, 86, 87, 87n, 88, 91, 92, 97, 98, 108, 113-120, 129-131, 134, 137, 139, 142-146, 148-150, 152, 153, 158, 160, 162-164, 166-170, 176, 177, 179, 209-211, 217-219, 229, 246, 251, 252, 254, 255, 258, 262, 263, 269, 273, 276
Roman Empire (29)   36, 76, 76n, 77, 84, 96, 103, 104, 131n, 133, 156, 171, 174, 178, 195, 197, 204n, 207, 210, 231, 233, 236, 258, 260, 263
Roman Kingdom (3)   76, 263
Roman Republic (5)   76, 249, 263
Rome (65)   xxv, xxvi, 1, 5, 28, 72, 76, 77, 81, 85, 91, 93, 96, 97n, 99-102, 104, 117n, 118, 126, 148, 159, 172, 203, 207, 207n, 209n, 211-216, 226, 229, 234, 252, 255, 263
Samaria (47)   xxv, 15, 17, 27, 33-35, 37, 38, 40-42, 84, 92, 95, 98, 107, 175, 180, 190, 191, 193, 195, 218, 246-248, 251, 254, 259, 263-265
Sanhedrin (5)   203, 205, 248, 264
Saul (27)   9, 15, 18, 44, 82, 103, 188, 190, 193-196, 235, 249, 265, 265
Scourge (5)   3, 53, 70, 251, 264
Second Coming (7)   xxiv, xxx, 58, 84, 155, 264, 270
Seventy (35)   xxv, 13, 15, 28, 29, 45, 62, 65, 67, 74, 76, 77, 96, 115, 145, 163-165, 184, 196, 210, 247, 264
Sight of the Lord (11)   11, 19-22. 30, 244, 265
Snare (9)   6, 7, 13, 87, 265
Socrates (4)   252, 260, 265, 267

Sodom (13)   24, 33-35, 265
Solomon (26)   15, 44, 66, 78, 84, 163, 187-189, 249, 255, 261, 262, 265, 266, 272, 276
Sophocles (2)   260, 265
Spiritism (3)   9, 265
Spiritist (2)   9, 265
Standard (7)   69, 104, 179n, 223, 266, 267, 276
Stephen (43)   94, 102, 118, 131, 178-183, 188-190, 193-195, 201, 202, 209, 210, 212, 216, 217, 235, 251, 252, 264
Tabernacle (6)   8, 187, 253, 266
Temple (203)   xvi, xxv, xxx, 1, 8, 27, 28, 40, 41, 44, 45, 47, 49, 52, 53, 55, 56, 60, 62, 65, 66, 69, 75, 77, 84, 85, 87, 90-93, 95, 97, 98, 101, 104, 105, 110, 116, 118, 121-124, 126, 127, 131, 133, 135, 137-141, 144, 146, 153, 158, 161, 172, 178, 182, 183, 188, 189, 191, 201, 202, 204, 211, 215, 217, 245-250, 253, 255, 257, 258, 260, 263, 264, 266, 267, 275, 276
Tertullian (14)   101, 102, 213, 214, 214n, 215, 218-221, 225, 266
Testament (New) (29)   xxiv, xxvi, 5, 57, 76, 90, 117n,, 129n, 173, 174, 194, 201n, 252, 253, 255, 256, 259, 270, 275, 276
Testament (Old) (21)   xvi, 1, 59, 61, 78, 90, 114, 173, 174, 179, 209, 242, 247, 252, 255, 262, 276
Testify (8)   xxviii, 18, 51, 52, 199, 266
The Books (2)   62, 266
Theology (9)   xix, xxix, 117n, 266, 273
These Things (38)   xxviii, 29, 32, 37, 42, 53, 56, 106, 107, 109, 110, 116, 118, 150, 154, 160, 162-164, 169, 183, 187, 198, 207, 213, 227, 229, 266
Those Things (18)   xvii, xxvi, xxviii, 10, 54, 58, 62, 81, 137, 159, 166, 178, 188, 266
Time of Distress (11)   xxx, 68, 69, 75, 100, 177, 191, 192, 235
Titus (22)   xxv, 69, 85, 105, 131, 136, 172, 178, 209, 216, 217, 245, 249, 255, 266, 267
Two Witnesses (4)   18, 84, 256, 267

Subject Index

Tyre (5)   28, 200, 267
Vespasian (17)   105, 105n, 131, 131n, 172, 178, 216, 217, 255, 267
Wilderness (15)   7, 10, 31, 44, 89, 185-187, 189, 250, 266, 267
Wing of Abominations (3)   27, 67, 267
Witnesses (13)   89, 90, 103, 113, 150, 180, 188, 190, 218, 254n, 263, 269
Woe (26)   33, 49-51, 108, 109, 267
Woman (28)   xxvi, 18, 34, 89, 90, 92-94, 103, 132, 163
Xenophon   267
Xerxes (5)   165, 251, 258, 267
Ziggurat (12)   xvii, xxvii, 80, 82, 124-126, 138, 146, 157, 227, 267

Gospel and Prophet entries are separated between Scripture and non-Scripture Verses.

Numbers in parentheses are number of times entry is found in the text, less Table of Contents and Page Headings